Europe, Globalization, and the Coming Universal Caliphate

Other Works by Bat Ye'or

Les Juifs en Egypte, 1971. Revised and enlarged Hebrew edition: *Yehudiya Mizrayim.* Foreword by Hayyim Ze'ev Hirschberg. Translated from the French by Aharon Amir, 1974.

Le Dhimmi: Profil de l'opprimé en Orient et en Afrique du Nord depuis la conquête arabe, 1980.

The Dhimmi: Jews and Christians under Islam. Revised and considerably enlarged English edition. Preface by Jacques Ellul. Translated from the French by David Maisel, Paul Fenton, and David Littman, 1985. (Seventh printing, 2005.)

Ha-Dimmim: B'nai Hasoot. Enlarged Hebrew edition. Translated by Aharon Amir. Preface by Jacques Ellul. Introduction by Moshe Sharon, 1986.

The Dhimmi: Jews and Christians under Islam. Russian edition. In 2 vols. 1991.

Les Chrétientés d'Orient entre Jihâd et Dhimmitude, VIIe-XXe siècle. Preface by Jacques Ellul, 1991. 2nd ed., 2007.

The Decline of Eastern Christianity under Islam: From Jihad to Dhimmitude. Seventh-Twentieth Century. With a Foreword by Jacques Ellul. Translated from the French by Miriam Kochan and David Littman, 1996. (Fifth printing, 2005).

Juifs et Chrétiens sous l'Islam: Les dhimmis face au défi intégriste, 1994. (Second printing, 2005.)

Der Niedergang des orientalischen Christentum unter de Islam. German edition. With a preface by Heribert Busse. Translated from the French and English by Kurt Maier, 2003. 6th ed., 2006.

Islam and Dhimmitude: Where Civilizations Collide. Translated from the French by Miriam Kochan and David Littman, 2002. (Fourth printing, 2005).

Eurabia: The Euro-Arab Axis, 2005. (Eleventh printing, 2010, with new preface, postscript, and appendix.)

Eurabia: l'Axe Euro-Arabe, 2006.

Eurabia: Come l'Europa è diventata anticristiana, antioccidentale, antiamericana, antisemita, 2007.

Europe, Globalization, and the Coming Universal Caliphate

Bat Ye'or

FAIRLEIGH DICKINSON UNIVERSITY PRESS
Madison • Teaneck

Published by Fairleigh Dickinson University Press
Co-published with The Rowman & Littlefield Publishing Group, Inc.
4501 Forbes Boulevard, Suite 200, Lanham, Maryland 20706
http://www.rowmanlittlefield.com

Estover Road, Plymouth PL6 7PY, United Kingdom

British Library Cataloguing in Publication Information Available

Library of Congress Cataloging-in-Publication Data

Bat Ye'or.
Europe, globalization, and the coming universal caliphate / Bat Ye'or.
p. cm.
Includes bibliographical references and index.
ISBN 978-1-61147-445-9 (cloth : alk. paper) — ISBN 978-1-61147-492-3 (pbk.: alk. paper) —
ISBN 978-1-61147-446-6 (electronic)
1. Muslims—Europe—Politics and government. 2. Muslims—Government policy—Europe. 3. Europe—Relations—Islamic countries. 4. Islamic countries—Relations—Europe. 5. Islam and politics—Europe. 6. Organisation of Islamic Conference. 7. International agencies—Europe. 8. Civilization, Western—Islamic influences. 9. Culture and globalization—Europe. 10. Multiculturism—Europe. I. Title.
D1056.2.M87B38 2011
305.6'97094—dc22
2011014646

Printed in the United States of America

Contents

Foreword

Michael Curtis

By her stream of books and articles over the last thirty years, Bat Ye'or, an independent scholar not connected with any ideological or political group nor identified with any partisan organization, has made a singular and challenging contribution to the discussion of the historic and present role of Islam in politics and society in Europe and elsewhere. Throughout that long literary career she has written on various subjects, but most important have been the works on the treatment of non-Muslims, or "dhimmis," in countries under Islamic rule, and on the nature and impact of that Islamic rule.

Her writings are commentaries of a scholarly character and strong observations of an original kind, but are also very much interrelated with and emanate from her personal history. This is the poignant story of a young Jewish woman forced to leave her native Egypt as the Jewish community which had existed in that country for over 2,600 years came to an end. Bat Ye'or chronicled that community in an early book in 1971, *Les Juifs en Egypte*.

If Bat Ye'or has been a formidable and courageous figure in discussion of Islamic activities, she has also been a controversial and politically incorrect one, whose work has sometimes been found by more conventional critics to be strident. It is understood that not everyone will agree with her assertions and her resolute conclusions and policy recommendations. It is equally clear that her arguments and analysis are presented strongly and clearly, sometimes emphatically, and with exact references, accumulation of accurate data, and a scholarly apparatus. In the present age of political correctness when criticism of Islamic activities or even commentary on them have been subjected to various forms of censorship or denial, and even violent personal assault, in Western countries, it is refreshing to read Bat Ye'or's well-presented, stimulating, and insistent thoughts, and frequently her unfashionable views. Even if one is not always in agreement with them, it is salutary to read, consider, and take them into account.

Bat Ye'or began her original approach with the first of her major works, *Le Dhimmi*, published in 1980. In this and further works, she examined the texts of Islamic theologians and jurists and testimonies of eyewitnesses in various Islamic countries on the treatment of their non-Muslim populations, challenging the mainstream position on the question held by many scholars. One of them, Mark Cohen, expresses this position in a number of writings, especially in his book, *Under Crescent and Cross: The Jews in the Middle Ages*. The general argument by Cohen and others is that non-Muslims under Muslim rule were tolerated, though not treated in benign fashion, and were considered "protected people" who were guaranteed security of life and property, communal autonomy with their own leaders and judges and able to abide by their own laws in personal and family matters, and having relatively free practice of religion. Though dhimmis were treated unequally in relations between them and Muslims, it is often argued that Jewish individuals were treated with more toleration in Islamic countries than in countries under Christian rule. The orthodox view is that both Jews and Christians in return for being "protected people" by Muslims accepted their subordinate status as second-class subjects and the restrictions, taxes at higher rates than those for Muslims, tolls, and customs duties.

Bat Ye'or, on the contrary, though agreeing that the condition of Jews in Islamic countries has varied, takes a more negative view of that condition and argues that the mainstream view is largely a myth. She argues that the myth started in the nineteenth century when the Ottoman Empire, self-described as a tolerant Islamic regime, proclaimed it was the most suitable regime to rule the Christians of the Balkans. Providing source data and analysis of that data, she holds that the condition of Jews was in general one of insecurity, humiliation, and subjection to a repressive system of rule over them. In rejecting the usually accepted view of the tolerant treatment of Jews under Islamic rule, she put forward and made familiar the term "dhimmitude," the institutional subjection throughout history of non-Muslims to Islamic power and discrimination against them, in her path-breaking book, *Islam and Dhimmitude: Where Civilizations Collide*, published in 2002.

That subjection, she argued, involves fear and insecurity on the part of non-Muslims who were obliged to accept their condition of humiliation. She sees that condition as the outcome of Islamic belief and law that stems from the eighth century on. At its basis is the doctrine and jurisdiction of jihad, defined differently as struggle, striving, or holy war. This flows from three sources: the Koran, the Hadiths (the words and deeds attributed to the Prophet Muḥammad), and the biographies of the Prophet. For Bat Ye'or, jihad is central to the development of Islamic countries and to the requirement to spread Islam through the world by peaceful means or by war. She emphasizes this requirement for Muslims that the *Dar al-Islam* (the House of Islam) in which Islamic law prevails must, according to doctrine, overcome the countries containing infidels, the *Dar al-Harb* (the House of War).

Perhaps more important and pertinent for readers today than the historical argument in Bat Ye'or's writings is her assertion that the condition of non-Muslims remains the same and is still apparent in present-day practices in Muslim countries that apply or are inspired by *shari'a* (Islamic) law. Those practices are qualitatively different from Western conceptions of human rights and equality. Her challenging conclusion is that the Islamic emphasis on *shari'a* law and on jihad implies and even demands perpetual war against those who will not submit to Islam.

Bat Ye'or applies this line of thought to current affairs, concentrating on Europe. In her previous book, *Eurabia: The Euro-Arab Axis*, published in 2005, she began an intensive study of the complicated and intense relationship between the countries of the European Union and Arab states, using the term "Eurabia" as a shorthand description of that relationship to indicate the increasing influence of Islam on European political and social life. Others may have been aware of this influence, but Bat Ye'or was the first scholar to dwell on and point out the exact details of that relationship. This began as a political reality in 1973 with informal alliances between the then nine countries of the European Community (soon to be renamed the European Union) and the Mediterranean Arab states. The relationship became more formal with the creation of the European-Arab Dialogue (EAD) in Paris in 1974 and the establishment of the Parliamentary Association for European-Arab Cooperation with over 600 members from European political parties who would consult with Arab representatives to provide an agenda for policy proposals by both sides.

The proposals led to cooperation and collaboration by Europeans and Arabs, through specially created organizations, diplomatic, parliamentary, and economic, on a wide range of issues: trade, media, culture, school text-books, youth associations, tourism, immigration, and foreign policy. This interaction has resulted from a mixture of economic, political, and ideological factors: mutual concerns about oil supplies, Arab markets, European interest in Arab industrial development, political support in general for the Palestinians in the conflict with Israel, which they have criticized disproportionately, and a frequent anti-American viewpoint.

At the heart of Bat Ye'or's line of reasoning is her criticism of the Islamic voice and presence in Europe and her warning of its pernicious influence and of the resulting subservience of a considerable number of European politicians and media outlets. She envisages, not the hoped-for moderation of Islamic extremism or the Europeanization of Islam that some anticipate, but rather the Islamization of Europe, reflected in current European behavior and way of thinking. She does not sanitize the character of Islamic political culture. Nor does she minimize the extent of the appeasement currently displayed by European personalities in deference to Islamic interests.

At its harshest this point of view would suggest that Europe, if its present activities continue in this same direction, will be lost to Islam. Europe, for her, is being transformed into "Eurabia," a term first used in the mid-1970s by a French publication pressing for common European-Arab policies and advocating European support for Arab anti-Israeli policies. Eurabia is thus the enemy of Europe, though she holds that it is not agreeable to the majority of Europeans. It is however an ideology and a strategy for promoting an alliance between the European Union (EU) and the Arab world, which affects EU foreign and security policies and encourages automatic criticism of Israel. The danger today is that Islam is having an increasing impact on European life, not only in policy matters but also in the establishment of Islamic cultural and political centers in European cities and in promoting the maintenance of the ties of Muslim immigrants with their homelands. Fashionable European concepts of multiculturalism have aided this by suggesting that Muslims not become integrated into EU societies but rather remain participants in coexisting parallel communities.

This new work, *Europe, Globalization, and the Coming Universal Caliphate*, continues, brings up to date, and expands the essential argument and analysis of the previous book, *Eurabia*, that Europe is not only being subdued and is on the way to succumbing to Islamic authorities and concerns, but is also acquiescing in its own subordination. She now argues that Europe has lost its moral compass in its apathy and reluctance to defend liberal democracy or unwillingness to recognize the true nature of Islamic terrorism and to act against it. Europe is renouncing or caring little for its Judeo-Christian identity. Though this work is relatively short it contains a detailed presentation and a wealth of precise information not readily available else where of the statements, activities, the political and diplomatic pressures by Islamic organizations and activists, the ambitious and unceasing proposals and intentions, and the supine response, with rare exceptions, of European leaders, groups, and media.

Bat Ye'or points out the various methods employed by Islamic bodies to achieve their objective, implanting Islamic values and traditions on Europe, and the West generally, fostering the increasingly large Muslim immigration into the EU, and working ultimately to achieve the conversion of Europe into the Islamic orbit. She also makes clear the way in which globalization and concepts such as multiculturalism and relativism have helped the growing Islamization. She has challenging passages on the Islamic denigration of both Christianity and Judaism and on the Islamic threat to the state of Israel. It is also welcoming to find that she indicates the deliberate use made by Muslims to ascribe an attitude of "Islamophobia" to those who are critical of Islamic activities.

Even more welcoming is Bat Ye'or's portrait of contemporary affairs. The EU has allowed large and increasing Muslim immigration into its countries, paid large sums of money to the Mediterranean Union and to the Palestinian Authority (PA), which it generally supports. She indicates the significance of the creation in December 2003 of the Dialogue between Peoples and Cultures in the Euro-Mediterranean Area, a Dialogue that is being implemented by a foundation purportedly reinforcing mutuality and solidarity. The EU has not taken heed of the prominent role of the Organization of the Islamic Conference (OIC), a religious and political organization representing 56 countries and the PA, and one which nominally has a community of 1.3 billion throughout the world. Bat Ye'or sees the OIC as attempting to restore the caliphate, which, deriving from the feud over the succession to the Prophet after he died in 632, became in medieval times the supreme sovereign of the Islamic empire, the head of both the religion and the state. She regards the intended universal caliphate as the supreme controlling authority, one inspired by the *shari'a* and Islamic culture and values and aiming at the

Islamization of the world. The OIC is concerned with Muslim immigrants in the EU and it interacts with European authorities through a variety of mechanisms, including the Alliance of Civilizations.

In assessing the value of Bat Ye'or's work it is useful to put it in the context of contemporary life. The West has witnessed and been subjected to many Islamic assaults against critics, including attempts to limit free speech and death threats, sometimes carried out. Some of the more egregious examples include the assassination of the Dutch politician Pim Fortuyn in 2002 by an individual claiming he was denigrating Muslims; the death sentence imposed on the novelist Salman Rushdie in 1989 for being "disrespectful" of the Prophet; the prosecution of another politician, Geert Wilders, for critical remarks about Islam and the Koran; the murder of Dutch filmmaker Theo van Gogh in Amsterdam in 2004; and the attacks on the Danish newspaper that had published cartoons of Muhammad. There were also the cancellation of the production in Berlin of Mozart's opera *Idomeneo* because it included a scene indicating the severed head of Muhammad; the self-censorship by Reuters and the Associated Press in refusing to refer to the perpetrators of 9/11 as "terrorists"; and the introductions in the United Nations and other international bodies of resolutions banning "defamation of religion" in the attempt to prevent criticism of Islam.

Bat Ye'or's work has noteworthy contemporary significance as the West confronts the danger of jihad and the fear of dhimmitude. Her work is a virtual call to arms as she sees Western civilization in danger, a danger that many Westerners do not fully comprehend. She warns that if the process of Islamization continues in Europe, the US will be challenged by an emerging Euro-Arab continent linked to the Muslim world and with considerable political and economic power. If she occasionally overstates her case there is no gainsaying her honesty, intellectual courage, and scrupulously accurate scholarship in confronting what she perceives as the myths of conventional wisdom and indicating the mindset of reluctance and apathy of those who ought to be more aware of present danger.

It is good to ponder her argument that people hold on to destructive myths as if they were the only guarantee for their survival when, in fact, they are the path to destruction.

Michael Curtis
Distinguished Professor Emeritus of Political Science
Rutgers University

Introduction

This book was intended to be short, with few references and for the general public, but as the topic became more complex than expected—and being unfamiliar to most people—greater development was needed. The central research focuses on three issues:

1. The European Union (EU) policy of globalization, which consists of reinforcing the United Nations world power, weakening both American influence and European cultural/national identities through multiculturalism. Globalization, combined with the European Common Security and Defence policy, induced the EU Mediterranean partnership with the southern Arab-Muslim countries—and Israel nominally—based on two new mechanisms: multilateralism and multiculturalism.

2. The multileveled geo-strategy of the Organization of the Islamic Conference (OIC) conceived for the West on Muslim immigration; the penetration of Muslim influence and culture in the West; academia and the media; "Islamophobia"; globalization, and the establishment of a world Muslim body rooted in the Koran and the Sunna in anticipation of the coming universal caliphate.

3. The instruments, mechanisms, and networks created by the EU, and now also the US, binding them with the OIC in a policy aiming to enforce security, defense, and globalization. These instruments provide the channels and cogs for the progressive Islamization of the West; they establish the major elements of a new global system of totalitarian social and political domination impervious to Western democratic institutions. As

they are linked to the UN—where OIC power is increasingly predominant—the Islamization of the West represents a dynamic triggered by the globalization that the EU is sponsoring.

As for the universal caliphate, it refers to the significance of the OIC in nearly all UN institutions and its policy to increase its world influence as stated in its new 2008 charter.

Without a better knowledge of those mechanisms, free societies will be crippled in their fight for survival and strangled by the various octopus-like networks. The analysis provided for Europe applies also to North America since the US and Canada are targeted by the OIC and brought into its sphere of influence through Muslim immigration as well as economy and oil interests. In fact, it can be shown that most declarations on Islam by EU officials and President Obama, as well as other political commitments in domestic and foreign policy, originate from the OIC through these numerous networks and instruments that frame the global governance of the future.

Chapter One

The European Union and the Organization of the Islamic Conference

A Common Struggle

CONCEALED KNOWLEDGE

Few terms are as significant to the understanding of current events as "dhimmitude." Yet this term, which offers an explanation for historical events and processes leading up to contemporary issues, is not only unknown to the general public, it is taboo in academia. Professors reprimand students who refer to the concept and to the author who gave it life by defining its specific characteristics. However, any attempt to understand our times without fully grasping the meaning of dhimmitude would be like analyzing the twentieth century while ignoring the ideologies—communism, fascism, and Nazism—that shaped it.

Dhimmitude designates the civilizations of peoples conquered by jihad over the past thirteen centuries and subjected to *shari'a* law. A "dhimmi" is a non-Muslim belonging to the civilization of dhimmitude. Having surrendered to the armies of jihad, the dhimmi loses his territorial rights and his sovereignty, but in exchange he is protected by a contract (*dhimma*) *against jihad*—the obligatory and irrevocable war against the infidels. This protection provides some relative security, conditioned upon a series of demeaning restrictions and discrimination.

1

The geographical setting of dhimmitude expanded across three continents according to the vagaries of victorious jihad wars waged in Africa, Europe, and the heartlands of the Indian subcontinent. Its population (*ahl al-dhimma*) shared similar characteristics of dhimmitude despite its heterogeneity. This uniformity imposed on widely diverse peoples, religions, and cultures, geographically and chronologically distant from each other, stems from the uniformity and permanence of the Islamic laws that governed them. These laws are determined by the Koran and the Sunna,[1] the two pillars that, to this day, sustain Muslim governments and dictate their domestic and foreign policies.

Dhimmitude, prescribed by Islamic jurisdiction exclusively for non-Muslims, is inherent to the geographical expansion by jihad. Conquered non-Muslims were thereafter defined by religious rather than ethnic criteria. They were governed by the religious, political, economic, and legal structure of dhimmitude, which affected them to varying degrees. Interaction between Islam and the vanquished (now dhimmis) was set in an exclusively religious vision that is still operative today.

We might ask how the concept of dhimmitude is relevant today. The answer is that the jihad ideology of world conquest, propelled by billions of petrodollars and facilitated by the complacency of European governments and the rivalry between Western powers, is flourishing in every corner of the world. The driving force of this process is the Organization of the Islamic Conference (OIC), which has been dedicated since its creation in 1969 to the elimination of the State of Israel and the eventual implementation of *shari'a* over the West. The OIC, today composed of 56 Muslim or predominantly Muslim member states, is based in Jeddah (Saudi Arabia) and includes a large number of subsidiary bodies. It seeks to unite the various parts of the Islamic Nation (*Ummah*) and to represent it on the international stage. Its traditionalist view leads it to cooperate with the Muslim World League (co-founded by Egyptian Said Ramadan), which follows the Wahhabi ideology. Ali Merad sees in these two organizations "the political and religious infrastructure that is indispensable for operating a modern caliphate."[2] The OIC issued the Cairo Declaration on Human Rights in Islam (1990), based upon *shari'a*; it supports Muslim separatist wars and approved the takeover of Gaza by Hamas (2006), the Palestinian branch of the Muslim Brotherhood (MB), founded by Amin al-Husseini, the Grand Mufti of Jerusalem.[3] This movement was created in Egypt by Hassan al-Banna in 1928.

The condition of dhimmitude transformed populations that were once free, self-governing majority nations, boasting the most refined, powerful civilizations of their times into amnesic survivors, living as humiliated, terrified, insecure minorities in their Islamized countries, strewn with the ruins of their history. The destruction of indigenous cultures and nations by Islamic colonization from the seventh and eighth centuries was accomplished by jihad conquests and dhimmitude—a body of humiliating, discriminatory laws verging on servitude. The dynamics and ideology that drive these transformations, which are still active at every level today, are barely detected as they continue to operate in Europe's current changes because of ignorance of their history and mechanisms.[4]

The history of dhimmitude, with an analysis of the chain of political, economic, and social events that ineluctably drove nations targeted by jihad into decadence and disintegration, is a taboo subject in Europe today. This is because Muslim states refuse to take responsibility for their history of imperialism, colonization, enslavement, and oppression, unlike European and American historians and politicians who acknowledged the dark pages of their past. European leaders, fearful of irritating the OIC countries, have adopted the Islamic view of history in which concepts of war, peace, and justice do not have the same meaning as in Judeo-Christian civilizations.

In his essay on war and peace in Islam, Bassam Tibi emphasizes that in Islam peace only exists between Muslims, and not between Muslims and non-Muslims.[5] The word "peace" applied to non-Muslims requires conversion or submission (dhimmitude). Citing the Koranic duty to Islamize the planet (Kor. 34:28), Tibi explains that for a Muslim, striving in the path of Allah to spread Islam in the world is not war but a pious, just action and a religious duty. Non-Muslims who obstruct the Islamization of their nations are the aggressors. They are to blame for the wars caused by their opposition to Muslim conquest; if they had not resisted them, the massacres incurred in this struggle (jihad) could have been avoided. Peace would reign if non-Muslims complied with the call of Islam (*da'wa*) by converting or submitting to Islam. Jihad, writes Tibi, is considered beyond reproach because it is an obligation and submission to the will of Allah. Non-Muslims bear all the guilt for provoking war by resisting Allah's will and forcing Muslims to wage jihad against them.

The explanation of jihad by Hassan al Banna, founder of the Muslim Brotherhood, is currently posted on the Brotherhood's website:

Jihad is the means of spreading the Islamic call and of preserving the sacred principles of Islam. This is another religious duty imposed by Allah on the Muslim, just as He imposed fasting, prayer, pilgrimage, alms, and the doing of good and abandoning of evil. He has imposed Jihad upon them, and entrusted them with it. He did not excuse anyone possessing the strength and ability from performing it, for it is a Koranic verse which is imperative a warning, and an exhortation which is binding: *"March forth, light and heavy, and strive with your wealth and your persons in Allah's way!"* (Surat-at-Tauba (9), ayah 41)[6] The Muslims have travelled to the furthest countries of the earth with the Koran on their chests, their homes on their saddles and their swords in their hands, and with the clear proof on the tips of their tongues, inviting mankind to accept Islam or the paying of jizya, or else face combat. Anyone who accepted Islam became their brother; what was theirs became his too. Anyone who paid the jizya was under their protection and liability, they stood by his rights, observing the pact made with him, and faithfully keeping to the conditions accepted by him. Anyone who remained unyielding was fought by them until God granted them victory.[7]

For Islam the whole earth is a *wakf*, a territory belonging to Allah and promised to the Muslim community that will bring it under the reign of the Islamic order revealed to the Prophet. Jihad is the striving to recover those *wakf* lands illegally held by infidels that must be *returned* to the Muslims. The conquest of non-Muslim territories is described in Muslim legal and historical texts on jihad as the *return* of lands by Allah to the Muslims, implying the *recovery of a prior possession* and the illegality of any non-Muslim sovereignty. This sense of re-appropriation by jihad of territory belonging to Islam qualifies jihad as a defensive, just, and legitimate Muslim war because it reinstates the will of Allah and brings peace through the submission and humiliation of the non-Muslim. The very existence of disbelief is an aggression against Allah. Jihad confers "the justice and peace" of Islamic order.

According to this vision of religious politics, Islamic conquest is deemed beneficial for vanquished populations because defeat offers them the opportunity to convert to Islam. This positive interpretation of Islamic wars against non-Muslims precludes negative criticism that might tarnish jihad, defined in Islam as a just, defensive war fought to liberate lands from unlawful infidel appropriation and promised by Allah to his community. The re-appropriation of their lands by indigenous non-Muslim nations (Spain, Armenia, the Balkans, India, Israel) is considered an unjust attack on Islam. Muslims can never be guilty of occupation or oppression because Allah granted them the whole world; jihad *returns* to them what *belongs* to them as true believers. Islam cannot be the oppressor because Islam dominates according to divine order and is not dominated (Kor. 9:33; 4:144). To criticize or challenge this supremacy is an infringement of the Divine Will.

This view explains the Muslim denial of the dark pages of their history. Research conducted according to Western criteria and based on objective examination of the facts about jihad, its progression, conquest of territories, and treatment of the vanquished is deemed unacceptable or even blasphemous by Islamic religious dogma. Jihad ideology, strategy, and praxis, being inspired by the life, words, and deeds of the Muslim Prophet, are an integral part of the Koran and Sunna, the holy Islamic texts. As an emanation of divine infallibility, jihad stands as a sacred category of Islamic thought and civilization that is beyond criticism. The European scholar and the Muslim believer can observe the same events without ever agreeing, because they operate within systems of thought that are worlds apart.

Today Europe is blocked in an impasse by the unofficial ban on studying jihad according to Western standards for fear of offending expanding Muslim immigrant populations within their midst. Europe not only betrays the foundations and standards of critical thought on which its culture stands, it denies itself an understanding of contemporary phenomena by ignoring the past.

And yet EU leaders are well acquainted with this past. They are informed, through their embassies and various intelligence services, about the ordeals of dhimmitude endured in Muslim countries today by the vanishing indigenous Christian communities and any remnants of ancient Jewish populations. Europe's silence and denial until the carnage in Baghdad and Alexandria in 2010–2011 was a deliberate strategic and security choice. For the past forty years, it provided the basis of its rapprochement policy with the Arab and Muslim world, shaping its systematic hostility to Israel and the United States. To implement this policy, Europe has developed new instruments—multilateralism and multiculturalism—that undermine the democratic decision-making processes in European states with subversive forces and impenetrable networks.

This development leads to instability, in a climate of latent terrorism, urban violence, justification of antisemitism, and hatred of Israel. Rejecting the Jewish roots of Christianity, which are the foundation and basis of Europe's spirituality, a self-hating Europe mutilates itself and works for its own destruction.

Historians know that the course of history is punctuated by key dates. Unnoticed by contemporaries, these dates appear retrospectively as defining moments that mark decisive political transformations and lead to inescapable long-term consequences. October 1973 is the date of the Yom Kippur War, which after initial losses was a brilliant Israeli victory over the Egyptian and Syrian armies that joined in a surprise attack against Israel. And October 1973 is a key date in the projected defeat of Europe, when Europe closed its air space and NATO bases to American aircraft to prevent them from flying needed supplies to Israel at a crucial moment. By so doing, Europe definitively took sides with the Arab League's jihad against the Jewish state.

THE CENTRALITY OF ISRAEL IN ISLAMIC-CHRISTIAN RELATIONS

Who would not be surprised by the relentless determination of Arab and Muslim countries to appropriate a tiny piece of land in which no town, village, or hamlet is mentioned in the Koran or in biographies of Muhammad, who spent his whole life in Arabia? Given the immense territories conquered and Islamized over thirteen centuries of expansion and war, marked like all wars by genocide, large-scale massacre, expropriation, enslavement, and deportation of the vanquished, why would Muslim countries keep plotting to destroy Israel?

The Muslim world knows full well that the dhimmitude it imposed on the Jewish people—and with most cruelty in their own land—was a state of humiliation, exploitation, and poverty tantamount to servitude. Why does the immense oil wealth of Muslim nations nourish a flood of hatred that poisons the heart of humanity against such a small nation? Why is Israel considered so alarming?

What Israel possesses is the Bible; the book that Muhammad claims was the unaltered version of the Koran uncreated and consubstantial with Allah, before Jews and Christians falsified it. The history of the Hebrews, according to the Koran, is the history of the Muslims before Muhammad. The Prophet maintained that the biblical characters are Muslim prophets, and that the Bible—both First and Second Testaments—is simply a falsification of the story of these biblical prophets who, in the Koran, were Muslims and preached Islam. They appear in the Koran, like Abraham, Moses, David, and Jesus, with Arabized names. But they are flimsy disembodied figures floating in fragments of undefined space-time, and featured in homilies.

The crime of the people of Israel is the creation of a compilation of books written over a period of centuries recounting the vagaries of their history, faith, legislation, and aspirations—completed more than a thousand years before the Koran was written and excoriated by Muslim orthodoxy as a falsification of the Koran. The same charges are brought against the Four Gospels assimilated with a different Koran, supposedly written by Jesus himself, who appears in the Koran as Isa and a great Muslim prophet and Islamic preacher. The Muslim designation of Jews and Christians as "People of the Book"—in the singular—derives from this assimilation of religion with a book, an object endowed with exceptional status in the illiterate pagan Arabia of the seventh century.

Jews and Christians, guilty of falsifying Islam, the one true religion taught by their Muslim prophets, are condemned to ignominious dhimmitude to expiate their stubbornness until they return to Islam, their first faith. Islam is true Judaism and true Christianity, the first and only monotheistic faith, preached for the good of all humanity.

Muslims proudly claim to venerate and respect the prophets, including Jesus, without revealing that the objects of their veneration are Koranic versions of the originals that they reject. Though these Koranic figures wander in uncertain space with no geographical or temporal references, Muslims claim they lived in "Palestine," on the basis of Jewish and Christian scriptures that they reject. It follows that biblical history is Islamic history usurped by Jews and Christians, and the land in which it took place—though inexistent and never mentioned in the Koran—is a Muslim land, and Jewish and Christian holy sites are all Muslim. Any Judaization of parts of Judea, Samaria, and the Galilee where every region, town, and village is mentioned in the Bible with historical and chronological precision, is sacrilegious to Muslims. They observe with destructive rage this unfolding return of history that they claim as their own, though they know nothing about it because it is not told in their Koran and sacred books. Any confirmation of the veracity of the Bible is seen as an attack on the Islamic authenticity of the Koranic figures taken from the Bible. Israel, in the land of its history, towns, and villages, resuscitates the Bible, the book the Koran must supplant. Determined to destroy Israel's history and recover its Islamized past, Muslims construct, with the help of their European acolytes, Arabizing fables of the biblical past, including early fictive Christian history.

This is the foundation of the war against Israel. As for the Christians, Islam teaches that they have gone astray by placing themselves in the lineage of the Hebrew Bible, because their real origin is Islam, with Isa, the Muslim Jesus mentioned in the Koran and the Sunna. Christians who betray Isa by rejecting his Koranic message, inventing the concept of the Trinity, are as diabolical as the Jews. Jesus belongs to Islam, not to Judaism, so Christianity too belongs to the Muslim world. This Muslim-Christian relationship drives the hateful, outraged rejection of the term "Judeo-Christian" that ties Christianity to the Jewish Jesus of the Gospels—"born in Bethlehem of Judea"— and of the Bible. Jesus, they insist, belongs to Muslims and the Koran.

This doctrinaire position informs a policy of provoking and sustaining hatred between the peoples of the Bible. By destroying Israel and eliminating the Jewish people, Islam could thus eliminate the Bible and bring Christianity back to its Islamic origin. The destruction of Christianity's sustaining Jewish roots will facilitate its Islamization. This leads to constant efforts to force Churches in Muslim countries to spread in the West a Christian doctrine purified of Judaism. From the 1970s, a new crypto-Islamic Christianity, shaped by "Palestinian liberation theology," is becoming today a majority current, very much in vogue in Europe. Separating Christianity from Judaism opens the way to its Islamization by assimilating Jesus with Isa, the Muslim Palestinian prophet as affirmed by Arafat at the United Nations in 1983.[8] The common battle of the Arab and the European Palestinized Churches against biblical Judeo-Christianity fed the EU's fevered hatred of America and George W. Bush for daring to profess a natural "Zionist" biblical faith that horrifies Europe and its Churches, drowning in Palestinianism and debilitated by Palestinolatry.

The policy of dejudaization of Christianity is not new. Based on prejudice and ignorance of Judaism, it reached its paroxysm in Nazism and served as a binding force between, on the one hand, Nazis and antisemites in Europe, and on the other hand, their faithful allies in the Muslim world—including the Arab Churches and Christian Arabs, particularly Palestinian. Betraying the solemn vow of "Never again," pronounced in the wake of the methodical extermination of Jews throughout its territory, Europe has thrown its political support behind Palestinianism and re-established the 1940s networks between former Nazi Germany and its European collaborators and their Arab allies. Since 1973, European propaganda has sought to delegitimize Israel—with all that it entails for Christian theology. Its justification of Palestinian terrorism thereby integrates jihadist logic that classifies any non-Muslim who defends himself as the aggressor. Steeped in hatred of Israel, some European Churches collaborate with their Arab counterparts to strip Jesus of his Jewishness and cut him off from his biblical roots, thereby Islamizing their own faith, roots, culture, and civilization. Today's most active proponents of the crypto-Islamic Palestinian theology are two Christian theologians, the British Stephen Sizer and the Arab Naim Ateek.

Over the past forty years Europeans have been calling Israelis "colonizers" and "occupiers," although Europe's Christianity teaches that Israel's homeland is the "Holy Land." Moreover, Europeans manipulated by the EU-OIC networks are forcing Israel to engage in a "peace process" that is in fact the antechamber to its death, an extermination previously initiated in Europe. It would seem as if Euro-communism and Euro-Nazism have regained control of Europe. Singing the praises of fraternity to a Mediterranean tune, portraying America and Israel as the villainous enemies of peace, the EU leaders have opened the gates of Europe to the jihadists and pledged allegiance to them for fear of fighting them. Here we see the renewal of the strong old alliances between Hitler, Mussolini, and the Arab world, now cemented by love for Palestinians and hatred of Jews.

But most Europeans reject this Eurabian policy. In the following pages we will try to establish the origin and causes of Europe's deterioration.

FROM EUROPA TO EURABIA

Who can deny the benefits of European unification? The elimination of wars, ease of movement, and discovery of so many rich and varied cultures within Europe inspires wonder and stimulates learning. European integration, with its reconciliation between nations, has brought economic advantages, wide and varied improvements contributing to a new era of peace. Old animosities have given way to respect, friendship, and solidarity between former enemies. Numerous programs give young people an opportunity to travel and study in different European countries and broaden their relations and knowledge. After so many wars Europe is one, unified yet diverse.

The great achievements of European integration are incontestable, and yet Europe today is wavering and its future seems irremediably doomed. To their horror, young intellectuals and politicians discover that the Europe of the Enlightenment, of human rights and freedom—that Europe for which so many celebrated and anonymous heroes sacrificed their lives—is effaced and dissolved into a totalitarian European Union governed by an omnipotent centralizing organ, omnipresent in every cultural sector and media, a cauldron of virulent antisemitism and anti-Americanism until Obama's election. Lockstep thinking and political correctness stifle hard-earned freedom of opinion, while a state-imposed curriculum in schools and universities substitutes falsehood for truth on taboo subjects and corrupts reason.

A growing number of citizens reject this Europe. Pockets of resistance are mobilized here and there. The ruling group that has brainwashed Europeans and used their taxes to build a hegemonic censorship system destroying them is now felt as oppressing those it should be protecting. In a word, there is a breakdown of trust between the governed and the faceless, globalist bureaucrats that govern them. Maneuvering in anonymous circles of networks within networks, this bureaucracy imposes directives dictated by the foreign powers that control it by means of terrorism and economic retaliation inside and outside Europe's borders.

In December 2002 an article entitled "The Euro-Arab Dialogue and the Birth of Eurabia" was posted in several languages on the Internet. Published in a serious Parisian Jewish periodical by an author unknown to the general public, the article situated the European Community's Arab policy in a precise, strategic, coordinated framework called the Euro-Arab Dialogue.[9] Constructed from agreements concluded between the nine EEC governments and the countries of the Arab League in 1973–1975, this framework defined a semi-official, quasi-secret policy that would trigger the transformation of Europe. Two years later, in a book published in the United States, the author analyzed the structural composition of Eurabia.[10]

Substantial documentation was cited to show how Muslim immigration fits into a European ideological approach to politics, economics, and security, aiming at the establishment of a Euro-Arab-fused Mediterranean civilization (Eurabia) through a program of coordinated measures. This analysis contradicted the prevailing belief that immigration from Arab countries was a fortuitous phenomenon in a remorseful Europe riddled with guilt for the genocide of the Jews and now charitably opening its doors to the downtrodden. Saddling itself with this moral stance, European Community leaders[11] justified a campaign blaming hesitant Europeans, accusing them of harboring the same kind of racism against millions of Muslim immigrants that led to the extermination of European Jewry.

But there are no similarities between the genocide of the Jews in 1940–1945 and the mass migration of Muslims to Europe from the 1970s. Eurabia grew out of a Euro-Arab alliance against Israel, cemented by European support for an Arab policy aimed at Israel's elimination. It generated a fundamentally Judaeophobic policy and culture, punctuated by anti-Jewish attacks, perpetrated within Europe by Palestinian terrorists under the protection of European police forces and secret services, at a time when a former SS officer had become Interpol's president.[12] This campaign, focused on hatred of Israel, became particularly virulent under the European Commission presidency of Romano Prodi (1999–2004) and Chris Patten, then European Union Commissioner for external affairs.

The realization that Eurabia resulted from an ideology developed by the European Council[13] and implemented by European Commission bodies helped their opponents refine their political analysis and their struggle. Who was in charge of the Eurabian project? How was it being carried out? The problem became an inter-European conflict focused on the very meaning of the European Union, its identity, its institutions, and its future. Actually, Eurabia encompasses an ideology that draws on various devices to achieve its objectives. These strategic, political, and cultural instruments aim to replace nation states with an order of world governance managed by international bodies. This concept is based on multilateralism, a policy of concessions and appeasement between diverse states with diverging interests.

THE ORIGIN OF EURABIA

The impunity of the secrecy enveloping the negotiations of the Euro-Arab Dialogue (EAD) and the scarcity of publications on the subject hinder the study of the development of the Eurabian movement. The extent of its representation within the various political parties of the EEC/EU and within the Churches remains obscure. It was nevertheless this movement that established Europe's structural changes and shaped its irreversible characteristics today. Patronized by France, this trend included among its members well-known officials, intellectuals, and ministers close to Marshal Pétain, like for instance Maurice Papon.

In the 1960s, the Quai d'Orsay and the French Catholic Left sponsored numerous pro-Palestinian demonstrations in Europe, Lebanon, and Cairo.[14] These movements revived those Euro-Arab currents, Palestinian in particular, which from the 1930s had fostered active collaboration between the European Nazi and fascist regimes and the religious and political leaders in the Arab lands. Their activism went back to the use made of Islam by the Axis regimes in their struggle against the Soviet Union.

In 1941 Nazi theoretician Alfred Rosenberg was appointed Reich Minister for the Occupied Eastern Territories. His colleague, Gerhard von Mende, director of the Ostministerium, the Ministry for the Occupied Eastern Territories, became the architect of the collaboration between the Wehrmacht and the battalions made up of defector Muslim soldiers from Soviet Turkestan. This activity was bolstered by the help provided by Hitler's Arab agent, Amin al-Husseini, Grand Mufti of Jerusalem. Al-Husseini was the religious and spiritual head of the Arabs of Palestine during the British Mandate, and took refuge in Berlin following the failure of his pro-Nazi insurrection in Iraq, which ended in a pogrom (*Farhud*) against the Jews in June 1941. Al-Husseini cooperated with von Mende and indoctrinated the Muslim SS troopers from Asia and the Balkans and Arabs in the beliefs of the Muslim Brotherhood. Numbering about 250,000, the Muslim SS served as auxiliary forces in Poland, Yugoslavia and the extermination camps. Representatives of the Ostministerium attended the Wannsee Conference at which the Final Solution was decided upon.[15]

After the war the Muslim soldiers, still sponsored by von Mende and a group of ex-officers of the Wehrmacht and SS that he had set up, regrouped in Munich and Hamburg. As naturalized Turks they obtained student status and during the 1950s were recruited by various sections of the CIA against the USSR. Von Mende maintained his contacts with the Mufti, the MB and Nazi criminals who had found refuge in Arab countries. These durable relationships between European supporters of the Third Reich and their Arab networks in the postwar period split off into European, pro-Arab groups against America and Israel. When Said Ramadan, son-in-law of Hassan al-Banna, founder of the Muslim Brotherhood, fled Egypt in 1954, he managed with CIA support to take control of the mosque in Munich to make it a center for MB influence throughout Europe. Using this base he set up a network of Muslim communities and centers spread across Europe, and from there, aided and abetted by European ex-Nazis, relaunched the war against Israel. According to Ian Johnson, "Munich was the bridgehead from which the Brotherhood spread throughout Western society."[16]

The denazification process in Federal Germany, full acknowledgment of the Shoah, rejection of antisemitism, and support for Israel particularly stressed under Chancellor Willy Brandt (1969–1974), a noted opponent and victim of the Nazi regime, opened the way for an Israel-German reconciliation. However, in the postwar period, in Germany as well as in the rest of Europe, especially in the countries under the communist yoke, former Nazis and their followers peopled the various government ministries. Some were even elevated to the highest positions of state, such as Chancellor Kurt Georg Kiesinger, former member of the Nazi party; Theodore Oberländer, an ex-pogrom inciter who was head of the German Ministry for Refugees; Hans Globke, co-author of the Nuremberg race laws who was appointed Secretary of State by Chancellor Konrad Adenauer (1953–1963), becoming his *eminence grise*; Walter Hallstein, professor of law in Nazi Germany and an officer in the Wehrmacht, who became architect of the European Community and first president of the European Commission from 1958 to 1967.

This deep-rooted solidarity between European adherents to the Third Reich ideology and their Arab networks continued after the war in their shared collaboration against America and the Jews. From the mid-1960s, French policy revived these latent networks. The Quai d'Orsay endeavored to build a common EEC foreign policy tied in solidarity with the PLO of Yasser Arafat. On January 25–28, 1969, in Cairo, France sponsored the Second International Conference in Support of the Arab Peoples.[17] On November 22, 1970, in the Dar es Salaam area of Cairo, Georges Montaron, editor of the French weekly *Témoignage chrétien*, gave a lecture on "The Arab World and Western Opinion" to a crammed room. He deplored Europe's ignorance of the Arab world, which he attributed to the effectiveness of Zionist propaganda. "Zionism can make use of anything; it has an army of propagandists, rabbinical Judaism, which identifies itself with Israeli policy, so that the majority of authentic French Jews double up as authentic Zionists. If you manage to make authentic Frenchmen or authentic Englishmen be at the same time authentic Eastern Arabs, how great will then be your influence!"[18]

The Quai d'Orsay attempted to build solidarity with the PLO, a movement created in 1964. It strived to bring the European states into this alliance, which would become the fulcrum of the foreign policy of the EEC in the Mediterranean region, thwarting American ambitions.

Great Britain's joining the European Community (January 1973) strengthened the French project. According to unpublished sources from the Euro-Arab Dialogue movement,[19] in November 1973 the British Member of Parliament Christopher Mayhew and Raymond Offroy, member of the French National Assembly, envisaged the setting up of an association. Its mission consisted of bringing together their European colleagues who wished to improve Europe's relations with the Arab world. The two men met during meetings of the Parliamentary Assembly of the Council of Europe and shared a common vision. The launch of this initiative coincided with the EC's Brussels Declaration (November 6, 1973), which called on Israel to return to the 1949 armistice lines and for the first time recognized the rights of a newly created people, the Palestinians. France had succeeded in unifying European Community policy against Israel and rallying it on behalf of Israel's enemies.

Mayhew and Offroy, now supported by the EC, organized on March 23–25, 1975, a conference in Paris that brought together 33 parliamentarians from seven countries of the Europe of Nine (West Germany, Belgium, Denmark, France, Great Britain, Italy, and Ireland). This is the origin of the Parliamentary Association for Euro-Arab Cooperation (PAEAC) and of the political processes leading to the concept of Eurabia.

The Secretary General of PAEAC, Robert Swann, a former Foreign Office diplomat, had been a Secretary General of Amnesty International. The funds for PAEAC came from a Swiss foundation, the ANAF, set up in 1969 and managed by an administrative committee made up of European political personalities.[20] The origin of this funding was Arab, mainly Palestinian, but European parliaments also made contributions. PAEAC benefited from the financial aid and support of the European Commission and its networks, in liaison with the Council of Europe. Research into the membership of this association would provide information on the extent of its representation within the various parties.

This policy was not limited to supporting the pro-Arab political movement officially initiated by President Charles de Gaulle after the June 1967 Six Day War. Its scope extended to a new policy which de Gaulle would most certainly have disapproved, as it innovated a strategy opening Europe's doors to the aims of the OIC and sketched the outlines of Eurabia.

Members of PAEAC belonged to the national parliaments of European Community member states and also countries outside the EC. The Association maintained a section in the European Parliament; its Executive Committee met twice a year in a European city. Recruited from within the principal European political parties, committee members elected the Association's two co-presidents and vice presidents for two-year terms. The Euro-Arab Dialogue (EAD) is an offshoot of PAEAC.

EAD was a founding body of Eurabia but escaped the usual right-left wing classification and, like its parent cell the PAEAC, brought together parliamentary members of all the European political parties. Its central organism, PAEAC, provided the channels through which Arab interests were communicated within European parliaments. It relied on Christian Arab advisers, representatives of dhimmitude who enjoyed the trust of Muslim Arab dictators, their masters, and promoted their anti-Zionist policies and expansionist aims in Europe.

Christians in Iraq, Lebanon, Syria, and Palestine, including many Christian PLO members, strove for Europe's rapprochement with the Arab world, hoping in this way to avert any threat to Christianity's existence in its Eastern lands of origin, by destroying the State of Israel. Eulogists, and yet victims of Muslim "greatness and tolerance," these Arab Christians switched from Nazism to communism and became the main instrument of the Euro-Arab alliance, thereby contributing to the transformation of Europe into Eurabia.

This activism reconnected, reinforced, and modernized the web of collaboration, synergies, and sympathies that existed between the European fascists and Nazis and their Arab Christian and Muslim supporters in the period 1920–1945. As early as the 1970s its members had revived this platform within the new structure, PAEAC, with responsibility for standardizing the policies of the EC and the Arab League across various fields and in foreign policies, particularly against Israel.[21]

No one has done more to destroy the fundamental basis of Western understanding of Islam than Edward Said, a Christian of Egyptian origin operating under a false Palestinian identity and an active member of the PLO. Said disseminated a racist theory restricting the right to write about Islamic history and culture to Muslims alone.[22] This Christian dhimmi engagement, enhanced by a scathing antisemitism that was well received in Europe, introduced the cultural and psychological facets of dhimmitude. It played a predominant role in modifying Europe's demography and religions and in the Islamization of its political leanings.

PAEAC, created in 1974 in response to Palestinian terrorism and the oil boycott decreed by the Arab League after the Yom Kippur War, injected Eurabia into the very heart of Europe. In effect, to its initial anti-Israeli and anti-American program the association added a new element relating to the internal politics of the EEC: the promotion in European countries of an extensive Muslim immigration on which would be conferred the same social, political, and national rights as the indigenous populations. This political activism complied with the requirements of Arab countries and their insistent and repeated claims for the propagation of Islam and the Arabic language in Europe in view of an integrationist rapprochement between the two shores of the Mediterranean (Eurabia). [23]

PAEAC, with a membership then totaling 650 parliamentarians, henceforth required a new mechanism for social coexistence, the concept of multiculturalism. In order to pursue a combined Euro-Arab policy, the Euro-Arab Parliamentary Association and the Arab Inter-parliamentary Union (AIPU) were simultaneously set up in 1974. [24] According to the AIPU website, this association "parallel to the Euro-Arab governmental Dialogue which also started in 1974," was the replica of its European sister organization, PAEAC, born the same year with the aim of reinforcing total cooperation between Arab countries and Western Europe. AIPU was successful in establishing good relations with the Parliamentary Assembly of the Council of Europe (forty-seven member states) and the European Council of the EEC. Its website also states that Euro-Arab parliamentary meetings dealing with political, economic, and cultural matters served to strengthen the cooperation between Arab and European countries. The continuing and irreversible evolution of twenty-first-century Europe results from the European Union's pursuit of this political convergence, called multilateralism, in both domestic and foreign policy, which has been unknown to its peoples for the past forty years.

THE CORE PROBLEM

It can be said that present-day Europe results from decisions taken in October 1973 in reaction to PLO terrorism and the OPEC oil boycott of countries friendly to Israel. These two pivotal factors altered Europe's course and determined its political choices, the consequences of which can be assessed today. Before the Egyptian-Syrian war against Israel in 1973 the EC had no uniform policy on Israel or the Israeli-Arab conflict—it did not even have a common foreign policy.

Despite France and Germany's assiduous efforts to unify EC policy on the Israeli-Arab conflict in line with the wishes of its Arab and Palestinian allies, certain EC member states refused to align themselves with the French position, which they judged unilateral and pro-Arab. But repeated Palestinian terrorist attacks on European soil, punctuated by plane hijackings, raised the specter of jihad that had held Europe in a vice-like grip from East to West for fourteen centuries. The leaders of the nine countries of the European Community (West Germany, France, Belgium, Luxembourg, the Netherlands, Denmark, Italy, the United Kingdom and the Republic of Ireland) concluded alliances with the Arab League countries on the following points: [25]

- The EC recognized the PLO and agreed to support Arafat. This policy brought Europe to legitimize the ideology of jihad and cemented its choice of Palestine over Israel. By supporting the PLO whose charter rejected the existence of Israel, the EC was challenging the Jewish people's right to a free and sovereign life in its homeland. Yet it granted that self-same right to an Arab population group that until 1967 had not troubled the Jordanian government or the Egyptian rule in Gaza. It also created the conditions for permanent conflict, which allowed it to constantly intervene as protector and ally of the Palestinians.
- The EC was also aligned on Arab bloc policy that demanded hostility or cooling of transatlantic links between the EC and America as a condition of Euro-Arab rapprochement.
- Furthermore, a policy of Muslim immigration in Europe began in line with agreements between the European Commission and the Secretary-General of the Arab League. Western countries outside the EC signed these agreements for reasons of national economy and security. This immigration, probably linked to the granting of Arab industrial contracts, was an integral part of an economic, ideological, and political strategy dominated by anti-Zionism and the promotion of Palestinianism, Arabism, and Islam in Europe, in line with the strategy of the OIC.

Such political choices triggered the development and dissemination of an antisemitic/anti-Zionist and pro-Palestinian culture propagated by the very organs of the EC. Further, the USSR and Socialist International support for the Palestinians was echoed on the Israeli left. Incitement to hatred—integrated in Palestinian mythology—was transmitted vertically from leaders to the population, whose reticence required certain precautions. The Palestinization of Europe on the basis of a replacement doctrine, the indoctrination of contempt and hate, and a terrorist praxis merged within Euro-Arab relations.

EUROPEAN DOMESTIC POLICY

This new context, as it evolved during the 1970s and 1980s, called for the elaboration of political concepts such as multiculturalism that justified fostering friendly and close relations with totalitarian states and terrorist organizations, which were looked upon kindly in Moscow and collaborated with Western communist parties. For its part, the CIA strengthened its links with the Muslim Brotherhood, with America combating the Soviet Union through its international support of fundamentalist Islam. The European-Arab rapprochement was rooted in both parties' economic interests, especially in oil and major industrial projects for the modernizing and arming of Arab countries.

Mass immigration from Africa and Asian Muslim countries, sustained by the promotion of Arabism and Islam, induced the social construct of multiculturalism. This concept, conducive to the relativity of cultures and values, is essential to Europe's demographic and religious merger. At the same time, the EU planned a common defense and security policy with regard to the Mediterranean region, hoping that close links between Arab Mediterranean countries and Europe would prevent a "clash of civilizations." This policy, as initiated by the Euro-Arab Dialogue (1974), was strengthened following the Khomeini revolution (1979), resulting in the Venice Declaration (1980) that adopted the position of the PLO.

The disintegration of the Soviet Union (1991) marked the end of the Cold War between the major Western blocs, facilitating a historic, ideological calming down on a global scale. This development changed the strategy of the alliances, revealing the emergence of new dangers that the Cold War had hidden and promoted, such as America's alliance with Arab oil kingdoms, its support for Islamism, the MB, for the extension of *madrassa* in Pakistan and to the Taliban in Afghanistan, together with its relentless pressure to allow Turkey into Europe. Taking advantage of the conflict between the two Superpowers, Islamism put down the milestones of its conquering march toward the West and America. The unilateral NATO destruction of Serbia (1995) redeemed the First Iraq War of 19991 to liberate Kuwait. The European Union Constitution (1992) and the Oslo Accords (1993) gave a new impulse to Mediterranean policy, which was pursued through the Barcelona Process (1995) and the Union for the Mediterranean (2008).

The conflicts between Europe and Eurabia concern the politics and criteria that define European history and culture. These are contested by the tide of Islamic immigration, sustained by European government leaders at the helm of an EU now comprising twenty-seven countries. This situation gives rise to conflicts between the EU oligarchy on the one hand and large discontented sections of Europe's populations, as well as liberal and democratic movements opposed to Eurabia. Deprived of national and transnational political structures, this vast array of opinions cannot yet impact EU policy. Through Islamic immigration and its integration problems, these trends become aware of the political, demographic and cultural modifications imposed on European countries by the EU supranational power. Brussels' encroachment on national sovereignty and democratic freedom provoked an outcry from those intellectual and political circles defined as "racist" by the Eurabian pro-immigration and pro-Palestinian movements.

After September 11, 2001, "the war on terror" launched by George W. Bush revealed to European consciousness the reality of political Islam, previously hidden by the EU's anti-Israeli propaganda. During the following years, the emergent Islamic European terrorism forced Europe to adopt immigration and security measures, risking upsetting the entire policy pursued by the EU for the past forty years, thereby lining up Europe within the sights of jihadist terror.

On the domestic level the conflicts over cultures and civilizations intensified between European populations, including Muslims, who on the one hand subscribed to secularity, democracy and the Universal Declaration of Human Rights, and on the other hand the majority of immigrant Muslim populations, followers of the Koran's precepts, *shari'a* and the Declaration on Human Rights in Islam (Cairo, 1990). In reaction to multiculturalism, European movements concerned with national and cultural identity grew in size and substance. The consequences of the combined policies of immigration and Euro-Arab fusion in the Mediterranean region, as pursued for forty years in the semi-secrecy of the Euro-Arab Dialogue lobbies, became progressively obvious and provoked hostile reactions.

The Mediterranean strategy omnipotence on the EU developed powerful networks linked to international organizations such as the Organization of the Islamic Conference (OIC) representing fifty-six Muslim countries and the Palestinian Authority. These faceless networks of a huge administration uniting the EU and OIC countries administered Europeans through directives, creating a Kafkaesque world functioning as a totalitarian and anonymous system maintaining political correctness and censorship.

The EU drift toward a type of totalitarianism, rejected by a large section of its population, risks destroying European integration's positive achievements and the very basis of its edifice. The conflicts between Europe and Eurabia hinge on the modalities of multilateralism and multiculturalism, human rights, freedom of expression and religion, European identity, Islamophobia, rivalry between the EU supranational ambition and member states' sovereignty. These aspects are discussed below.

EUROPEAN UNION FOREIGN POLICY: THE ARAB WORLD

The standardization of EC/EU foreign policy set in motion in 1974 required coordination between every member state and the transfer of their sovereignty to the EU, a supranational body which established its power by eliminating local nationalisms. The European Union set its policies according to its strategic choices. Undoubtedly, the implementation of multiculturalism secured the success of Muslim population shifts from Asia and Africa, as these heterogeneous elements would only concur with the emergence of a mixed European society. The EU's supranational power and global strategy would gain from a multicultural policy undermining local nationalisms and cultural identities.

After the attacks of 9/11, a sequence of crises prompted by President Bush's commitment to the "war on terror" and the 2003 Iraq war provoked feverish and violent anti-Americanism in the EU, bound as it was to the Arab world. Under the presidency of Romano Prodi the European Commission derided America and strengthened its allegiance to Arafat in the hope of defusing the Arab terrorist threats. Massive self-flagellating marches honoring two criminals, Arafat and Saddam Hussein, took place in European capitals. Common institutional mechanisms between Europe and the Arab countries were stepped up, aiming at greater Euro-Arab political and cultural integration. Simultaneously a campaign of boycott and defamation of Israel unfolded.

These measures complied with the directives of the *Common Strategy on the Mediterranean Region* adopted in June 2000 by the European Council till 2004 and extended till 2006. The document recognizes the strategic importance for Europe of the Mediterranean and advocates a policy of partnership with the Southern shores, meaning the Islamic countries. Article 26 states that the Council and the Commission and all the Union Member States must ensure the consistency, unity and effectiveness of the Union's action:

> The effectiveness of this Common Strategy will be optimised by ensuring the greatest possible coherence between the various instruments and areas of activity undertaken by the Union, and between the activities of the Union and those of the Member States.[26]

This paragraph explains the brutal and totalitarian nature of the EU's campaign of hatred against Israel and its orchestrated support for the *intifada* unleashed by Arafat in autumn 2000. It highlights "the greatest possible consistency" against Israel, enhanced by the joint activity of NGOs affiliated to the Commission, the media, university and academic boycotts and even "artistic" displays and films,[27] as well as antisemitic attacks in EU schools and streets. The policy enacted against Israel was repeated in the anti-American campaign opposed to the Iraq war of 2003. Such mechanisms reveal the totalitarian structure integrated within the domestic and foreign policy sectors and their inner links. The process put in place by the European Council and the Commission subverted and standardized information and reporting by applying a dominant and politically correct ideology throughout the Union.

This situation follows from the commitment by Union Member States to build a Common Foreign and Security Policy (CFSP) which constitutes the second pillar of the European Union in line with the Maastricht Treaty:

> In order to improve the coherence and effectiveness of the foreign activities of the Union, the Commission and the Council are committed to a deeper coordination with respect to foreign policy. In effect, as the CFSP is currently situated at the hinge between the "Community mode" and the purely "intergovernmental," its development (as well as that of ESDP)[28] is evolving toward an "inter-pillar" treatment of issues.[29]

By the same token, Member States are required to ensure that their national policies are in line with the common positions they defend both in terms of foreign policy and within the international organizations. "A State should no longer depart from a common position."[30] The CFSP covers "all areas of foreign and security policy."

Several EU documents on the subject of foreign policy stress the principles of "consistency," "unity," and "effectiveness" between the instruments and areas of activity of the Union, and of its Member States, in order to bestow the highest possible level of effectiveness on the Mediterranean strategy. The centrality of the Mediterranean to the EU defines every aspect of its foreign policy as is apparent in article 26 of the *Common Strategy*, referred to above, which states: "The Union will ensure complementarity between its Mediterranean policy and other policies."

The following article emphasized the standardization for every Member State of a foreign policy. It requires all Member States to contribute to achieving the common Mediterranean strategy's objectives by making appropriate and coordinated use of all the instruments and means at their disposal. In 2000–2004 these objectives consisted in deriding the United States and providing massive and complete support to Arafat, while organizing a defamatory campaign against Israel and the European Jewish community in order to force them to accept the PLO's conditions.

Article 29 prompts Member States to increase their effort to coordinate activity with regard to the Mediterranean region, the "Mediterranean" being a euphemism for the Arab-Muslim states and the PLO:

> Member States shall make additional efforts to coordinate their actions vis-à-vis the Mediterranean region, including within regional and international organisations such as the Council of Europe, the UN, the OSCE,[31] and the IFIs.[32]

Articles 30–32 stipulate that Member States participating in activities regarding the Mediterranean in other circles must ensure that their actions are consistent with the objectives of the *Common Strategy*. Their representatives and the Commission's representatives in partner countries are required to coordinate their activity on the ground. The European Council, the Commission and EU Member States must endeavor to secure more effective cooperation with regional and international organizations and those countries sharing the same beliefs in order to achieve the *Common Strategy*'s objectives. To ensure coordination, Article 30 states:

Member States participating in other forums, engaging either as their principal objective or as a collateral activity in activities related to the Mediterranean, shall do so in a way consistent with the objectives of this Common Strategy.

With the collaboration of the press and its international organs during the second *intifada* (October 2000 to August 2005), this strategy which coordinated the overall domestic and foreign policies of the EU and of each Member State targeted Israel with an unprecedented vehemence. Such a forceful propaganda war stifled all dissidence and revealed a hitherto unknown framework of totalitarian EU mechanisms. Its relative and temporary failure due to an international scandal,[33] and the very nature of its excesses should not conceal the structural totalitarianism integral to the networks and instruments of the EU, nor the indifference and, for some, active collusion in this hate campaign displayed by the media, intellectuals and the public.

Setting these EU directives in the context of contemporary events explains the uniform force and aggressiveness of the combined European action against Israel with its academic boycotts in European cities and universities, its campaigns of disinvestment, the attacks on Jews and Israelis in numerous public places and schools. Like in its allied Muslim countries, Europe suffered again from a wave of desecration of cemeteries and synagogues, constant incitement to hatred spread by the media and some Churches, notably the accusation of apartheid against Israel leveled and upheld by Archbishop Desmond Tutu, chairman of a powerful international network: The Elders.

This intimidation campaign to terrorize small and peaceful European Jewish communities throughout the EU went in tandem with considerable pressure from Commission delegates on the Bush government to enlist it in the Euro-Arab jihad. It combined with the victimization of Palestinians and the sanctification of Arafat, the originator of international terrorism and suicide bombers. As all these factors emerged at once with the same uniform violence throughout the whole EU, they point to a *policy of consistency* availing itself of all the instruments of the EU in every sector and every European country.[34] It revealed the totalitarian structure of the EU and the control it wields over all sectors of domestic and foreign policy by means of a hegemonic ideology and control, blocking any opposition.

In December 2003 the European Council adopted the *European Security Strategy* drawn up by Javier Solana as a viable basis of collective action for the EU. This document envisages, among other measures, the creation of synergies between all the diplomatic resources of the Union and of its Member States as well as the coordination of their civil and military powers.

TERRORISM AND EUROPE'S MEDITERRANEAN POLICY

According to an EU declaration of 2003, "[Terrorism] arises from complex causes. These include the pressures of modernization, cultural, social and political crises, and the alienation of young people living in foreign societies."[35]

The stated official objectives of the European Union's Common Foreign and Security Policy (CFSP) encompasses the development of democracy, respect for human rights and fundamental rights, reinforcement of security for the Union and Member States, keeping the peace, and promoting international security and cooperation:

> These objectives represent the basic principles but also the spirit in which the member states organize their cooperation with respect to foreign policy as well as their relations with third countries. [36]

It would be safe to say the CFSP has not really been a success. A climate of fear, tension and self-censorship, spurred by the constant threat of terrorism against Europe, is aggravated by the violation of Europeans' fundamental rights to security and freedom of speech and opinion. The failure of the CFSP lies in the refusal of the EU to recognize the cause of terrorism and take adequate measures to counter it.

The Euro-Arab partnership policy was organized in the wake of a spate of airplane hijackings and terrorist attacks in European cities perpetrated by the PLO in the late 1960s. From 1968 to 1971 Palestinian organizations hijacked nearly fifteen planes yearly, a statistic that increased and reached fifty in 1973.[37]

Far from combating this terrorism, the EEC complied with PLO demands and conferred on Arafat the dignity and legitimacy of a statesman. At the instigation of France and later Germany, the EEC adopted a concept of terrorism that exonerated the perpetrators by incriminating the victim—Israel—by means of metaphors such as "underlying causes" and "injustice."

The existence of the Jewish state became an injustice and not vice versa. Using Palestinian ideology Europe could again blame Israel. This political reversal allowed the EC to drop its former support for Israel—that some deemed to be against nature—and restore ties with the Arab world formerly cultivated by Vichy, fascist and Nazi regimes.

Suspicions were aroused in the early stages of multilateralism (1970–1980) about the complicity of EC leaders with Palestinian terrorists in exchange for immunity for their countries and their interests abroad. These suspicions were confirmed in 2008 for Italy by eighty-year-old Francesco Cossiga, who served as minister of the interior (February 1976 to May 1978), prime minister, president of the Senate, president of the Republic, and senator for life. As undersecretary for defense, Cossiga had restructured the Italian police, civil protection, and secret services. Without the slightest tinge of bad conscience, Cossiga unambiguously corroborates the Christian Democratic Party's collusion with crime. In a *Corriere della Sera* interview Cossiga cites the agreement made in the early 1970s between then Prime Minister Aldo Moro and Yasser Arafat's PLO and its affiliates.[38] Palestinian terrorists were free to come and go in Italy, circulate freely under the protection of the secret services, stock weapons and set up bases, in exchange for immunity for Italy's domestic and foreign interests. Cossiga, who knew Giulio Andreotti and Bettino Craxi well, says they were among the most pro-Palestinian leaders in Europe. Craxi transferred billions to the PLO and eventually was forced to flee Italy and retired in Tunisia, headquarters of the PLO (1982–1993). In his book, the magistrate Rosario Priore confirms this agreement, known as the "Moro agreement," with the Palestinian terrorists.[39]

Cossiga revealed that Italian Jews were not included in the protection agreement. On October 9, 1982, six terrorists opened fire on members of the congregation as they left the Great Synagogue in Rome. Dozens of Jews were wounded and a two-year-old child, Stefano Tache, was killed. Several hours before the attack, Italian policemen on guard at the synagogue disappeared.[40]

Cossiga admitted for the first time that the explosion at the Bologna train station in July 1980 that killed 85 and wounded 200 was perpetrated by the PLO-affiliated terrorists of George Habash's PFLP.[41] The bomb, explained Cossiga, which accidentally exploded in the baggage check area, was not intended to kill non-Jews. Cossiga, who was prime minister at the time, exonerated the Palestinians by blaming the attack on neo-fascists.

In an interview with the Rome correspondent of *Yediot Aharonot*,[42] Cossiga admitted that the Italian government tolerated attacks against Israeli and Jewish targets, and continued to protect the terrorists despite the large number of casualties.

The hijacking of the Italian cruise ship *Achille Lauro* in October 1985 offers further evidence of state collusion with terrorism. Palestinians led by PLO leader Abu Abbas boarded the ship, terrorized the passengers, shot a handicapped American Jew—Leon Klinghoffer—and threw him overboard, still alive, in his wheelchair. The terrorists made their escape in an Egyptian plane, but it was intercepted by American fighter planes and forced to land at a NATO base in Sicily. They were tried and sentenced in Italy but Abu Abbas was liberated. In December 1985, Palestinian terrorists opened fire at a Rome airport El Al ticket counter, killing eighty and wounding thirteen. In a similar attack at the same time, they killed three people and wounded forty at an El Al ticket counter at the Vienna airport.

Cossiga admits he always knew about these agreements between Italian officials and Palestinian terrorists. His revelations were confirmed by Bassam Abu Sharif, representative of the Popular Front for the Liberation of Palestine. "Aldo Moro," he declared, with a touch of cynicism, "was a great man, a true patriot. He wanted to spare Italy some headaches." At the cost of massacres and hundreds of casualties. . . . The Palestinians, he said, had to inform the secret services of their plans and refrain from launching attacks from Italian territory.[43] Today Cossiga revealed he is sure that Italy has made a similar agreement giving Hezbollah free reign and total freedom to rearm in southern Lebanon. It is what the EU calls a common security policy aimed at reinforcing human rights.

Cossiga's disclosure, which could be corroborated by other European leaders, shows that European governments choose to ignore these terrorist activities. Palestinian terror organizations have benefited from enthusiastic empathy and encouragement among the countless ex-Nazis and collaborationist officials, former ministers, diplomats, officers, propagandists and intellectuals who recycled themselves in influential positions in postwar European society. Maintaining their links with the war criminals exfiltrated to the Arab countries, they established a complex network of political solidarity and economic interests that contributed to the building of a future Eurabia. The war against the Jews waged in World War II did not stop in 1945, for its ideology and tactics continued through other channels converging in Palestine.

Among endless other examples, the case of Paul Dickopf illustrates such a situation. Dickopf, a former SS officer in German military intelligence (the Abwehr, intelligence gathering from 1921 to 1944), after the war became one of the directors, and then the president of West Germany's Criminal Police

(Bundeskriminalamt, BKA). On June 29, 1971, Hans Dietrich Genscher, West German Minister of the Interior, complimented Dickopf on his professional qualities.[44] At an EAD symposium in Hamburg (1983), Genscher, who later became Foreign Minister, recalled in his opening speech that shared political objectives cemented Euro-Arab solidarity.[45]

Karl Laske and Pierre Péan mention the warm contacts of this former senior Gestapo officer with the international Nazi networks and the Palestinian terrorist organizations. In October 1968, with the help of the Nazi-Arab axis, Dickopf—supported by the votes of Arab states—became president of the Organization of the International Criminal Police (Interpol). Under his mandate, Interpol did nothing to stop terrorism, nor the wave of hijacked planes and the 1972 Munich massacre of the Israeli athletes.[46]

The security of European territory was obtained in exchange for anti-Israel and anti-American policies. Even before the advent of widespread terrorism, de Gaulle's France had adopted such a policy. According to Jean Bourdeillette, former French ambassador to Israel (1959–1965), "[In June 1967] the world discovered that Paris had crossed into the camp of the USSR and the Arab nations. . . . Israel was sacrificed to the demands of a conjugated anti-American pro-Arab policy."[47] According to Raymond Kendall—three times elected Interpol General Secretary—the meeting of the International Criminal Police Organization (Mexico, October 1968) refused by a majority vote to consider a report on hijacking planes. After the Munich massacre (1972), Jean Nepote, himself an Interpol General Secretary (1963–1978) and former collaborator with the Nazis in the Vichy Government, refused to gather information on Arab terrorists on the pretext that the Munich crime was political and that Interpol should not interfere. The Report of the Interpol General Assembly in Frankfurt (September 1972) does not mention the Munich massacres although it had been heatedly discussed by the assembly.[48]

The EU's entire Mediterranean security strategy was later built on exonerating Palestinian terrorism by accusing Israel or America of double standards. Terrorism was not considered a criminal act but a political factor "with underlying causes." These causes—Israel's existence—had to be eliminated. France's imperialist ambitions, and what Bourdeillette calls its "Great Muslim policy,"[49] together with the Nazification of the International Criminal Police Commission (ICPC), and the cogs of EC institutions, provided the "underlying causes" of this European policy. Deprived of world power by the loss of its colonies on four continents, France turned to European integration and its alliance with the Arab-Muslim world as a means of regaining what it had lost in international affairs.

To protect its southern flanks, Europe adopted multilateral policies of concession and appeasement dictated by the structure of the Euro-Arab Dialogue. In 1995 the European Union launched the Barcelona Process that established close relations, synergies, and solidarity with the Palestinians and Arab countries through a network of association agreements, while Israel—though nominally included in the process—was treated like the plague. In 2008 the Barcelona Process was renamed the Union for the Mediterranean.

THE PALESTINIZATION OF THE EUROPEAN UNION'S POLICY

Relations between the European Union and southern Mediterranean countries were inscribed in the framework of the Euro-Mediterranean (Euromed) partnership. In fact, as explained in the CFSP Guide, the process was originally designed to allow EU Member States to support their southern neighbors with all the economic and cultural instruments at their disposal, within "the dynamics of peace established by the Oslo Agreement."[50] In fact, Europe, acting as spokesman for Arab interests, obstructed American policy and defended the war strategy of Arafat, its favorite ally, protector, and mascot of its Arab policy.

The *Common Strategy on the Mediterranean Region* plan adopted in June 2000 by the European Council stated that EU policy for the Mediterranean region—that is, the Muslim countries on its southern shores—was animated by the principle of partnership. This text, adopted for four years, was extended till 2006. The EU objectives cited in the document mention:

- to establish a common area of peace and stability through a political and security partnership,
- to create an area of shared prosperity through an economic and financial partnership,
- to establish a partnership in social, cultural and human affairs: developing human resources, promoting understanding between cultures and exchanges between civil societies,

- to promote the core values embraced by the EU and its Member States, including human rights, democracy, good governance, transparency and the rule of law,
- to pursue, in order to fight intolerance, racism and xenophobia, the dialogue between cultures and civilizations.

However, Arab nations do not share the fundamental human rights values of the Union: they subscribe to the OIC's 1990 Cairo Declaration on Human Rights in Islam and discriminate against their own minorities and religious dissidents. Animosity against non-Muslims is a normal, endemic condition in these dictatorships. Despite its good intentions, a policy based on such a fundamental misunderstanding is doomed to failure; it has in fact failed miserably in the autonomous Palestinian territories where *shari'a* law is imposed. Christians continue to flee Gaza, Iraq and Lebanon, and Copts are persistently persecuted in Egypt; Syria and the nations of the Maghreb are dictatorships. Despite these infringements of human rights, the EU steadily increases and enlarges the network of associations with Mediterranean Arab countries and pours large financial support into their economies. In 2003, the Proximity Policy was incorporated into the Barcelona Process, with bilateral action plans in five spheres: political and security cooperation, sustainable socio-economic development, education, culture and migration.

One could of course retort that good relations are better than bad ones, even with dictatorships, and this opening could stimulate improvements on the ground. However, in that case the policies would have to include honest criticism, which alone could encourage reforms. Such honesty is excluded by the practice of censorship and stifling of free speech in Europe in the hopes of staving off terrorist threats.

In December 2007 French President Nicolas Sarkozy launched his Union for the Mediterranean project with the approval of the European Council. In fact, this project incorporates and develops the principles of the Barcelona Process, encompassing EU Member States and non-members on the shores of the Mediterranean. Its stated aim is to develop this partnership, reuniting Europe and Africa to make the Mediterranean a zone of peace, prosperity, and tolerance. To develop solidarity, the project will adopt and transfer to the Euro-Arab context the process applied in the construction of Europe.

The Union for the Mediterranean (UfM) launched various concrete economic and cultural projects to reinforce cooperation between Europe and its southern neighbors. Its counter-terrorism strategy is based on strong alliances involving a substantial cash flow and operating through numerous coordinated networks. The greater the danger of jihadist terrorism and religious fanaticism, the greater the EU relies on strategies of North-South synergy and solidarity. The Partnership, based on the assumption that poverty, humiliation, frustration, and "injustice"—synonymous with Israel—provoke terrorism, has developed a strategy aimed at ministering to those ills. EU members assure Arab partners who want to blackball Israel that, in fact, keeping that rogue state in their "assembly of democrats" will lead to the creation of the Palestinian state. Contrary to Arab members of the Partnership on whom Europe makes no demands, not even respect for human rights and democracy, Israel's membership is posited on its demise.

The UfM includes various projects for the environment, the development of solar energy, emergence of new enterprises, financing of co-development of infrastructure and facilities for investment along with increased regional cooperation. These activities represent sustainable development, reduction of immigration and counter-terrorism by means of economic exchanges.

The Euro-Mediterranean Parliamentary Assembly (EMPA), established in Naples (December 2003) and confirmed in Dublin (March 2004) created an additional Euro-Arab network to exert pressure on Israeli and European domestic and foreign policy. Convened in Brussels on October 13, 2008, EMPA asked the Union that EU Mediterranean Foreign Ministers increase the Assembly's powers and provide a legal base authorizing it to represent the UfM in the political sphere. EMPA decisions are not binding, but they force ministers and heads of state of the Union for the Mediterranean to take into account resolutions and recommendations on the agendas at its meetings.[51] EMPA is a perfect example of a body conducting multilateral policies—unknown to the general public—that funnels the Arab world's injunctions to feckless European leaders.

POLICY AMBIGUITIES OF THE COMMON STRATEGY IN THE MEDITERRANEAN REGION

The EU Mediterranean policy is designed to neutralize dangers from Arab countries by relying on alliances, substantial economic aid, and especially political support from EU Member States at the international and regional levels for the Arabs' anti-Israel policy (principle of coherence). We can already observe here how EU foreign policy infringes on the sovereignty of

Member States by imposing compliance with directives formulated by Brussels. However, the Member States' leaders are precisely those who set the EU policy. They based the Mediterranean policy on a deliberate lie fabricated to exonerate the jihadist terrorism from which Europe tries to protect itself by denying it. Until 2008, both Javier Solana, EU High Representative (HR) for the Common Foreign and Security Policy, and the Romano Prodi, President of the EU Commission, repeated the OIC statement that poverty, injustice, and frustration breed conflict and terrorism. They pretended that peace could be achieved by pouring the billions earned by the industrious European populations into the bottomless pit of Palestinian corruption with jihadists and their allies—in other words, it could be bought.

Muslim states and their European followers make excuses for jihadist terrorism on all continents, blaming it on the criminal policies of the United States and Israel. This strategy of denial, integrated into the European Union's common security and defense policy along with unilateral European support for Palestine, forms the foundation of the Euro-Arab alliance, the Mediterranean Union, and short-term European security.

One could naturally question the future of a policy that denies reality and replaces it with fallacious arguments. Believing that stronger ties with Arab countries and their terrorists is the best guarantee of security for a continent that refuses to defend itself when attacked, the EU waves the banner of multilateralism and compromises with criminal forces and ideologies that contradict Europe's proclaimed values. The more Europe persists in this direction, the more it weakens and saps its own foundations.

In the sphere of foreign relations, it is important to note that Judeo-Christian and Muslim civilizations do not share the same interpretation of the concepts of peace and security. The Islamic concept of defensive war, already mentioned, also leads to confusion. According to *shari'a*, peace with infidels is no more than a truce between two wars in the ongoing battle that will not end until Islam dominates the whole world. Armistices are permitted only to recoup and strengthen Islamic forces. The EU Mediterranean policy accepts this jihadist interpretation of truce with its substantial financial contributions to its southern neighbors, lax immigration policy, unilateral support for Palestine, and promotion of the myth of an Islamic civilization of tolerance and peace. Europe is a perfect ally, serving the expansionist ambitions of the Ummah, the universal Muslim community.

September 11—attributed by a majority of Muslims and certain European circles to the CIA and the Israelis—is qualified not as an attack but an act of Muslim self-defense against aggressive American policy. Muslim public opinion also sees it as the starting point of an aggressive Islamophobic campaign in the West, and condemns Western anti-terror measures as an assault on Muslims. The source of conflict is not from this viewpoint an anti-Western jihadist ideology, but the West's self-defense that is an aggression against Muslims; the definitions of aggressor and victim have been switched. Infidels are always guilty of opposing Islamic peace, that is of rejecting the choice between the Islamization of their country, conversion or dhimmitude. Europe has assimilated this viewpoint on Israel, accused by its very existence of attacking Islam, and summoned to excuse itself when in fact it is the victim of jihad. Europeans readily ascribe to the jihadist tactics against Israel, even though they are themselves targeted by the same conceptual and political ideology where the infidel's world is just a reprieve in Islam's timetable.

Two radically different visions of international relations are generated by these concepts. While European integration is based on striving for peace, secular law and separation of powers, the Muslim world sees peace only as submission or elimination of the adversary in a context where religion, law, and politics are inseparable. This is illustrated by the way the Muslim world and its satellite, the European Union, always present Israel as the occupation force and aggressor in the Arab-Israeli conflict when in fact Israel is the victim of jihad in its own land. For the same reasons, Europe and the Muslim world incriminated President Bush's anti-terrorist policy rather than global jihad in current conflicts. Thus, Europe is pursuing a suicidal policy based on denial.

The European Union states in paragraph 23 of the declaration of *Common Strategy*, with regard to its Mediterranean partners—that is, the Arab-Muslim countries and Israel:

> The EU will continue to encourage Mediterranean partners to adhere to the UN's international conventions on terrorism, and to follow the principle that the fight against terrorism must be firmly based on the principles of international law and the respect for human rights.

However, the Arab-Muslim partners only recognize laws and human rights in conformity with *shari'a*. They subscribe nominally to the United Nations' international conventions to the extent that they serve Islam's objectives. Western principles of international law and human rights are not compatible with *shari'a* law in Muslim countries. Moreover, Western nations and Muslim countries do not agree on the definition of terrorism. Westerners define terrorism as murderous attacks that blindly target civilian populations or individuals, committed by criminal gangs that act outside of recognized military formations and do not respect the laws of war. They consider terrorism as unacceptable warfare.

Muslim states judge terrorism by its motives not its methods. Any enterprise aimed at extending Islamic territory is considered "resistance." Palestinian jihadists, who popularized all modern terrorist methods, are always called "resistants" in official OIC documents. However, Muslim attacks against other Muslims in Iraq, Afghanistan, Pakistan, Morocco, Algeria or other Muslim countries are labeled terrorism. In other words, terrorism is defined by motives and not by the violation of a universal humanitarian law. This definition is generally accepted with regard to the Arab-Israeli conflict where Europe condemns Israel's defensive actions against terrorism as aggressive or disproportionate.

Taking pride in its own integration process, Europe is using it as a model for its Mediterranean Union policy in the hopes of restoring a form of Roman-Byzantine Empire that once united the shores of the Mediterranean in a single civilization. However, Europe, with its one-way immigration policy, is in fact rebuilding the Arab Empire of the Western Mediterranean and the Ottoman Empire to the east. Its strategy aimed at defusing jihad through the integration of a large-scale Muslim immigration into Europe ends up determining its entire domestic and foreign policy.

THE EUROPEAN UNION, MULTILATERALISM, AND INTERNATIONAL ORGANIZATIONS

To favor multilateralism and weaken American power, the EU has been active since the 1990s promoting projects and initiatives that increase the power and influence of international organizations—UN, UNESCO, the Arab League, the Muslim World League, the OIC and others—thereby weaving powerful networks of world governance.

The multilateral strategy is an outgrowth of unofficial pacts concluded since 1973 that sought to protect European security through EC alliances with—and allegiance to—Arab dictatorships and terrorist organizations. Immigration would favor the symbiosis of cultures and populations and the union of both shores of the Mediterranean, creating a new civilization in the new Muslim-Christian continent of Eurabia.

This strategy, which has involved significant European funding for the economic development of Arab countries, worked through powerful state-connected networks to achieve close collaboration between Europe and Arab countries at all levels and in all sectors. In the 1950s and 1960s the Nazi worldwide diaspora, particularly in the Middle East, provided the cogs of these interwoven, high-level connections which remained discreet. As bankers, industrialists, diplomats, jurists, academics, journalists and politicians, even rising to the top in the police as in the case of Interpol, these former high officials—often converted to Islam—pursued common objectives with their Muslim allies. Postwar governments cautiously used their connections to improve their relations with the Muslim world.

While working on European integration in a range of economic, social, monetary, legal and educational spheres, the Union tried to develop a common foreign policy that would place it on equal footing with the great powers. Europe also promoted an international order based on a body of rules that would be applied by international organization as stated in the CFSP *Guide*:

> Overall it is the promotion of an international order founded on an effective multilateralism, on international institutions (the United Nations foremost) and on regional organizations, that is at the heart of the European security strategy.[52]

The EU stated:

> the development of a stronger international society, well functioning international institutions and a rule-based international order is our objective. . . . Strengthening the UN, equipping it to fulfill its responsibilities and to act effectively, is a European priority.[53]

One of Europe's priorities is to strengthen the United Nations. In fact the EU's multilateral policy sought to undermine American power.[54] In a document drafted under the authority of Javier Solana, High Representative (HR) of the EU for foreign policy –dated December 12, 2003, but not published in the official journal—the EU states that its security strategy aimed at achieving a secure Europe in a better world, identifying the threats facing the Union, defining its strategic objectives, and setting out the political implications for Europe.[55]

The EU Council adopted this program at its Brussels meeting on December 12–13, 2003. Among other measures, the HR planned the promotion of an "international order founded on effective multilateralism." The EU strategy on the international level is set forth:

> The Union aims to develop a stronger international society, well-functioning international institutions—such as the United Nations, whose Charter constitutes the fundamental framework for international relations—and a rule-based international order. The best protection of our security is a world of well-governed democratic States. European Union policies are aimed at bringing this about.[56]

Solana advised the EU to adopt active policies and assume increased responsibilities that would give it greater authority on the international scene. Seeking improved coherence that would make his strategy more effective, he worked to bring together various EU instruments and means, such as international aid programs and diplomatic efforts. The goal was to make the European Union a factor of worldwide influence.

It should be noted that this ambitious EU policy, aimed at increased power in international bodies and world politics, responded to reiterated demands from its Arab League partners. Flattering Europe's imperialist ambitions, the Arab states incited Europe to compete with the United States and enticed it with hopes of a powerful Euro-Arab bloc built on solidarity with Palestinians, whose cause is based on jihad values and consequently on universal conquest.

THE EUROPEAN UNION AND THE UNITED NATIONS: GLOBAL GOVERNANCE

A communication posted on the Europa website on September 10, 2003, sets forth the European Union's ambitions within the UN and its mechanisms for cooperation. The Commission—then directed by Romano Prodi—offered a program by which the European Union would help the UN impose its decisions and establish the global governance of international society.[57] The document explains how multilateral cooperation, as a basic principle of the Union's foreign policy, should develop and improve means of action of global governance.

Since the UN—states the document—is precisely the essential element of this multilateral cooperation, the European Union should imperatively work to strengthen its authority. The Union was to take a leading role in the negotiation and implementation of UN initiatives and contribute to the elaboration of international instruments to reach this goal. It should be the front-runner of the UN movement and form, together with its partners, the "critical mass" necessary for the realization of UN decisions.

The document explains:

> The challenge currently facing the UN is clear: "global governance" will remain weak if multilateral institutions are unable to ensure effective implementation of their decisions and norms—whether in the "high politics" sphere of international peace and security, or in the practical implementation of commitments made at recent UN conferences in the social, economic, and environmental fields. (p. 5)

> Acting as front-runner implies the earliest possible ratification of UN instruments by member-states (and where appropriate, the Community), and then taking decisive action at an early stage to implement key UN measures at the EU level—thus setting an example and demonstrating a "clean record." On the external front, it means identifying where possible specific EU initiatives to build on, taking forward objectives agreed in the UN, and ensuring that important multilateral institutions have the means to deliver results effectively. (p. 9)

This strategy of unmitigated support for the UN implies substituting national sovereignty and democratic process by an association of states and ideologies that are frequently anti-democratic. Nevertheless, the Commission recommends unifying all EU partners in a single policy. To this end, the Union should "consolidate and reinforce the practice of establishing concise orientation notes, guidelines or position papers for selected UN events and meetings" (p. 19). The EU would thus speak with one voice within the UN. According to Javier Solana, one of the three strategic objectives of this policy was "to build an international order based on effective multilateralism" (p. 4). Addressing the European Council on June 20, 2003, in Salonika, he declared:

> The fundamental framework for international relations is the United Nations Charter. Strengthening the United Nations, equipping it to fulfill its responsibilities and to act effectively, must be a European priority.[58]

The European Union flatters itself on its ability to influence UN bodies and through its privileged relations with the 56 Muslim states of the OIC to influence world politics. During the terrorist campaign launched by Arafat in 2000, the Union energetically worked to multiply UN condemnations of Israel. Disregarding the incompatibility between Western and Islamic policies, the EU was busy creating legal mechanisms for world governance despite the fact that their normative and obligatory nature is rejected by nations that recognize *shari'a* as sole source of legitimacy, law and politics.

By so doing, the EU weakened rule-of-law states by transferring their sovereignty to international organizations. Moreover, it is concocting transnational structures that tomorrow will bring a worldwide caliphate to power as a result of the OIC's preponderance at the UN and in all international organizations—especially through the 118-state Non-Aligned Movement (NAM). Considering the ideology of jihad that determines the policies of Muslim countries and the Islamic penal code relating to women, apostates and non-Muslims, one wonders what motivates the EU to foster the domination within the UN of values antithetical to universal human rights. As the EU does its utmost to reduce American power by building up a UN counter-force, it is paving the way for domination of the UN by a universal caliphate.

OIC POLICY: DIALOGUE AND DA'WA

The Organization of the Islamic Conference (OIC) is an umbrella organization created in 1969, now bringing together fifty-six Muslim or Muslim majority states and the Palestinian Authority. The number of member states, which will increase, makes it, according to its representative, the second largest intergovernmental organization after the United Nations. At the 11th Islamic Summit held at Dakar on March 13–14, 2008, the OIC adopted a Charter stipulating its principles and objectives. The first of them promotes the unification of the Ummah (the world Islamic community) by rooting it in the Islamic values and religion, and proclaims solidarity in the defense of Muslim causes and interests.

The OIC seems to have modeled its organization on that of the EU. Its principal organs include: (1) an Islamic Summit composed of kings and heads of state that constitutes the Organization's supreme authority; (2) the Council of Foreign Ministers; and (3) the General Secretariat working as the OIC's executive body. Since its creation, the OIC has founded many committees to coordinate its activities and its policy at Muslim inter-state and international levels in numerous sectors, including the political, economic, social, religious, media, educational and scientific.

On October 4, 2005, Professor Ekmeleddin Ihsanoglu, OIC Secretary General, addressed the European Parliamentary Assembly in Strasbourg, reminding them that the OIC was the largest international organization after the United Nations.[59] In classic Muslim fashion, he affirmed that multicultural and inter-religious dialogue emerged from the edifice of human tolerance and Islamic values fourteen centuries ago in the Pact of Medina and the final sermon of Prophet Muhammad. Since its birth, he declared, "Muslim society advanced with the core values of respect for human dignity, regardless of color, creed, faith, social status, or ethnic origin." He asserted that Andalusian culture in Spain and "the cultural heritage of the Ottomans in the Balkans furnished the most successful examples of peaceful coexistence between the three religions, and produced brilliant models of human values." For fourteen centuries, Ihsanoglu went on, "the adherents of Islam developed a radiant civilization that stood for international values of human rights, justice, tolerance, compassion, and peaceful co-existence with other civilizations and faiths."

Naturally, historians reject such assertions as do the numerous peoples who have been victims of the Arab and Turkish yokes, of slavery, dhimmitude, and often of genocide. In the twentieth century alone, one could recall the genocides in Turkey and in Iraq of Armenians, Greeks, and Assyrians, and that of non-Muslims in Southern Sudan; the repeated massacres of Jews and Kurds in the Middle East and in North Africa and that of Christians in Egypt and Indonesia. One could even assert that the denial of the sufferings of jihad victims and Islamic imperialism is a kind of racism that treats them as sub-human.

The speaker developed the classic theme of the transfer of Greek science, philosophy, and the arts from the Muslim world to Europe, totally ignoring the Byzantine channels. Muslim contributions, he stated, clearly demonstrated the common roots and sources of universal civilization, a theme inculcated in Europeans by the programs of the Anna Lindh Foundation.[60]

Having vaunted the perfection of Islamic history, the OIC representative attributed Muslim grievances to the historical and political injustices of imperialism and colonialism and to the unresolved issues from which Muslim victims suffer, such as unjust borders and the illegal occupation of Muslim territories. He evoked the harsh treatment of Palestinians, their continued misery, and the lack of recognition of their fundamental rights, which have constituted overarching injustices.

It is legitimate here to wonder on what grounds a dialogue could take place with a person who considers the liberation of the Jewish people in a tiny portion of its homeland, Israel, as an injustice of indescribable proportions, whereas he considers a model of ethics the Muslim wars of invasion across three continents, with their continuous successions of massive destruction, despoliation, expropriation, slavery and massacres.

The orator called for a community of values with the West if the latter, rid of the prejudices of the old and new Islamophobia, realized that Islam had since its inception developed the best in human nature. Islam, he went on, "laid down the foundations of human rights and dignity, and asserted the supremacy of the values of justice and equality among all beings . . . Islam had taught for centuries the principles that later became the basis for international legislation on humanitarian law." Given these common points with the West, Ihsanoglu argued for an open and critical dialogue. Such an exchange would allow addressing the roots of misunderstandings and conflicts, and lead to a convergence of opinions and a historic Pact of Reconciliation. To realize these objectives, the OIC secretary general proposed the following steps to Europeans:

1. Give Islam in Europe official recognition equal to that of the other main religions of European states, which would infuse confidence and interfaith harmony.
2. Revise the educational syllabuses at all levels on both sides, particularly in key disciplines such as history, philosophy, and the human and social sciences, aimed at presenting a balanced view of other cultures and civilizations.
3. Establish a real intercultural dialogue at the local, national, regional and international levels and in all the media, news reporting, literary work, and "even cartoons."
4. Promote tolerance and encourage debate with the intelligentsia and media about their responsibilities "to avoid perpetuating prejudices."

5. Develop campaigns to stimulate and disseminate respect for culture, religious pluralism, and cultural diversity.
6. Address the root causes of terrorism, including political conflicts.
7. Try to encourage positive feelings of belonging and responsible citizenship among Muslim youth in Europe, and give them more incentives to participate in mainstream public life. This requirement refers to social and political promotion or "positive discrimination."
8. Strengthen existing legislation, adopted by EU council directives, on hate crimes and discriminatory and unequal treatment.

Yet Muslim countries have not implemented this list, especially where religious or ethnic minorities surviving from the pre-Islamic period reside.

The enforcement of these measures intended for immigrant Muslims into European countries required—according to the speaker—joint action and structured cooperation between the Council of Europe and the OIC. He acknowledged the OIC's awareness of the important work undertaken over the past fifty years in Europe by its ongoing dialogue with the Council of Europe. He concluded with the remark, "For centuries, Muslims, Christians and Jews lived together in harmony and peace in the lands of Islam, giving the world an example of fraternity among faiths." Such assertions evade the fact that all these Islamic lands were once non-Muslim lands where today some remnants of persecuted indigenous communities still survive. A fine program for the future . . .

In the space of three years, although most Europeans ignore it, every measure proposed by Ihsanoglu entered into the framework of cooperation between Europe and the OIC, which advises and acts within the numerous Euro-Arab collaboration networks. These latter contained some recycled, former European leaders who created the current situation. Disavowed by their own citizens they are now rescued by their OIC friends for whom they generously open Europe's doors.

OIC: THE MARCH TOWARD THE UNIVERSAL CALIPHATE

At the end of September 2005, the cartoons in the Danish newspaper *Jyllands-Posten* raised a wave of fury organized in the Muslim world, intended to terrify European leaders. On December 7–8, 2005, the heads of state of OIC's fifty-six countries met in Mecca for the Third Extraordinary Session of the Islamic Summit Conference.[61] They examined the issue of Islamophobia in Europe, the rights of Muslim immigrants in non-Muslim host countries, the policy of dialogue in the West, and Israel. Other subjects dealt with the Muslim world economic and cultural recovery, concerns for its solidarity, and the unity of its activities in world geopolitics.

The sages and ulamas gathered in Mecca for this summit expressed their worries about Islamophobia in the Western countries, which they likened to forms of racism and discrimination.[62] They "highlighted the necessity to fight and eradicate it as a way of raising the level of mutual understanding between different cultures." They invited Western countries "to legislate against Islamophobia and use educational and media channels to combat it." Their recommendations included "enhanced coordination between the OIC institutions and civil society groups in the West to counter the phenomenon" (§11). These proposals could not suit better the numerous associations involved in Euro-Arab dialogues, sponsored by both the European Commission and the OIC.

In his report, Secretary General Ihsanoglu requested the solidarity of the OIC—the organ representing the entire Muslim world—with Muslim minorities living in "non-OIC Member States," that is, non-Muslim countries (§5). The ulamas participating in the summit had examined the political and human rights of these Muslim minorities and "the challenges faced by them in their countries of residence" (§12). Speaking on behalf of these minorities, they insisted on their entitlement to basic human rights, including protection for their cultural identity, respect for their laws, their participation in the building of their nations and their protection from all forms of discrimination, oppression and exclusion.

The Islamic scholars underlined the need to accelerate and coordinate efforts to safeguard the cultural heritage of Muslims in non-Muslim states. They called on the OIC to protect these cultural and religious rights and the cultural identity of Muslim immigrants (§49). They also recommended internationalizing the fight against Islamophobia through cooperation between the OIC and other international organizations such as the United Nations, the European Union, the Council of Europe, OSEC, the African Union, etc. (§12) to ensure the protection of Muslim immigrant minorities in the West and preserve their identity. It is worth recalling that OIC countries refuse these same historic and cultural rights for indigenous pre-Islamic religious minorities in their own countries, Islamized after the Muslim conquest.

In his report on the recommendations of the various commissions, Ihsanoglu stressed the prime need for Islamic solidarity and activity in all political,
economic and religious domains. Real solidarity, he explained, necessarily
implied the strengthening of institutions and the deep conviction of a community of destiny, based on common values as defined in the Koran and the
Sunna (§4), which provide the parameters of good Islamic governance (§7).

As for terrorism, he claimed that its root causes should be addressed while
excluding military operations as they only breed more violence (§10). Opposing foreign occupation in self-defense was not terrorism—as the OIC had
always maintained; moreover, any link between Islam, Muslims and terrorism should be opposed. It is clear that this vision was dictated by classic jihad
theory, in which self-defense by non-Muslims constitutes aggression, which
could be avoided by their surrender.

Naturally, the harmful power of the Western media was examined, as
well as the means of using it to "project a positive image of Islam and to
promote the interests of the Ummah" (§13). In the Dialogue of Civilizations,
judged a necessity, the OIC should play a central role and insist on revision
of textbooks and teaching in the West (§45). Continuation of the dialogue
was important but it required equality among partners, mutual respect, reciprocity and dignity.

The OIC Conference planned a "Ten Year Program of Action" to set the
internal domestic policy of the world Ummah and its foreign policy with
non-Muslim nations. The plan promotes the consolidation of Islamic solidarity to allow Muslims to speak with a single voice in international politics[63]
and recommends fighting Islamophobia, which is likened to racism. To succeed in criminalizing Islamophobia, states should involve regional and international institutions and organizations. The OIC would strive to obtain from
the United Nations a resolution prohibiting Islamophobia and inviting UN
member states to promulgate laws combined with dissuasive sanctions.

The final communiqué of the Ten Year Program recommended the use of
the Western media to promote and sustain the cause of the Ummah and
Islamic values. It stressed the OIC commitment to solidarity with Muslim
minorities and immigrant communities in non-Muslim countries. The Organization would cooperate with international and regional organizations to
guarantee their rights in these foreign countries. In view of this, it recommended close contacts with the governments of states hosting Muslim communities on their soil. OIC organs specialized in the Dialogues of Civilizations and Religions should pursue the Dialogue of Religions.

The final communiqué of the conference[64] confirmed the validity of the 1990 Cairo Declaration on Human Rights in Islam and stressed the urgency of working with the international community to impose constraints on Israel. It reaffirmed previous OIC resolutions and decisions on Jammu and Kashmir in India, Cyprus, Nagorno-Karabakh and Somalia, while confirming its solidarity with the rightful causes of Muslim peoples fighting in these countries (§5). Five years later, it would be interesting to know how many of these measures, planned by the OIC, were adopted by the EU and international organizations.

The OIC conference in December 2005 condemned the fight against terrorism by solely military means, alleging that this only intensified violence; it advocated addressing its root causes (§10).[65] The EU approved the OIC stance and based its policy and its anti-Bush propaganda on a condemnation of the military combat against terrorism, forcefully stressing its "underlying causes." We have seen that the 1972 Munich massacre of the Israeli athletes by Palestinians gave rise to the same arguments by the ex-Nazi heads of Interpol. It served as a pretext for the EU to overlook PLO terrorism for decades. This was the refrain of Chirac, Prodi, Chris Patten, and others to blame the victim, Israel. Clearly this argument seeks to neutralize the defenses in the war against terrorism, and replace them by political surrender.

The OIC cited the inadmissibility of all attempts to establish a link between Islam and Muslims with terrorism—a tenet strongly upheld by the EU and President George W. Bush, and recently totally endorsed by the United States.

Ihsanoglu had asked Javier Solana to establish a code for the media that would take into account specific Muslim sensibilities. In March 2007, the EU and the US established a list of forbidden words for their diplomats, in response to Muslim susceptibilities. Among them figured the terms *jihad*, *fundamentalists*, and *Islamic terrorism*. This list became longer under Barack Obama, to the point of causing confusion about anti-terrorist operations— since there were no longer any terrorists, but only "activists" and "militants." On the other hand, the word "settler" became a generalization for Israelis. According to an EU civil servant, the common Union lexicon containing the forbidden words is kept secret. It claims that precautions in the usage of certain words are necessary to prevent terrorism.[66] This implies that if Europeans abstain from provoking Muslims through their bad habit of taunting their holy beliefs, they would not be attacked and terrorism would cease!

Henceforth, the fight against terror includes "respect" for the religion and customs of Muslim immigrants, and the adoption of a prudent language which avoids irritating them. Respect for Islam has now entered into the security arsenal of Europeans. Hence a London *Times* article in 2008 reported that hundreds of booklets written in 2007 instructed town hall officials and police on how to talk about terrorism without offending Muslims. A guide, written by British Home Office civil servants, suggests avoiding the words *Muslim* or *Islamic extremism* and *jihad*, using instead "violent extremism." Speaking of the West and Muslim communities should also be avoided because it reinforces the concept of a homogenous Muslim world and should be replaced with "diversities."[67] Such proposals recall those of the Anna Lindh Foundation, which seek to base Europe and Islam within the same geographic and conceptual civilization.

WESTERN DOMESTIC RULES BASED ON OIC DIRECTIVES

(*Recommendations applied in Europe; author's emphasis throughout)

Another document from this OIC summit in Mecca has particular importance, for it directly influences Eurabia's domestic policy. Presented by an OIC Commission made up of eminent Muslim personalities, it lists final recommendations for the OIC's approval. Although drawn up by Muslim thinkers, this OIC document would become a normative treatise of European domestic policy if European governments were to adopt its proposals. Today the majority of these recommendations have been accepted and integrated into the domestic and foreign policies of the European Union countries.

The document[68] includes recommendations for domestic policy concerning the Ummah on issues such as the fight against poverty, child labor, illiteracy, encouragement of creative, innovative and critical thinking within the education system, and the fight against religious extremism and terrorism. Concerning the foreign policy of OIC member countries, it advocates a set of measures arranged for the short-, medium- and long-term, organized below by theme.

OIC recommendations with international organizations:

1. *Strengthen OIC relations with major international and regional organizations** and make use of them to enhance the Islamic voice and advance Islamic causes.
2. Urge OIC member states to play a more active role within international organizations. *OIC members should support the candidates from member countries for positions in international functions.*
3. Urge more *proactive coordination* to promote the just causes of occupied Muslim peoples.

OIC recommendations in international relations:

1. Strengthen the existing EU-OIC relationship and forge OIC-Japan, OIC-Korea, OIC-China, OIC-South America relationships and dialogues.
2. Encourage the OIC to develop a standard high school curriculum in order to remove all prejudices about each other [Muslim countries] and ask the Secretary General to approach Western countries to remove the bias against Islam and Muslims from their curricula.*
3. Endeavor to improve the situation of Muslim communities/minorities in non-OIC countries.*
4. Address the *moral obligation of Western powers*, which directly or indirectly contributed to the injustices, oppression, aggression and long-standing disputes involving Muslim peoples, and assist in raising the socio-economic standards of the poor countries in the South.*
5. Creation of a conducive environment or incentives for the West or East Asian countries *to provide assistance, funding or transfer of technology* for the amelioration or acceleration of the socio-economic development of Muslim countries.*
6. *Promotion of the positive contributions of Islamic civilization in Spain to the West* and to humanity *in terms of tolerance, peaceful coexistence* of the three Abrahamic faiths (Islam, Christianity and Judaism) and the development of science and technology by Muslim scholars and scientists.*
7. Enlighten Western leaders and the public on: (a) *the positive role played by Islam in the rise of modern Western civilization*, and (b) *the moral obligation* they have to promote the socio-economic development of the South.*
8. Promotion of *inter-religion and inter-civilization dialogue* between East and West.

9. Drawing the attention of the international community to the dangers posed by the influence of *Zionism, Neo-Conservatism, aggressive Christian evangelicalism, Jewish extremism, Hindu extremism, and secular extremism* in international affairs and the "War on Terrorism."*

10. Anchor the principles of international solidarity in order to bridge the economic and cultural divide between rich and poor, North and South.*

11. *Promotion of the notion of peaceful jihad* in its many dimensions, such as economic jihad, educational jihad, intellectual jihad, ecological jihad, moral jihad, jihad against poverty, crime, drugs, AIDS, etc.*

12. Avoid confrontation and capitulation in dealing with Western powers.

13. Persuade the great powers to *address the root causes of terrorism*, and intensify coordination within the OIC for combating terrorism [between Muslims?].*

14. Rejection of the *equation of Islam with terrorism.**

15. Promote the idea that the campaign against terrorism can only be won through comprehensive and balanced measures, in particular by squarely *addressing the root causes of terrorism including, poverty, intolerance, injustice and foreign occupation.**

16. Promote a radiant and balanced image of the true values and principles of Islam *by all available means and channels.**

17. Publish books on the heritage of the Islamic civilizations in Spain, the Balkans, Central and South Asia, and other regions of the world *that focus on inter-religious harmony and tolerance*, Muslim economic development, and the *Muslim contribution to the development of modern science and technology.**

18. Promote and propagate the positive aspects of *shari'a* compatible with modernity and modernization, to be clearly distinguished from negative or repugnant aspects.*

19. Undertake research and studies to demonstrate that *Islamic principles and values* are not in conflict, but in fact are compatible *with the human values* used in current international discourse.*

20. Promote the Islamic principles of *respect for cultural, religious and civilizational pluralism*, as well as the practice of strictly adhering to these principles over the ages. It should be highlighted that *Muslim thinkers were pioneers of dialogue between civilizations and of comparative religion.*[69] *

In the realm of the media:

1. Promote Islam and the Muslims as a contemporary civilization recognizing and respecting the diversity of cultures, religions, and civilizations.
2. Work together to counter anti-Islamic propaganda in the international media.*
3. Consider an appropriate media strategy, including the recruitment of professional bodies, to improve the image of Islam and Muslims in the West and in the rest of the non-Muslim world.*
4. Engage international journalists in intellectual and humanist exchanges.*
5. Worldwide diffusion of the universality of the teachings and values of Islam.*

These recommendations have been successfully implemented in international and regional organizations for promoting Islamic interests worldwide, especially with the constant condemnations of Islamophobia at the UN General Assembly and UN Human Rights Council, the world condemnation of Israel's self-defense "Cast Lead" reaction in Gaza (January 2009), the world support for the pseudo-humanitarian flotilla for Hamas, and the boycott war against Israel backed by the Group of Elders chaired by former Archbishop Desmond Tutu. The enforcement in the West of the other decisions will be examined next.

THE OIC CONFERENCES: JEDDAH (2006), DAKAR (2008), KAMPALA (2008)

On March 15, 2006, the Executive Committee of the OIC held its first Ministerial Meeting in Jeddah.[70] The agenda included the publication in Denmark and elsewhere of defamatory cartoons, the Palestinian problem and the situation in Iraq. Regarding the cartoons, the meeting declared that the conclusions of the Foreign Ministers of the Council of the European Union on February 27, 2006, were extremely disappointing to the Islamic world. It deplored that the EU Council had only recognized that "freedoms come with responsibilities" and that "freedom of expression should be exercised in a spirit of respect for religious and other beliefs and convictions. Mutual tolerance and respect are universal values we should all uphold." OIC ministers regretted that the EU Council had not planned collective measures to prevent the recurrence of such acts of defamation in the future.[71]

The ministerial committee in Jeddah decided that the OIC Member States and its secretary general ought to pursue efforts to achieve the following objectives:

1. Adoption of a resolution at the 61st session of the UN General Assembly to proscribe defamation of religions and religious symbols, blasphemy, denigration of all prophets, and the prevention in the future of other defamatory actions.
2. Planning of a global strategy to prevent the defamation of religions with the implementation of effective and appropriate measures.
3. Intensification of contacts with the international community, particularly Europe, the EU-OIC Joint Forum, and the Alliance of Civilizations, to encourage the Dialogue of Civilizations.

The committee decided to intensify contacts with the international community, in particular the countries of the European Union and international organizations, to urge greater cooperation with Muslim NGOs. Muslim NGOs should initiate a constructive dialogue, offer their good offices "and follow up this issue with their European counterparts with a view to promoting the true values of Islam and underlining the tolerant and humanitarian message of Islam"(§8).

On the subject of Palestine, the committee commended the democratic elections in Gaza that carried Hamas to power (January 2006). In its usual racist and defamatory language toward Israel—falsely accused of attacking sacred Muslim and Christian sites—the committee decided to pursue its pressure on the international community to strengthen measures against Israel, while maintaining political and materiel support to the Palestinians so they could establish their state, with Jerusalem as its capital.

In March of 2008, the OIC Summit Conference met again, this time in Dakar, Senegal, and it confirmed its adherence to the guidelines of the Ten-Year Program of Action adopted at Mecca in December 2005. The Dakar Declaration[72] stresses the importance of uniting the Islamic Ummah to achieve a political unity founded on common values and interests. In Dakar, heads of state proclaimed their determination "to make sure that the Ummah's causes prevail in accordance with resolutions adopted in this regard by the Islamic Conference and the United Nations." This affirmation refers to the determination of the OIC to retrieve from Israel both Judea and Samaria (the West Bank) and to substitute the name *al-Quds* for the three-thousand-year old name, Jerusalem (Yerushalayim). As in the Christian countries where jihad effaced their entire pre-Islamic history, the Islamization of Israel would eventually suppress all Jewish and Christian history prior to the Koran.

The OIC proclaimed that from this region of the world came the spiritual messages "that advocate love for one's fellow human being, [it] illustrates our strict adherence to the values of Islam, a religion of peace that forbids all forms of exclusivity and extremism." Yet it fails to mention that the commandment "You will love your neighbor as yourself" appears for the first time in the Hebrew Bible (Leviticus 19:18)—not in the Koran. Moreover, the refusal to recognize the legitimacy of Israel in its historic homeland, and the determination to expel it through terrorism, expresses precisely exclusivity and extremism.

The struggle against Islamophobia is once again proclaimed, along with the necessity of a Dialogue of Civilizations to fight it. The idea of Islamic solidarity is reaffirmed:

> The Leaders of Muslim countries hereby renew their pledge to preserve world peace and security, one of the OIC's objectives, and thus to fully adhere to the United Nation's [sic] key mission in this regard as well as international legality as a rule for all without any political double standards.
>
> This is the reason why we proclaim, once again, our resolve to make sure that the Ummah's entire causes prevail in accordance with resolutions adopted in this regard by the Islamic Conference and the UN. [. . .]
>
> Based on this deep conviction, we the Kings and Heads of State and Government of the Organization of the Islamic Conference, renew our pledge to work harder to make sure that Islam's true image is better projected the world over in line with the guidelines contained in the Ten Year Programme of Action issued by the Third Extraordinary Summit of Makka Al-Mukarramah, which seek to combat an Islamophobia with designs to distort our religion.
>
> Consequently, we continue to strongly condemn all forms of extremism and dogmatism, which are incompatible with Islam, a religion of moderation and peaceful co-existence. It is in this vein that we support the dialogue of civilizations, and we believe that it is important to plan along such lines a preparatory phase by organizing a major international gathering on Islamic-Christian dialogue that involves governments, among other players.

The synod of October 2010 that brought together the Eastern Churches and the Vatican would be a step in this Muslim-Christian encounter. The glorification of Islam's perfection impregnates the Dakar Resolution, hoisted like an Islamic flag over the world:

> We are proud to proclaim, once again, to the entire world that the Ummah is fortunate, in the face of such challenges, to find in the Holy Quran's lofty teachings the right solutions to the problems currently besetting human societies. Islam, a religion of total devotion to Allah the Almighty, is also an irreplaceable vector of progress in this world, in that its message of human salvation encompasses all walks of life.

Such declarations of religious politics where religion impregnates politics are unthinkable in Judaism and Christianity. The saturation of all realms of life with Islam heightens the difficulties of integration for Muslim immigrants, supported by the OIC, in Western societies. As a result, multiculturalism becomes imperative.

Reference to the Koran as a source that provides solutions for every problem is a fundamental principle of the Muslim Brotherhood. Thus, in a 1997 study, the MB Deputy Chairman, Mohammad Ma'mun El-Hudaibi, wrote:

> The two basic sources of Islam are the Glorious Qur'an and the Sunna which is both a theoretical explanation and a practical application of the Glorious Qur'an. These two sources have become the sole reference point for everything relating to the ordering of the life of the Muslim family, individual, and community, as well as [for] the Muslim State all economic, social, political, cultural, educational, and also legislative and judicial activities. The Islamic creed and *Shari'ah* have ruled over the individual and society, the ruler and the ruled. They have had supreme authority and neither a ruler nor a ruled people could change anything they contained. [73]

In his speech at Dakar (2006), Secretary General E. Ihsanoglu confirmed this impression of monolithic force, prior to the US elections:

> The OIC General Secretariat gave utmost support to the roles of the OIC Ambassadorial Groups particularly in Geneva and New York towards more concerted action. Our Organization has assumed, with a deep sense of responsibility, the role of the legitimate representative and voice of the Muslim World on issues of dialogue among civilizations, interfaith dialogue, and combating the dangerously increasing trend of Islamophobia through dynamic

interaction with the international community, particularly with the UN, OSCE, Council of Europe, EU and Western governments. We have established strong ties with the centers of "think tanks" in Europe and the US to expose our views and values and defend our causes. [We have also succeeded in consolidating their vote in international bodies in a way that Muslims form a block on issues of crucial importance for the Islamic Ummah.] We have laid down bridges of communication with international media and press centers to project and propagate the voice of the Muslim world to Western societies in particular and to world public option in general.[74]

According to Ihsanoglu, it is Israel that provokes successive crises in order to block the peace process—it is not the election by Gaza residents of Hamas, which vows to destroy Israel and whose genocidal charter calls for killing all Jews:

> The situation in Palestine remains deplorable, due to the successive crisis fabricated by Israel to stall the peace process and to thwart the many peace plans and initiatives proposed by the international community. We have condemned these practices. We firmly believe that it is becoming indispensable that these aggressions and heinous crimes be officially documented and that their perpetrators be brought before international justice authorities designed for this kind of act committed in impunity, such as the International Criminal Court.

This decision took the form of intensive and indiscriminate rocket attacks by Hamas on Israel. It lasted seven years and provoked Operation Cast Lead, during which armed Hamas fighters hid among the civilian population. Consequently, a committee presided by Judge Richard Goldstone presented its biased report to the UN in October 2009, which he later regretted.

In June 2008, OIC foreign affairs ministers gathered in Kampala, Uganda. Their resolutions reasserted the centrality of the al-Quds cause for the Ummah and demanded the withdrawal of Israel to the 1949 armistice lines.[75] The ministers asked the OIC Secretariat to plan conferences and seminars with international and regional organizations on the historic Islamic boundaries of al-Quds and on the means of foiling the attempts by the "Israeli occupiers" to modify them. But neither Jerusalem nor any town or region of Palestine is mentioned in the Koran or Sunna. Only the Bible recounts the history of this land linked to the people of Israel, beginning more than two millennia before the Koran and the birth of Muhammad. This reality, perfectly well known in Europe, should bar calling the Israelis "occupiers" of Jerusalem or anywhere else in their country.

At this 2008 meeting the OIC ministers declared their support for the Arab League resolution to consider al-Quds as the Arab cultural capital for the year 2009. They invited the Vatican, Eastern churches and other Christian congregations to participate in the struggle against Judaization, on the principle of "land for peace." In fact, this principle is the foundation of jihad, since non-Muslims obtain the peace of dhimmitude only by ceding their country to Muslim aggressors. UN General Assembly Resolution 242 of November 29, 1967, cited here, does not mention "occupied Arab territories"—a phrase appearing later— and neither does it demand the creation of an Arab Palestine nor even mention the Palestinian people.

On the subject of Cyprus, the OIC ministers recalled a resolution on the situation in Cyprus adopted by the 31st session of the Islamic Conference of Ministers of Foreign Affairs (ICMFA) held in Istanbul (June 14–16, 2004). This resolution approved the participation of the "Turkish Muslim people of Cyprus in the OIC under the name of the Turkish Cypriot State." It is clear that the model of Palestine is being applied to Cyprus, Armenia, Kashmir and other regions that had been Islamized and subsequently liberated by their pre-Islamic indigenous peoples. Thus, the creation of a Palestinian people from 1968, the incarnation of imperialist Arab-Muslim irredentism, is repeated in the context of the Turkish conquest:

> **Reaffirming** the previous resolutions of the Islamic Conferences on the question of Cyprus which express firm support for the rightful cause of the Turkish Muslim people of Cyprus who constitute an integral part of the Islamic world;
> 4. **Calls upon** the Member-states to strengthen effective solidarity with the Turkish Muslim people of Cyprus, closely associating with them, and with a view to helping them materially and politically to overcome the inhuman isolation which has been imposed upon them, to increase and expand their relations in all fields. [. . .]
> 7. **Reaffirms** its previous decision to support (until the Cyprus problem is solved) the rightful claim of the Turkish Muslim people of Cyprus for the right to be heard in all international fora where the Cyprus problem comes up for discussion, on the basis of equality of the two parties in Cyprus. [76]
>
> **Gravely concerned** over the aggression by the Republic of Armenia against the Republic of Azerbaijan, which has resulted in the occupation of about 20 percent of the territories of Azerbaijan. [. . .]

3. **Strongly condemns** any looting and destruction of the archeological, cultural and religious monuments in the occupied territories of Azerbaijan.

4. **Strongly demands** the strict implementation of the UN Security Council resolutions and the immediate, unconditional and complete withdrawal of Armenian forces from all occupied Azerbaijan territories, including the Nagorno-Karabakh region and strongly urges Armenia to respect the sovereignty and territorial integrity of the Republic of Azerbaijan. [. . .]

7. **Urges all** States to refrain from providing any supplies of arms and military equipment to Armenia in order to deprive the aggressor of any opportunity to escalate the conflict and to continue the occupation of the Azerbaijani territories. The territories of the Member States should not be used for transit of such supplies.[77]

On the subject of India, the ministers noted "the Indian attempt to malign the legitimate Kashmiri freedom struggle by denigrating it as terrorism" and demanded that they be involved in the process of dialogue between India and Pakistan. The ministers called on India to cease its massive violations of human rights in the state of Jammu and Kashmir.

> **Expressing concern** at the alarming increase in the indiscriminate use of force and gross violation of human rights of [sic]committed against innocent Kashmiris and regretting that India had not allowed the OIC fact-finding mission to visit Indian occupied Jammu and Kashmir or responded favorably to the offer of the Good Offices made by the OIC;
>
> **Regretting** the restrictions imposed by the Indian government on the movement of the Kashmiri leaders in IoK [India occupied Kashmir];
>
> **Noting with regret** the Indian attempt to malign the legitimate Kashmiri freedom struggle by denigrating it as terrorism and **appreciating** that the Kashmiris condemn terrorism in all its forms and manifestations, including state sponsored terrorism. [. . .]
>
> 2. **Calls upon** India to cease forthwith the gross and systematic human right violations of the Kashmiri people and allow an impartial inquiry into the issue of more than 1000 nameless graves discovered in the Uri district of IoK.
>
> 3. **Further calls upon** India to allow international human rights groups and humanitarian organizations to visit Jammu and Kashmir.
>
> 4. **Affirms** that any political process/elections held under foreign occupation cannot be a substitute to the exercise of the right of self-determination by people of Kashmir as provided in the relevant Security Council resolutions and reaffirmed in the Millennium Declaration of the UN General Assembly. [. . .]
>
> 11. **Recommends** that OIC should initiate to issue annual report of the human rights situation in Indian occupied Jammu and Kashmir.

12. **Recommends** that Member-states continue to coordinate their positions in international forums and mandates the OIC Contact Group on Jammu and Kashmir to meet regularly alongside the session of the UN General Assembly, the UN Human Rights Council and the Sub-commission on Promotion and Protection of Human Rights, as well as at the OIC ministerial meetings. [78]

Three months later in Europe (October 2008), the second International Conference for Intercultural Education and Dialogue was held in Copenhagen, co-organized by the Danish Center for Culture and Dialogue, the Danish Ministry of Foreign Affairs, UNESCO, the OIC Secretariat, ISESCO (Islamic Educational, Scientific and Cultural Organization), the Alliance of Civilizations, the Anna Lindh Foundation, and the Council of Europe. In his speech, OIC Secretary General Ihsanoglu expressed hope that the conference would open a new era to promote intercultural dialogue, inter-religious understanding, and constructive dialogue. OIC participation in the conference, he explained, responded to the wishes of its member states desirous of curbing the growing current of prejudice, disinformation, stereotypes, discrimination and intolerance aimed at Muslims and their religion. They hoped to diminish or eliminate the sources of confrontation between the West and the Muslim world by means of intercultural and inter-religious dialogues, in cooperation with international and regional organizations and Western countries.

Ihsanoglu insisted on the importance of education and human rights for OIC countries without clarifying that these rights must conform to the prescriptions of *shari'a*, a principle that had been confirmed in Dakar. He affirmed that the countries of the OIC respected freedom of expression and human rights, and forbade incitement to religious hatred at the national level—an assertion that is verified neither in law nor by the facts. He declared that freedom of expression should not serve as an alibi for extremists in either the Muslim world or the West, for these extremists are opposed to diversity and to common peace efforts.

According to him, cooperation and consensus on this point required empathy, compassion, comprehension, respect, human rights and international law. He was very optimistic about the collaboration of the Islamic Educational, Scientific and Cultural Organization (ISESCO) [79] with UNESCO, and the cooperation of the Center for Research in Islamic History, Art and Culture (IRCICA) with the Council of Europe in the realm of history teaching. He declared,

> I am particularly interested in projects which will lead to the correct depiction
> of our common past in a way to clarify that Islam is not alien but an integral
> part of the past, present and future of Europe in all fields of human endeavor,
> and how Islamic civilization and culture has contributed to the creation of
> modern Europe. [80]

Repeated since 1967, such proposals aim at imposing on Europe a fully justifiable and legal immigration with its culture, customs, and jurisdiction. In a word, Islam is coming back into its own in Europe—and those Europeans who oppose its return are considered racists and Islamophobes who must be fought.

A year later, Denmark's former Prime Minister Anders Fogh Rasmussen became NATO's new Secretary General (August 1, 2009). Turkey opposed his nomination on the pretext that he refused to apologize for the Danish cartoons, although he disapproved of them. Ankara dropped its opposition after a guarantee that he would reach out to the Muslim world and a pledge from President Barack Obama that Turkish commanders would be present in the alliance's command, and that one of Rasmussen's deputies would be a Turk.

While in Turkey to discuss with Turkish Prime Minister Recep Tayyip Erdogan NATO operations in Afghanistan and to improve relations with the Muslim world, Rasmussen declared at an *iftar*, the evening meal breaking the fast during the month of Ramadan:

> Please see my presence here tonight as a clear manifestation of my respect for
> Islam as one of the world's greatest religions.

On this occasion Erdogan criticized terrorist acts carried out in the name of Islam and urged greater respect for Muslims in the West. Pushing for Turkey's EU membership, he said,

> If the European Union desires to be a global actor, the home for an alliance of
> civilizations, then Turkey must take its place within the Union.

Erdogan and Davutoglu, his minister of foreign affairs, proposed to Rasmussen that NATO establish close contacts with the fifty-six members of the OIC. They asked Rasmussen to organize a joint conference of NATO and the OIC to dispel misunderstandings between the Western and Muslim worlds. Ankara was also working on a proposal to establish an institutional communication mechanism between the two organizations. [81]

The Turkish newspaper *Today's Zaman* (Ankara) reported on October 1, 2010, that Rasmussen "suggested that the EU should conclude a security agreement with Turkey, give Turkey special status in the European Defence Agency (EDA) and involve it in decision-making on EU security missions." As Ankara wants to be consulted further regarding European security policy, Rasmussen, according to the newspaper, "has criticized the EU for its "unfair treatment" of Turkey, while urging the EU to give more say to Ankara on military matters.[82]

NOTES

1. Collection of acts and words attributed to the Prophet Muhammad, constituting a sacred source of Muslim law.

2. Ali Merad, *Le califat, une autorité pour l'islam?* (Paris: Desclée de Brower, 2008), 179.

3. Since 1974 the OIC has adopted the MB policy introduced by Said Ramadan of creating a network of Islamic centers in Europe's main cities, reveil-des-consciences.over-blog.com/article-dr-said-ramadan--les-prieres-avant-le-pouvoir-37316496.html (accessed September 19, 2010); see also Bat Ye'or, *Eurabia: The Euro-Arab Axis* (Madison, N.J.: Fairleigh Dickinson University Press, 2005), 68.

4. Bat Ye'or, *Islam and Dhimmitude: Where Civilizations Collide* (Madison, N.J.: Fairleigh Dickinson University Press), 2002.

5. Bassam Tibi, "War and Peace in Islam" in *Islamic Political Ethics. Civil Society, Pluralism, and Conflict*, ed. Sohail H. Hashmi, with a foreword by Jack Miles (Princeton, N.J.: Princeton University Press, 2002), 175–93.

6. Hassan Albanna, *To What Do We Invite Humanity*, Ikhwanweb—Cairo, Egypt, www.ikhwanweb.com/Article.asp?ID=804&LevelID=1&SectionID=117 (accessed September 19, 2010).

7. Albanna, *To What Do We Invite Humanity*; See also www.memriiwmp.org/content/en/report.htm?report=2877 (accessed September 19, 2010).

8. Bat Ye'or, *Islam and Dhimmitude*, 319.

9. Bat Ye'or, "Le dialogue Euro-Arabe et la naissance d'Eurabia," *Observatoire du monde juif*, Bulletin no. 4/5, December 2002, 44–55. Translated into English as "The Euro-Arab Dialogue and The Birth of Eurabia," at www.dhimmitude.org/d_today_eurabia.html (accessed September 19, 2010).

10. Bat Ye'or, *Eurabia*, published in English (2005), French (2006), Italian (2007), Dutch (2007), and Hebrew (2008).

11. In 1967 the European bodies founded during the 1950s by six Member States—the European Coal and Steel Community (ECSC), the European Economic Community (EEC) or Common Market, and European Atomic Energy Community (EURATOM)—were placed under a single European Commission and named the European Communities, which during the 1980s became known simply as the European Community (EC). Out of this, in 1993, the Treaty of Maastricht established the European Union (EU), currently composed of twenty-seven countries. In EU literature, there is a supersessionist tendency to refer to earlier forms by a current

term (e.g., speaking of the period 1945–1959, "The European Union [sic] is set up with the aim of ending the frequent and bloody wars between neighbours." See europa.eu/abc/history/index_ en.htm, accessed September 19, 2010). Herein, "EC" refers to pre-Maastricht Europe.

12. See section on "Terrorism and Europe's Mediterranean Policy."

13. Summit Meeting of the heads of State or government of EU member countries, including the EU Commission president.

14. Bat Ye'or, *Eurabia*, 41–46.

15. Ian Johnson, *A Mosque in Munich, Nazis, the CIA, and the Rise of the Muslim Brotherhood in the West* (New York: Houghton Mifflin Harcourt, 2010). All my information on this subject has been taken from this innovative and extremely well-documented book. The Hamburg mosque used by the 9/11 hijackers was closed on August 2010 as it remained a source of violent indoctrination.

16. Johnson, *A Mosque in Munich*, xvi.

17. Bat Ye'or, *Eurabia*, 44. In June 1967 Israel had just won the Six-Day War against its three neighboring countries, Egypt, Syria and Jordan. Incensed by this victory, de Gaulle promoted a full Arabophile policy.

18. *Bulletin de la Ligue Arabe. Centre d'Informations Arabes*, Genève, no date or number.

19. Document titled: *1974–1994 Association Parlementaire pour la Coopération Euro-Arabe*, coming from this Association's archives and provided to the author on a person's initiative. In 1994 the Association was reorganized in Brussels within the organization Medea, supported and financed by the European Community. See its site.

20. In 1958 François Genoud, a Swiss Nazi, founded in Geneva the Commercial Arab Bank which managed the business of key German Nazis, the Algerian leaders of the Algerian National Liberation Front (FLN), and Palestinian terrorists supported by the FLN. Admirer of Hitler and the Nazi war criminals, especially those responsible for the genocide of the Jews, he devoted his life after the war to help the Palestinian terrorist gangs. See Pierre Péan, *L'Extrémiste, François Genoud, de Hitler à Carlos* (Paris: Fayard, 1996).

21. Two French books examine in detail the postwar connections of European ex-Nazis and Arab leaders and their funding of the Palestinian terrorists movements through a Swiss banker, François Genoud. See Karl Laske, *Le banquier noir: François Genoud* (Paris: Seuil, 1996); and Pierre Péan, *L'Extrémiste, François Genoud de Hitler à Carlos* (Paris: Fayard, 1996). See also Klaus-Michael Mallman and Martin Cuppers, *Nazi Palestine. The Plans for the Extermination of the Jews in Palestine* (New York: Enigma Books, 2010); see also in German the recent publications of Klaus Gensicke and Gerhard Hopp.

22. Edward Said, *Orientalism* (London: Routledge & Kegan Paul, 1978). Two recent books examine Edward Said's work: Ibn Warrak, *Defending the West: A Critique of Edward Said's Orientalism* (Amherst, N.Y.: Prometheus Books, 2007) and Michael Curtis, ed., *Orientalism and Islam* (Cambridge: Cambridge University Press, 2009).

23. Minutes of these meetings are reproduced in *Documents d'Actualité Internationale. Ministère des Affaires Etrangères*, Paris. A larger bibliography will be found in Bat Ye'or, *Eurabia*, and since 1994 at www.medea.be.

24. *Arab Interparliamentary union (UIPA)* Arab Inter-parliamentary Union–News, at www. arab-ipu.org/english/(accessed September 19, 2010): "The Arab Inter-parliamentary Union (AIPU) is an Arab parliamentary organization composed of parliamentary groups representing Arab Parliaments . It was born in the wake of the October war of 1974, as a result of the atmosphere of Arab solidarity and Arab joint action, which encouraged Arab cooperation through political, professional and other institutions. "

25. Joint Resolution of the Nine countries of the EEC in Brussels November 6, 1973, followed by the Declaration of the Nine, London June 29, 1977 and the Venice Declaration, June 1980.

26. "Common Strategy of the European Council of 19 June 2000 on the Mediterranean Region (2000/458/CFSP)," *Official Journal of the European Communities*, 22.7.2000, pp. L 183/5-/10. eur-lex.europa.eu/LexUriServ/LexUriServ.do?uri=CELEX:32000E0458:EN:HTML (accessed September 20, 2010).

27. In January 2004, an exhibition in Stockholm glorified, through subway posters, a female suicide bomber who had massacred twenty-one people in a Christian restaurant in Haifa. See Bat Ye'or, *Eurabia*, 259.

28. ESDP: European Security and Defence Policy. Parentheses in the text.

29. Translated from the French at *Les institutions communes aux trois piliers—La Commission des Communautés européennes*. See www.diplomatie.gouv.fr/fr/europe_828/union-europeenne-monde_13399/politique-etrangere-securite-commune_851/fonctionnement-pesc_15060/les-institutions-communes-aux-trois-piliers_15061/commission-communautes-europeennes_40924.html (accessed September 20, 2010).

30. www.diplomatie.gouv.fr/fr/europe_828/union-europeenne-monde_13399/politique-etrangere-securite-commune_851/est-pesc_15055/les-objectifs-pesc_15102/les-objectifs-pesc_41284.html (accessed September 20, 2010).

31. Organization for Security and Cooperation in Europe.

32. International Financial Institutions.

33. The U.S. press had widely commented on the resurgence of antisemitism in Europe. American Congressmen and Senators intervened directly with Solana and Prodi in 2003, viz. Bat Ye'or, *Eurabia*, 127.

34. See Bat Ye'or, *Eurabia*, for the references to numerous articles detailing these events.

35. *. A Secure Europe in a Better World: European Security Strategy*, Brussels, 12 December 2003, 3, ue.eu.int/uedocs/cmsUpload/78367.pdf (accessed September 20, 2010).

36. *Guide de la PESC*, Ministère des Affaires Etrangères, Paris, p. 11.

37. Laske, *Le banquier noir: François Genoud*, 264. See also Xavier Rauffer, *La Nébuleuse: le terrorisme du Moyen-Orient* (Paris: Fayard,1987).

38. Aldo Cazzullo, *Corriere della Sera*, July 8, 2008. See also Menahem Ganz, *Israel News*, August 17, 2008.

39. Interview book by journalist Giovanni Fasanella and Rosario Priore, *Intrigo Internazionale*, Chiarelettere, Milan 2010.

40. Caroline B. Glick, "The Ironies of the West's Collusion with the Arabs and Iran," July 10, 2008, www.jewishworldreview.com/1008/glick100708.php3 (accessed September 20, 2010).

41. Popular Front for the Liberation of Palestine, founded in 1967.

42. Glick, "The Ironies of the West's Collusion with the Arabs and Iran." For collusion with France, cf. Enyo, *Anatomie d'un désastre, l'Occident, l'islam et la guerre au XXIe siècle* (Paris: Denoël, 2009), 238.

43. Davide Frattini, *Corriere della Sera*, August 14, 2008.

44. Laske, *Le banquier noir: François Genoud*, 277.

45. Bat Ye'or, *Eurabia*, 89.

46. Laske, *Le banquier noir: François Genoud*, 277.

47. Jean Bourdeillette, *Pour Israël* (Paris: Seghers, 1968, 246.

48. Laske, *Le banquier noir: François Genoud*, 278.

49. Bourdeillette, *Pour Israël*, 242.

50. *Guide*, 32.

51. Med Union: Empa Asks Foreign Ministers for More Powers (Ansamed), Brussels, October 13, 2008.

52. *Guide*, 13, parentheses in the text.

53. *A Secure Europe in a Better World*, 9.

54. Hubert Védrine, former Socialist minister of Foreign Affairs, notoriously called the United States a hyper-power. "To Paris, U.S. Looks Like a 'Hyperpower.'" *The International Herald Tribune*. February 5, 1999, www.nytimes.com/1999/02/05/news/05iht-france.t_0.html (accessed September 21, 2010).

55. Europa, Activities of the European Union, Summaries of Legislation, europa.eu/legislation_summaries/justice_freedom_security/fight_against_terrorism/r00004_en.htm (accessed September 21, 2010).

56. Europa, Activities of the European Union, Summaries of Legislation.

57. Communication from the Commission to the Council and the European Parliament, "The European Union and the United Nations: The Choice of Multilateralism," Brussels, October 9, 2003 [COM(2003) 526 final—Not published in the *Official Journal*], 5. eur-lex.europa.eu/LexUriServ/LexUriServ.do?uri=COM:2003:0526:FIN:EN:DOC (accessed September 21, 2010).

58. Communication from the Commission to the Council and the European Parliament, "The European Union and the United Nations," 4.

59. Council of Europe, assembly.coe.int/Main.asp?link=/Documents/Records/2005/E/0510041500E.htm#7 (accessed September 21, 2010). In fact the NAM (Non-Aligned Movement) counts 118 countries.

60. For the assertion of a universal civilization as opposed to differentiated cultural developments, see chapter 2.

61. www.oic-oci.org/ex-summit/english/prep-docs.htm (accessed September 21, 2010).

62. The Third Extraordinary Session, Secretary General's Report, "New Vision for the Muslim World: Solidarity in Action," Presented at the Third Extraordinary Session of the Islamic Summit Conference, www.oic-oci.org/ex-summit/english/sg-report.htm (accessed September 21, 2010).

63. Ten-Year Programme of Action to Meet the Challenges Facing the Muslim Ummah in the 21st Century, www.oic-oci.org/ex-summit/english/10-years-plan.htm (accessed September 21, 2010).

64. Final Communiqué of the Third Extraordinary Session of the Islamic Summit Conference—"Meeting the challenges of the 21st century, solidarity in action," www.oic-oci.org/ex-summit/english/fc-exsumm-en.htm (accessed September 21, 2010).

65. The Third Extraordinary Session, Secretary General's Report, "New Vision for the Muslim World: Solidarity in Action."

66. Bruno Waterfield, "Don't Confuse Terrorism with Islam, says EU." Telegraph.co.uk, March 31, 2007, www.telegraph.co.uk/news/worldnews/1547133/Dont-confuse-terrorism-with-Islam-says-EU.html (accessed September 21, 2010). See also Council of the European Union, *Partial Declassification—Annex*. register.consilium.europa.eu/pdf/en/07/st05/st05469-re03ex01.en07.pdf (accessed September 21, 2010); and European Parliament, *Parliamentary Questions — Reply*, www.europarl.europa.eu/sides/getAllAnswers.do?reference=E-2007-3587&language=EN (accessed September 21, 2010).

67. Stephanie Coudron, "Terrorism Phrase Book to Put Officials on Guard," *The Times*, London, April 2, 2008.

68. "Recommendations of the OIC Commission of Eminent Persons (C.E.P.)," Saudi Arabia, 5-6 Dhoul Qaada 1426/ December 7–8, 2005, www.oic-oci.org/ex-summit/english/em-persons-rep.htm (accessed September 21, 2010).

69. This assertion was made by a Palestinian, Ismail Raji al-Faruqi; see Bat Ye'or, *Eurabia*, p. 221.

70. OIC, The Executive Committee Meetings, www.oic-oci.org/page_detail.asp?p_id=193 (accessed May 3, 2009). The OIC Executive Committee is composed of: (a) The OIC Summit Troika comprising Malaysia; State of Qatar and the Republic of Senegal; (b) The OIC Troika of the Islamic Conference of Foreign Ministers (ICFM) comprising the Republic of Yemen; Republic of Turkey; Republic of Azerbaijan; (c) The Foreign Minister of the Kingdom of Saudi Arabia, the host country; and (d) The OIC Secretary General.

71. Final Communiqué adopted by the First Ministerial Meeting of the Executive Committee of the Organization of the Islamic Conference (OIC Troikas) Jeddah—Kingdom of Saudi Arabia, 15 Safar 1427h (March 15, 2006), §7, www.oic-oci.org/english/conf/exec/OIC%20TROIKAS%20-%20En.pdf (accessed September 21, 2010).

72. OIC, 11th session of the Islamic Summit Conference—Dakar Declaration, March 13–14, 2008, www.oic-oci.org/is11/english/DAKAR-DEC-11SUMMIT-E.pdf (accessed September 21, 2010).

73. *The Principles of the Muslim Brotherhood*, www.ikhwanweb.com/Article.asp?ID=813&LevelID=2&SectionID=116 (accessed May 3, 2009).

74. www.oic-oci.org/is11/english/SG-speech-sum.pdf (viewed May 3, 2009). Sentence in brackets from the French translation of the same quotation but omitted in the English.

75. "Resolutions on the cause of Palestine, The City of al-Qods Al-Sharif, and The Arab-Israeli Conflict," adopted by the Thirty-Fifth Session of the Council of Foreign Ministers (Session of Prosperity and Development) Kampala, Republic of Uganda 14–16 Jumadal Thani 1429H (June 18–20, 2008), www.oic-oci.org/35cfm/english/res/35CFM--PAL-RES-FINAL.pdf (accessed May 3, 2009).

76. Oic/Cfm-35/2008/Pol/Res/Final, "Resolutions on Political Affairs," adopted by the Thirty-Fifth Session of the Council of Foreign Ministers (Session of Prosperity and Development) Kampala Republic of Uganda 14–16 Jumada Al-Thani 1429H (June 18–20, 2008) Resolution No. 5/35-P on the Situation in Cyprus, 15–18, www.oic-oci.org/35cfm/english/res/35-CFM-%20RES-POL-FINAL.pdf (accessed May 3, 2009).

77. Oic/Cfm-35/2008/Pol/Res/Final, "Resolutions on Political Affairs," adopted by the Thirty-Fifth Session of the Council of Foreign Ministers (Session of Prosperity and Development) Kampala Republic of Uganda 14–16 Jumada Al-Thani 1429H (June 18–20, 2008) Resolution No. 6/35-P on the Aggression of the Republic of Armenia against the Republic of Azerbaijan, 19–22.

78. Oic/Cfm-35/2008/Pol/Res/Final, "Resolutions on Political Affairs," adopted by the Thirty-Fifth Session of the Council of Foreign Ministers (Session of Prosperity and Development) Kampala Republic of Uganda 14–16 Jumada Al-Thani 1429H (June 18–20, 2008) Resolution No. 2/35-P on the Jammu and Kashmir Dispute, 7–9.

79. See below for ISESCO publications.

80. Speech of His Excellency Prof. Ekmeleddin Ihsanoglu at the Copenhagen Meeting. 22 October 2008. www.oic-oci.org/topic_detail.asp?t_id=1548&x_key=(accessed May 3, 2009).

81. www.todayszaman.com/tz-web/news-185374-ankara-to-propose-joint-nato-oic-conference-in-talks-with-rasmussen.html (accessed August 28, 2009).

82. www.todayszaman.com/news-223147-rasmussen-pushes-eu-to-give-turkey-security-role.html (accessed October 1, 2010).

Chapter Two

Multiculturalism

DOMESTIC POLICIES OF THE EU

Multiculturalism developed within two different but interrelated European policies. The first was the European project in which multiculturalism represented an essential and positive instrument for constructing solidarity between member states of the European Community. Here multiculturalism referred to populations that shared the same values, the same culture and in particular the same desire for peace.

The second process was Euro-Arab integration around the Mediterranean. In this context, multiculturalism stemmed from the majority of Muslim immigrants' refusal to integrate into Western societies. Multiculturalism thus embodied a major element of Euro-Mediterranean common security and immigration policy, as it facilitated a way round that refusal. The modern notion of multiculturalism postulates the equivalence of all cultures (cultural relativism), and accordingly of the values they promote. It should be noted that this idea of equivalence exists solely in the West, whereas Islamic societies profess the superiority of theirs (Kor. III: 110),[1] which introduces asymmetry into the concept of multiculturalism, and effectively denies it.

Today multiculturalism is a fundamental element in inter-European and international policy. It determines the relations between Europe and Islam, while not doing so with other cultures, such as those of China, Japan, and India. The explanation lies in those verses of the Koran that prohibit Muslims from adopting the customs of non-Muslims, including Jews and Christians who are mentioned by name—and by the prohibition on accepting their ideas or becoming friendly with them (V: 51; 57). Multiculturalism allows Muslims emigrating to the West to retain their culture and customs on equal terms with those of the locals according to the principle of the equivalence of values and "diversity." This way they avoid an integration that is rigorously forbidden to them.

Ever since the 1970s, European countries and those of the Arab League have circumvented the obstacle of integration prohibited by the Koran by invoking multiculturalism. At the second Conference of the OIC in Lahore in 1974, the Secretary General of the Islamic Conference, Mohammed Hassan Mohammed al-Tuhami, had mentioned this problem. He spoke of an Islamic State that would endeavor to propagate Islam in non-Muslim countries, and he had invited Muslim experts to coordinate their efforts to create an intellectual renaissance that "would be a realization of our nation's hopes in building a broad solid base for this generation and coming ones."

He explained that this base would have to be built,

> of faithful and thoughtful men capable of leading the Islamic state in the various fields outstepping non-Muslim countries and saving future generations. Such leadership would set an example for those who wish to stem the tide of aberration and perdition and to protect the sons of our contemporary generation against the blind and meaningless limitation of the ways, customs and concepts of non-Muslims.[2]

Al-Tuhami had recommended at this conference Islamic finance regulated by *shari'a.* He had mentioned the creation of a European Islamic Council that would act as a coordinating body for all Islamic centers and institutions. It would help with the propagation throughout Europe of the true teachings of Islam and would reinforce the activities of *da'wa* and the establishment of Islamic cultural centers (p. 204).

Parliamentarians of PAEAC—loyal agents and disseminators of OIC policy in Europe—met in Strasbourg (June 7–8, 1975) and voted resolutions calling for:

> Recognizing the historical contribution of Arab culture to European development;
> Stressing the contribution that the European countries can still expect from Arab culture, notably in the area of human values. [. . .]

PAEAC demanded:

> [T]hat European governments make it possible for the Arab countries to create generous means to enable immigrant workers and their families to participate in Arab cultural and religious life [. . .]
> Asks the governments of the Nine to approach the cultural sector of the Euro-Arab Dialogue in a constructive spirit, and to accord the greatest priority to spreading Arab culture in Europe.[3]

The multiculturalism option was adopted by the EC following the massive waves of Muslim immigration that were encouraged by the official policy of the Euro-Arab Dialogue and expanded in the Barcelona Process (1995). The promoters of this social model extolled the example of the Arab and Ottoman empires where different ethnic and religious groups had coexisted. However, this argument is spurious because those Muslim empires applied solely Islamic law and only tolerated other religions in a form of servitude (dhimmitude) that attested to Muslim supremacy and the non-equivalence of cultures. Moreover, the existence of various ethnic groups within the Muslim empires was the result of Islamic conquests of foreign countries and their annexation as Islamic territory, with their populations expropriated and reduced to the status of dhimmitude. This situation, the result of jihadist wars for the Islamization of non-Muslim countries, differs totally from the current situation created by freely chosen immigration into sovereign European states.

At a less general level it should be noted that the European Union's adoption of multiculturalism contradicts its policy to standardize EU laws. The adoption of *shari'a* law introduces an alternative, religiously based jurisdiction into the EU, hostile to non-Muslims and contrary in its spirit and legislation to European laws.

In November 2000 at Doha, the OIC adopted a booklet entitled *Strategy of Islamic Cultural Action in the West,*[4] and re-titled after 2009 *The Strategy for Islamic Cultural Action outside the Islamic West.* There, ISESCO, one of the major organs of the OIC, states that "the Muslim immigrant communities in Europe are part of the Islamic nation," and that after the modification of the 1974 law,[5] "their second and third generations have made the existence of these communities permanent rather than temporary." The OIC considers it a duty to preserve the features of their places of origin and the special aspects of the identity of these immigrants in Europe (p. 5). On the strategic level, it recommends:

Strategic work: Aware that civilizational projects can materialize only when based on effective plans and strategies, the Organization [OIC] has laid down several guiding strategies for the Islamic world in the cultural, educational and technological fields. And knowing that the immigrant Islamic communities constitute part of the Islamic nation, the Organization has put forward this guiding policy for this community in the West so as to achieve certain objectives. (p. 7)

Thus, ISESCO works indefatigably to coordinate and unify the policies and attitudes about joint Islamic action to be undertaken in the West in the fields of education and culture, because

preserving identity requires a valid Islamic education. It also calls for carefully prepared programmes relating to education, guidance and social welfare from an Islamic perspective. (p. 10)

Muslims in Europe, then, should set up a uniform plan for the prospects of the Islamic presence there. This strategy should be targeted at providing the necessary conditions for individuals from the Muslim communities to occupy the key positions within host societies, in the economic, cultural, political or information fields.

These have been the main reasons which require setting up a strategy for cultural Islamic action especially designed for the Muslim communities in the West. (p. 16)

For ISESCO, the concept of different civilizations:

calls for awareness of the principles of Islamic civilisational peace, and for safeguarding Muslims' cultural identity against the pitfalls of ideological and political trends, which do not match our civilisational identity. [6]

The reference to an "Islamic peace" implies that it is somehow different from plain peace. ISESCO clarifies the link between culture and religion, which facilitates basing cultural strategy on faith:

the strategy concepts are based on *the Islamic referentiality* which views cultural actions as an act of worship, and not merely a set of skills and techniques, emphasizing thereby the spiritual dimension for the desired global development of Muslims. [7]

This ISESCO document will be examined in greater detail in chapter 4.

Multiculturalism is central to the policy of the Common Strategy of the European Council on the Mediterranean Region (June 19, 2000).[8] Although this document was officially valid till 2006, nevertheless it has implemented lasting cogs and mechanisms. Multiculturalism determines the EU's security strategy coordinated with the OIC and is integrated into an ideology that is being structured and imposed by lobbies created by the European Commission under the label of "representatives of the civil populations." Vested with a democratic appearance, these lobbies disseminate and implant within European populations the policies and action programs decided upon by the European Council and the Commission which concern them but about which they know nothing.

EUROPEAN CULTURE IN THE SERVICE OF *DA'WA*

The European Commission enthusiastically welcomed the recommendations of the OIC and its requests for cooperation and dialogue. European parliamentarians even anticipated its wishes. Strasbourg resolutions from the 1970s, extended by the many unofficial decisions of the Euro-Arab Dialogue, had already prepared the foundations for the Arab cultural penetration in the European Community. These policies were reinforced by the text and recommendations adopted by the Parliamentary Assembly of the Council of Europe on September 19, 1991.[9]

The Assembly called for wider cultural cooperation with non-governmental institutions and organizations such as the Western Institute of Islamic Culture in Madrid and the Institut du Monde Arabe in Paris. It requested the European Community Committee of Ministers to grant greater importance to the Islamic world in the intergovernmental activities program of the Council of Europe and in its recommendations to the governments of the member States (article 11). It also recommended increasing the number of Chairs in Arabic and Islam and the inclusion of Islam in the main university curricula. These requests were put into the Barcelona Declaration of 1995, which stated that the study of the Arab and Islamic sources of European civilization should appear in European school textbooks. Such steps would be accompanied by an increase in the number of translations and publications of Islamic works, both classic and modern. Museums should also play a major role in this context. As far as the media was concerned, the Assembly had decided that it must increase "the production, co-production and broadcast of radio and television programs on Islamic culture."

Ten years later at the Islamic Conference of Foreign Ministers in Istanbul (June 14, 2004), Walter Schwimmer, the Austrian Secretary General of the Council of Europe (September 1, 1999–August 31, 2004), declared: "The Islamic component is an integral part of the diversity of Europe." This was also the opinion developed in the ISESCO booklet on Islamic Cultural Strategy in Europe. Schwimmer proposed to the Foreign Ministers of the OIC countries to draw up joint projects on the topic of teaching history and religious diversity around the Mediterranean in order to contribute to the inter-cultural and inter-religious dialogue, adding that "the global threat of terrorism makes such dialogue more necessary than ever." It is clear that for the European Union the only response to terrorism is dialogue, which in the cultural field is understood as a European dhimmitude attitude for the servile promotion of Islamic culture.

In December 2004 the Council of Europe organized, together with UNESCO, the Arab League and Saudi Arabia a conference in Cairo on "The Image of Arab and Islamic Culture in European History Books." This Conference took place within the framework of the Euro-Arab Dialogue "Learning to Live Together," whose objective was an examination of negative stereotypes of Arab and Islamic culture conveyed by European history textbooks, with a view to removing them.

Worried about "the clash of civilizations," the European Commission favored a close association with the OIC. It launched the "Soul for Europe" among the large number of projects programmed for the media, television, literature and the arts. This project was conceived in 2002 and directly associated with the President of the European Commission at that time, Romano Prodi.[10] It brought together "civil society," scientists, academics, and representatives of the worlds of culture, politics and business with the objective of examining the European cultural scene. At the Berlin Conference (November 17–19, 2006), the participants, representatives of international cultural life, the economy and European politics, agreed upon the cultural dimension of Europe.[11]

Among the many objectives proposed, the initiators emphasized that Europe's cultural policy should provide support to its foreign policy in order to strengthen its position on the world scene. The cultural base would back up its strategy at the global level. It meant the subordination of culture to politics as with fascism, thereby emasculating culture of its attributes of freedom. In order to avoid a clash of civilizations, Richard von Weizsäcker, former German President, asked that Europe's cultural policy potentiality become the basis for its foreign policy. Quoting Javier Solana—Europe's High Representative for foreign policy and trustee of the conference—he stressed that Europe would do well to "act more intensively than in the past as a partner in the dialogue of cultures of the world." The conference adopted this position, in line with that of the OIC as stated in its ten-year action program. It deferred to Ihsanoglu's requests at its Wilton Park conference (March 2006) and to the Jeddah ministerial meeting the same month. The Berlin conference concluded that cultural action ought to be a basic factor in foreign policy and development, and that it would be promoted and applied as such.

Hans-Dietrich Genscher, the former German Foreign Minister, proposed the principle of "active tolerance" as a key value because it would ease the allegiance of immigrants to Europe and to its values rather than to the countries in which they settled. This idea, it was emphasized, had clear implications for naturalization.

In 1983 at the Hamburg Symposium of the Euro-Arab Dialogue, Genscher had declared that this Dialogue would be incomplete if its political aspect (European support for the Arab-Palestinian war against Israel) was ignored or treated lightly by the European Commission. He had then affirmed that the Joint Memorandum of the Euro-Arab Dialogue issued in Cairo in 1975 was the Dialogue's Charter. This Charter linked the two parties, the European Community and the Arab League, by a shared political will "which emerged at the highest level."[12] By that, he intended to confirm that the EC and the countries of the Arab League shared the same objectives in respect of Israel and America, and that the political part of the Dialogue, essential for the Arab side and on which all the Euro-Arab accords were based, should not be neglected in favor of the economic, cultural and social fields.[13]

The participants at the 2006 Berlin conference demanded the preparation of a European cultural charter. They wanted a program of actions and financing that would facilitate the permanent control of joint European policies and the resources allocated to culture. They stressed the role of culture in the maintenance of security and the need to improve measures for cultural inclusion and inter-cultural skills. Effectively this program confirmed the grip of security policy over culture.

Following this conference, the European Commission launched a rich program of cultural activities in all sectors. The Anna Lindh Foundation, associated with the Commission, was given the task of implementing it, and to prepare in 2008 the European Year of Intercultural Dialogue (ID). The Commission stated the unbreakable link between internal intercultural dialogue for member states of the EU and the promotion of dialogue between cultures and civilizations at the international level, and affirmed that the two fields complemented each other.

The Commission had already drawn up a long list of proposals that it had presented to the European Parliament and to the Council of Europe about the European Year of Intercultural Dialogue. [14] Among the scheduled initiatives in the cultural sections it mentioned citizenship, asylum policy, integration of immigrants, the fight against discrimination, social exclusion, racism, and xenophobia. It stipulated the importance of the Dialogue within the context of the Euro-Mediterranean Partnership on account of the countries of origin of many of the immigrants to the EU. This partnership included youth exchanges and programs about the cultural heritage. The highlight of these activities had been the creation in 2005 of the Anna Lindh Foundation, named after the Swedish foreign minister, who had been the most hostile European critic of Israel. At the Foundation's Alexandria headquarters, at the opening of the Library in November 2003, the Protocols of the Elders of Zion appeared alongside the Hebrew Bible to illustrate Jewish civilization.

In the summary of objectives and proposed activities, the Commission stated,

> To raise the awareness of European citizens, and all those living in the European Union, of the importance of developing active European citizenship which is open to the world, respectful of cultural diversity and based on common values in the European Union of respect for human dignity, liberty, equality, non-discrimination, solidarity, the principles of democracy and the rule of law as well as respect for human rights, including the rights of persons belonging to minorities. [15]

A note at the end of page 6 states that the target of this decision, the concept of "active European citizenship," does not only cover citizens of the EU as defined in Article 17 of the European Community Treaty, namely those belonging to member states, but also applies to anyone living permanently or temporarily in the European Union. The year would facilitate identifying projects that relate to the Intercultural Dialogue and to the development of synergies between these actions. It would be

> highlighting the contribution of different cultures to our heritage and ways of life; raising the awareness of European citizens and all persons living in the European Union, particularly young people, of the importance of seeking the means to use intercultural dialogue to realize an active European citizenship open to the world, respectful of cultural diversity and based on common values in the European Union. [16]

Allowing for the enlargement of the Union and the variety of cultures and peoples in the EU, the Commission stated that the Intercultural Dialogue was central to the European project. It authorized Europe to make its voice better heard in the world and to forge effective partnerships with neighboring countries—a formula that generally refers to the Mediterranean Arab countries. According to the Commission, the dialogue would allow the Union to extend the zone of stability and democracy beyond the EU and would influence the well-being and security of all those who lived there; it therefore represented an essential tool in various sectors, "combating discrimination and social exclusion, lifelong learning, combating racism and xenophobia, policy on asylum and the integration of immigrants, audiovisual policy and research."[17] Dialogue was a factor of increasing importance in the Union's "neighborhood policy."

The Commission's proposals were approved on December 18, 2006, and the European Parliament and the EU Council published a decision about the European Year of Intercultural Dialogue (2008).[18] Its contribution to achieve strategic and political priorities was stressed, as well as the importance in forging partnerships with the neighboring countries that would enhance Europe's well-being and security (§5). It was allocated a key role in the Community's policies and instruments in respect of various educational, social and political areas, in the fight against discrimination, social exclusion, racism, xenophobia, asylum policy and integration of immigrants (§6). The objectives of the Intercultural Dialogue would be achieved through the media, whose major importance would be reinforced by information and promotional campaigns aimed especially at young people and children at the national and Community levels. The carrying out of these activities was transferred to the Community (§19):

> Since the objectives of this Decision cannot be sufficiently achieved by the
> Member States and can therefore, by reason of the need, in particular, for
> multilateral partnerships and transnational exchanges on a Community scale,
> be better achieved at Community level, the Community may adopt measures,
> in accordance with the principle of subsidiarity as set out in Article 5 of the
> Treaty.

By these decisions the European Parliament confirmed the proposals of the
Secretary General of the OIC, especially those dealing with getting the media
and the new educational programs for children along the OIC's line. These
requests that introduced interference from the Muslim world into the fields of
information and education within the EU had already been formulated at the
Mecca Summit in December 2005.

The similarity of the OIC demands concerning immigration and the EU
decisions need to be emphasized. In Strasbourg in 2005, OIC Secretary General
Ihsanoglu had formulated a large number of demands, among which was
a revision of school syllabuses and the intercultural dialogue in all media by
means of information campaigns. He expressed the wish to stimulate a sense
of belonging and citizenship among Muslim youth in Europe, which matches
for example the concept of a European citizenship independent of that of the
EU member states and open to anyone. From this point of view, territoriality
vanishes within globalization, erasing ethnic, identity and cultural references
in the multiculturalism market. The High Level Advisory Group of the Anna
Lindh Foundation stated that the very concept of distinct, differentiated civilizations
needed to be abandoned in favor of an idea of global civilization that
values all cultures to the same degree.

Such cultural relativism is apparently demanded only of Europe, and can
be seen in an institutionalized form in Commission directives for educational
reform and the conceptualization of history. European culture and history,
scrupulously archived, examined and developed over millennia in scholarly
institutions, would lose their specific identity. This sell off was taking place
as the OIC announced in its ten-year program at its Mecca Summit (2005)
the strengthening of the world Ummah through the Koran and the Sunna, a
decision since reconfirmed at each of its subsequent Conferences. Further,
the OIC demanded that Europe recognize the immense contribution of Islamic
culture and civilization to Europe's development and to include it in
school and university syllabuses. Thus, on the one hand European history
and culture was minimized and erased, while on the other hand pride in an
Islamic mythical superiority led to cultural imperialism.

The obsession with dialogue as an antidote to all evils unites the EU and the OIC in a single cult. Hence, the statements and activity programs of the Commission could not satisfy more OIC claims, whose ten-year action program at its Mecca Summit quoted, as crucial elements of its strategy, the fight against both Islamophobia and Israel. Seizing on the Danish cartoons affair, OIC Secretary General Ihsanoglu succeeded in reversing the situation. He spirited away Islamic terrorism in Europe, creating from international podiums a campaign against Islamophobia in the West. Sacrilege practiced against the sacred symbol of Islam thus supplanted the terrorist crimes and threats against Europeans.

Several months before the Berlin Conference on the Intercultural Year, the OIC had organized a mega-conference at Wilton Park (London, May 2–3, 2006) to denounce Islamophobia in Europe. In his opening speech, Ihsanoglu declared that Muslims and their religion were being increasingly stereotyped, defamed, marginalized, discriminated and targeted by hate crimes since 9/11 and the terrorist attacks in Madrid (2004) and London (2005). In his opinion, there was a strong link between Islamophobia in the West and anti-Western feelings in the Muslim world. Through this false equivalence he erased the religious and historical bases of hatred against non-Muslims in both jihad and dhimmitude.

As part of the Muslim sense of being victimized, the speaker claimed that Muslims were victims of the Islamophobia of Westerners and their biased policy in favor of Israel. "In addition to the perceived biased Middle East policies of the U.S. and European countries, the rising trend of Islamophobia is giving a boost to the anti-Western sentiments in the Islamic world." Insensitive to the insecurity of Europeans struck by terrorist attacks, the speaker continued, "What is this terrifying stereotyping we suffer in the first decade of the 21st century? This is a phenomenon that reminds us of the horrible experiences of the anti-Semitism of the 1930s."[19] It would be hard to imagine a more cynical speech than this. In fact, not only the Arab world had supported Nazism and its anti-Jewish, genocidal policies, but the accusation of European and U.S. pro-Israeli bias in the Middle East reveals the enormous pressures the OIC is exerting on the West to impose its anti-Israeli policy.

MULTICULTURALISM AND THE ANNA LINDH FOUNDATION

Achieving the objectives of the Common Strategy on the Mediterranean Region's plan implied EU rapprochement with the Arab Mediterranean countries. In October 2003 in Brussels, a group of eighteen people called the High-Level Advisory Group (HLAG),[20] created by Romano Prodi, submitted its report entitled *Dialogue Between Peoples and Cultures in the Euro-Mediterranean Area.*

The report answered questions posed by Prodi as part of a policy that sought to create a prosperity zone characterized by peaceful Euro-Arab relations.[21] This study created a strategy that sought to structure a Euro-Arab symbiosis in all sectors of the EU. The general tone of the report suggested a sort of guilty feeling on the part of Europe regarding the Arab Mediterranean countries. It recommended that the EU adopt measures intended to link civil societies with the policies needed to put an end to "the discriminations from which European citizens of immigrant origin still too often suffer, and to the persistent situation of injustice, violence, and insecurity in the Middle East [. . .]." This sentence refers to the Palestinian-as-victim syndrome that the OIC blames on Europe, and whose solution it seeks through constant threats and pressure. On the other hand, the oppression of native Christians and other non-Muslims in Muslim countries, the almost daily incitement to genocidal hatred against the Jews—especially in the 1988 Hamas Charter and even in the media and on television—and the permanent violation by Palestinian terrorism of Israelis' basic rights to security, constitute human tragedies that are too trivial to deserve mention. Here can be noted the permanence of two, related formative themes of Eurabia: the claims of Muslim immigrants in Europe blended with increased condemnation of the State of Israel which allegedly creates antisemitism there.

The ambiguous term "civil societies" refers to European propagandists mandated by the EU to form public opinion through activities subsidized by governments to support their policy. Blaming Europe, which is repeated in the report, is justified by the Prodi approach, which consists of asking, "What can we do, as Europeans, to erase the hostility of the Arab-Muslim world towards us?" This effectively means accusing oneself of the hostility through which one is victimized.

The Report of the High Level Advisory Group recommends the merger of the two sides of the Mediterranean through the emergence of a multicultural, Mediterranean society that would create a joint civilization. This involves inculcating the people of both North and South with the awareness that they share a common destiny by providing them with a convergence of interests, values, and political priorities that would trigger the union of the two shores. To this end the Advisory Group proposed a program that would permeate every aspect of relations between the peoples around the Mediterranean with the spirit of the Dialogue between Peoples and Cultures. It would penetrate the social fabric and ensure a strong, real mutual commitment not just between governments and institutions, but also between citizens and peoples.

The question can here be asked if the Europeans want to feel solidarity with those who condemn women to being recluses, refuse equality with non-Muslims, deny historic rights to religious and ethnic minorities in their own Islamized countries, advocate the destruction of Israel, and are opposed to all Western political, social and cultural institutions, such as secularism, equality of rights and independence of the justice system. Does the Advisory Group want to make Europeans adhere to the hate-filled fanaticism of Hamas and Hizbullah and their crimes; to the anti-Christian and anti-Jewish racism in many Muslim countries; to the violence against apostate Muslims and free-thinkers; to the persecution of the Bahai whose pacifist religion is proscribed in Muslim countries; and to the justification for dictatorial systems and terrorism? Why should they associate with people who venerate jihad as a just holy war, and invoke religious precepts to destroy the West?

The report spells out the formative, key principles that will cement this Mediterranean civilization. These are equality, respect for others, freedom of conscience, social solidarity, and knowledge. However, the text does not explain the means to inculcate these marvelous principles in peoples governed by *shari'a*, with which they are incompatible. In these societies the non-Muslim is neither respected nor equal to a Muslim, while freedom of conscience and knowledge are determined by the standards of *shari'a*. Thus the Cairo Declaration on Human Rights in Islam adopted in August 1990 by the OIC states that all humans form a single family, they are united in submission to Allah, and descended from Adam. This is the definition of the Ummah, the Muslim community united by its submission to Allah, namely by Islam.[22] The article stipulates the rights and obligations of the members of this family, their equality without discrimination of race, color, sex, religion or other considerations, ending with the enigmatic statement, "True faith is the guarantee for enhancing such dignity along the path to human perfection." Yet Islam is the sole, true faith.

Article 2 stipulates that life is a God-given gift that should be protected "and it is prohibited to take away life except for a Shari'a prescribed reason." Safety from bodily harm is a guaranteed right protected by the state and "it is prohibited to breach it without a Shari'a prescribed reason" (2.d). Article 10 declares, "Islam is the religion of unspoiled nature. It is prohibited to exercise any form of compulsion on man or to exploit his poverty or ignorance in order to convert him to another religion or to atheism." Probably this sibylline phrase refers to the belief founded on the Sunna that every child is born Muslim (*fitra*), and hence his conversion to another religion is forbidden. As for freedom of conscience and knowledge, Article 16 states that any scientific, literary, artistic, or technical work is protected "provided that such production is not contrary to the principles of Shari'a." Articles 24 and 25 declare that "All the rights and freedoms stipulated in this Declaration are subject to the Islamic Shari'a," and "The Islamic Shari'a is the only source of reference for the explanation or clarification to any of the articles of this Declaration."

In 2000 the Muslim World League held an international symposium in Rome on February 25–27 on human rights in Islam, at which there were about 200 delegates from 43 countries.[23] It was stated that the symposium sought to offer improvements to existing legislation and that Islam, a religion founded on human rights and the duties of the individual, had a fundamental contribution to make to the international debate on human rights. After having studied current agreements, the delegates concluded that "their essence" was insufficient for the development of the world. By "essence" they meant a religious underpinning. They also launched an appeal to the governments of the world and to international organizations to modify international declarations and human rights conventions. They called on governments of the earth to bear in mind the following principles that were considered by the symposium to be an inherent guarantee of human rights:

- Human rights should respect religious beliefs and values ordained by God through his prophets and apostles.

This formulation is typically Islamic and does not exist in the two other monotheistic religions, where prophets and apostles do not have the role accorded them by Islam.

- Rights should be linked with duties, balancing man's functions and needs to build a family and society and "inhabit the earth" in a manner that does not contravene God's will.

This principle derives its inspiration from the Koran and presupposes that people are aware of this will in order to conform to it, apparently as stated in the Koran and the hadiths.

- Dialogue between different cultures and civilizations should be encouraged as a means of promoting a better understanding of human rights, protecting mankind against the horrors of armed conflict.
- Every effort should be made to eliminate discrimination based on race, color, language, or nationality.

This last principle does not mention religion. However, the following sentence explains this omission by stating the symposium's objective: to affirm that submission to Islamic law guarantees human understanding and international stability because human rights are truly rooted in Islamic law. Here it can be seen that human rights combine with religious and political proselytizing, a principle totally at odds with the Universal Declaration.

The Islamic symposium of Rome ended with twelve declarations, of which we summarize a few.

- "Islam is both a faith and a law (*Shari'a*). It provides a comprehensive framework for man's life on earth, establishing justice, protecting the dignity of man and assuring his peaceful coexistence with others" [sic].
- "The dignity of man is bequeathed by God. He is both the source of human rights and provides the benchmark by which man's behavior should be measured."
- "All mankind shares responsibility in trying to fulfill what is God's will on earth. Human beings must cooperate in defining legislation, rules, and charters to further the common good in accordance with God's will. [. . .]"
- "Respect for religious belief in God and living according to divine principles is a sound basis for achieving co-operation and peaceful co-existence, securing a better life for mankind." [. . .]
- "The establishment of justice [here Islamic justice] among all peoples, irrespective of nationality, religion, ethnicity, race or sex, is a fundamental tenet of *shari'a* that guarantees tranquility, stability and security for all members of society."

Article 12 professes that Islam utterly rejects international terrorism and violence, however, here terrorism is not judged by actions but by ideology. Certain causes, such as that of the Palestinians, justify terrorism, which in such a case is not deemed a crime. Finally, Article 14 declares that it is obligatory for all Muslims, whether leaders or nations, to apply *shari'a* in every aspect of their lives, to cooperate with the serious mass media to present Islam to a broad public and to strengthen relations with the various nations and cultures.

It is clear that the 1948 Universal Declaration of Human Rights and the Cairo Declaration on Human Rights in Islam emerge from two totally different concepts. This is an extremely important point because it involves contradictory meanings, principles, rights and laws and is never mentioned by the promoters of the Mediterranean Union. Practicing multiculturalism among populations where there is denial that their ideas are poles apart creates the conditions for civil war. If Muslims in Europe must live according to the precepts of *shari'a*, the life of their European co-citizens will become impossible and they will lose their freedoms for which they will fight.

The Report of the Foundation Advisory Group is mute on these essential contradictions. In order to develop this Mediterranean society built on an idealized model of Jewish and Christian dhimmitude in Andalusia and the Ottoman Empire, it advocates the creation of shared institutions and an overhaul of school, university and cultural syllabuses. The Report proposes the creation of a new organization whose networks would control the media, publications and teaching about Islam in order to purge them of their negative stereotypes.

In December 2003 the Council of Europe and the foreign ministers of the EU accepted this project and the creation of this organization for cultural control, which took the name the Anna Lindh Foundation. In this way the mechanisms were put in place for mental conditioning of the entire European culture under the control of a decision-making unit, the Anna Lindh Foundation. As a network of networks, this Foundation would manage the programs and activities in cooperation with Arab countries, in every sphere—social, cultural, audio-visual, educational, media, artistic and political, at both the national and international levels.[24]

A few months later, on May 5–6, 2004, the foreign ministers of the EU met in Dublin and approved the setting up of a Euro-Mediterranean Parliamentary Assembly (EMPA), which would act as an instrument for spreading democracy and for action throughout the Mediterranean Partnership. The EU expressed its desire to cooperate with regional initiatives by taking note of the demands of the Arab League Summit. The new EMPA was created in accordance with the recommendation of the High Level Advisory Group, the first step towards joint Euro-Mediterranean activism. The first session of the Euro-Mediterranean Parliamentary Assembly (EMPA) was held in Cairo March 12–15, 2005. In the final declaration the participants recalled that in accordance with the principles of the Barcelona Declaration, the Euro-Mediterranean partners had to:

> refrain, in accordance with the rules of international law, from any direct or indirect intervention in the internal affairs of another partner; Respect the sovereign equality and all rights inherent in their sovereignty; Develop the rule of law and democracy in their political systems, while recognizing in this framework the right of each of them to choose and freely develop its own political, socio-cultural, economic and judicial system. [25]

In other words, the legitimacy of *shari'a* must be accepted in those countries where it exists.

This renders quite useless any demand for reforms for the rule of law, equality of the sexes and of religions, freedom of opinion and of conscience or to change one's religion, respect for the Other, in particular non-Muslims, even though such measures represent the targets of the Mediterranean policy and the Anna Lindh Foundation. On the contrary, the parliamentarians asked the European Union to expand its efforts to increase the financial resources needed for the modernization of Arab countries, amounts that are already large, taken from the taxes paid by Europeans. Only Israel escaped the principle of non-intervention since the EU based its policy toward Israel on accommodating the Palestinian Arabs. The EU inserted itself into the Israel-Arab conflict as the ally of the Arabs and unconditional protector of the Palestinians, a strategy that has guided its entire policy since the late 1960s. Striving to undermine Israel, the EU earned Arab approval by promising to build Palestine, a second Protectorate after Jordan, on the disputed territories of Judea and Samaria it drags away from Israel.

As Europe was aligning itself increasingly closely with the Arab world, the war against Saddam Hussein broke out in March 2003, inflaming Arab hatred against the West. As a result, led by Prodi and Solana, the EU multiplied its projects to promote multiculturalism and tolerance and to combat "xenophobia" in Europe. It sponsored a solidarity campaign with the Palestinians and unofficially encouraged a climate of anti-Americanism, and extremely virulent Judaeophobic and antisemitic propaganda. The intimidation campaign of the Organization of the Islamic Conference (OIC) in international forums combined with a European strain of Islamic terrorism, unleashed in the EU a diversionary policy. It brought together antisemitic agitation orchestrated by the European Commission and racist defamation of the State of Israel, which was hit with a boycott and exclusion in European, pro-Palestinian academic milieus.

However, all the anti-Israel and anti-American venom expended in Europe could not prevent Moroccan Islamists from carrying out an attack on March 11, 2004, in Madrid, causing nearly 200 deaths and more than 2,000 injured. The Aznar government, allied with the Americans, fell in the subsequent elections, and was replaced by that of the socialist Jose Luis Rodriguez Zapatero, who hastened to comply with Arab and OIC demands on Iraq, immigration and dialogue. He withdrew his troops from the coalition forces in Iraq and adopted pro-immigration measures for Spain and thus for the EU. With Turkey, he then founded the Alliance of Civilizations complying with OIC demands.

In October 2004 the murder in Amsterdam of filmmaker Theo van Gogh created an atmosphere of insecurity and fear, heightened by the war in Iraq and the uncovering of European Islamic terrorist cells. On November 5, 2004, a few days following the assassination of van Gogh, Princess Maxima of Holland gave a speech at The Hague intended to calm down the widespread indignation. The princess underscored the importance of equal opportunities for women and immigrants and their active participation in society. She emphasized their talents and skills and on the need to trust the immigrants in a spirit of openness towards them and of respect for their different culture. Immigrants, she explained, were seeking their identity in their new country without repudiating their roots. This was in fact a skillful appeasement plea for multiculturalism in the wake of a crime.

In London on July 7, 2005, homegrown Islamists blew themselves up in the underground and on buses killing fifty-two and wounding more than seven hundred; two weeks later (July 21) a failed attempt by British Muslims followed, while three months later in France (October–November) the suburbs rose up in endless riots. In this atmosphere of hatred, terrorism and chaos, the Danish newspaper *Jyllands-Posten* published on September 30, 2005, twelve cartoons related to the Prophet Muhammad. Several months later they triggered unprecedented violent reactions throughout the Muslim world, causing over two hundred deaths and immense destruction. The Arab

League and the OIC, which had not been much concerned by the Islamist attacks that had caused hundreds of deaths and thousands of wounded Europeans, grasped this cartoons affair and turned it into a scandal at the Third OIC Conference of the Islamic Summit in Mecca on December 7–8, 2005.

MULTICULTURALISM AND ISLAMOPHOBIA AT THE UN HUMAN RIGHTS COUNCIL (GENEVA)

At that Mecca Summit, the OIC announced its determination to insist on the fight against Islamophobia in all international and national forums, namely at the state level. But how to define the manifestations and definitions of Islamophobia? Is it the refusal of unauthorized immigration? Is it freedom of opinion, expression and the press? Is it attachment to one's culture, country and human rights? Is it the wish to maintain one's country's security, and refusal of *shari'a*? Or Europe's resistance to Islamization? As shall be seen, all these elements are to varying degrees parts of Islamophobia, which has become the new battlefield of the OIC against Europe, especially via the United Nations.

With a great deal of skill the OIC has managed to inverse the situation created by Islamist terrorism against the West, which by sleight of hand has become the aggressor of Muslims who nonetheless immigrate there of their own free will. The turning of Islamophobia in the West into an international cause, discussed at UN forums, and even into "a crime against humanity" according to Turkish Prime Minister Recep Tayyip Erdogan, has eclipsed the crimes of terrorism.[26] In accordance with jihadist principle to transfer blame for being the aggressor onto the unsubdued infidel, Westerners protecting themselves against terrorism were guilty of Islamophobia.

This when Europeans are living under a permanent threat of terrorism, poisoned by an antisemitism imposed on them from outside by way of their own ministers as the price for their security. While they are obliged to live as in wartime, submit to searches on public transport and in public places, the OIC has been multiplying the number of international conferences and dialogues, including at the UN, complaining of Europeans' Islamophobia from which Muslim immigrants suffer as they continue to flow into Europe.

These repetitive charges fill the reports submitted by Doudou Diène, the Senegalese Special Rapporteur on Racism, Xenophobia and Related Forms of Intolerance, to the UN's Commission, later Human Rights Council in

Geneva. Diène demanded from the EU a strong political will to suppress "racist, xenophobic platforms" that appeal to insecurity and national identity to fight against immigration. His conclusions referred to the seriousness of the discrimination against the Muslim and Arab populations, the violence perpetrated against their places of prayer and culture, the hostility to Islam and its followers, and the intellectual legitimization of Islamophobia.

He denounced any association of Islam with terrorism, the security surveillance where Islam is taught, the monitoring of its places of worship, its mosques and its faithful. He recommends "the adoption of legal, political, and administrative measures" to combat racism and xenophobia.[27]

Naturally, at no time does Diène mention anti-Christian violence in Iraq, Gaza, in the territories run by the Palestinian Authority, Egypt, the Maghreb, Iran, Indonesia, Turkey, Saudi Arabia, and in all those Muslim countries governed by *shari'a*. He does not extend his brief either to the genocidal, fanatical hatred towards Jews and Israel in these countries, to incitement to hatred and violations of their human rights—especially in the Hamas Charter—nor to the limitations placed on women, liberal Muslims and apostates, the cult of terrorism and death against Westerners, maritime piracy and the ransoming of hostages. He ignores all the facts that explain the situation he is denouncing. He does not talk of the sense of invasion by Europeans, who are subject to massive waves of illegal immigration that undermine the right of asylum and put the State's services under strain, particularly in the fields of education, housing, health, employment, and security.

Diène considered controls on immigration to the West, anti-terrorist security measures and European cultural and national currents all to be Islamophobic. In his many reports to the Commission/Council and to the UN General Assembly he draws attention to two developments that he deems to be especially troubling: the emergence of racism and xenophobia in the West tied to national and cultural identity awareness, and the mistreatment of foreigners, asylum seekers, refugees and immigrants. He stresses the importance of Europe forging its new identity within ethnic, religious and cultural pluralism and denouncing racism,

> under the guise of combating terrorism, defending the "national identity," promoting "national preference," and combating illegal immigration.[28]

He condemns the impact of European xenophobic currents in the "legal, administrative and security practices that criminalize non-nationals, immigrants, refugees and asylum- seekers."[29] Diène appears to consider Europe to be a vast area for colonization, a continent in which nationalisms and native cultures should be eliminated, as were those of non-Muslim inhabitants of lands Islamized after jihadist conquests. The accusation of racism against attachment to European national cultures appears unbalanced in the light of OIC demands claiming protection for the cultural identities of Muslim immigrants in their host countries.

Diène's accusations became sharper in his report to the UN General Assembly on September 20, 2006, and August 21, 2007,[30] in which he denounced religious defamation and the violation of human rights of Muslims on account of security measures. He commented,

> A major negative impact is the trend and sometimes the ideological position of many Governments to consider that the security of the country and its people constitute the sum and substance of all human rights. (p. 4)

It can be observed here that Diène's criticism is identical to that addressed by Europe toward Israel, castigating it for its security measures against terrorism.

Diène denounces the new ideological context that undermines respect for human rights. He deplores discrimination against Muslims, which he attributes to two major problems, Europe's security imperative and European national identities. His reports appear to ignore the human rights of Europeans that are violated by jihadist terrorism, which legitimizes the right to kill European civilians indiscriminately or threatens them with collective terrorist reprisals if they do not submit to Islamic policies that are contrary to their laws and their freedom of opinion, especially with respect to Israel. In the same way, illegal immigration violates the laws of European states.

Diène seems to be urging European governments to break their own laws and ignore the wishes of their citizens and even to act against them in order to accord precedence to immigration. His unnuanced criticisms compare European national identities, anti-terrorist measures and the refusal to accept illegal immigration to a racist, xenophobic and Islamophobic obstruction to multiculturalism and immigration which ought to continue indefinitely, notwithstanding native opposition. Here can be found in a subtle manner with UN justification, the definitions of aggressor and victim in jihadist ideology, as provided by Bassam Tibi. The aggressor is always the one who puts up obstacles to the propagation of Islam in his country.

These accusations were taken up in the 300-page 2007 report of Amnesty International (AI), which attributes the deterioration in human rights in good part to the security obsession of Westerners and to the fight against terrorism.[31] In the preamble, AI's Secretary General, Irene Khan, taking up the argument of the OIC, reproaches in a moralizing tone, "We are prepared to compromise the rights of others to ensure our own security." She concludes, "No one wins." Wrong. The lives of innocents are preserved while the criminals are kept under surveillance. Amnesty International was indignant about fear of terrorism, which it accused of justifying security measures that encroached on human rights. It comes to replace the basic rights of Europeans to life and security with those of Muslim migrants to settle outside of the law and beyond any controls in European countries.

Diène's accusations are repeated in his many reports. He calls for the EU to impose severe sanctions to suppress movements antithetical to multicultural identity, which ought to be that of Europe and that must be accepted. But on which authority does Mr. Doudou Diène, a Senegalese, decide for hundreds of millions of Europeans their true identity? It can be noted that the picture he painted of Europeans is that of dhimmitude. Like dhimmis, Westerners are obliged to accept the demographic and cultural colonization of their own territory by massive immigration. They have to renounce their national history, identity and culture as well as the right to defend themselves against terrorist jihad, because these positions are those of Islamophobia. On the other hand, the OIC demands protection for the cultural and religious identity of Muslim immigrants, and the safeguard of their cultural heritage in states that are not members of the OIC,[32] namely non-Muslim countries.

In his report to the Council on Human Rights dated February 20, 2008,[33] Diène noted the growing scale of Europe's rejection of diversity and multiculturalism. He attributes this to racism and recommends the creation of European legal and administrative instruments to stifle the values, identities, and teaching of history that oppose multiculturalism. Such proposals overlook the fundamental rights of freedom of belief, thought and expression of the European populations. Again, Diène defines anti-terrorist security measures as forms of racism and xenophobia (§5); European racism and xenophobia arises from the ideological, cultural and political resistance to ethnic migration and cultural and religious multiculturalism (§62). The nation-state, he argues, represents the expression of an exclusive national identity that is opposed to the establishment of democratic, universal, egalitarian multiculturalism that respects ethnic, religious and cultural identities. These doctrinaire and theoretical considerations, which seek to eliminate European national cultures and memories that in turn are deemed to be racist and Islamophobic obstacles to the settlement in Europe of the religious cultures of Muslim immigrants, make multiculturalism a tool of soft-jihad.

In this context we note that Article 12 of the Islamic Declaration on Human Rights states:

> Every man shall have the right, within the framework of *shari'a*, to free movement and to select his place of residence whether inside or outside his country and, if persecuted, is entitled to seek asylum in another country. The country of refuge shall ensure his protection until he reaches safety, unless asylum is motivated by an act that *Shari'a* regards as a crime.

What is meant by the framework of *shari'a*? The Report of the Observatory on Islamophobia of the OIC dated July 24, 2008, 9th session—submitted to the UN Human Rights Council—presents even more serious charges against the West. Having stressed that Islamophobia is one of the major problems in the modern world, the Report states that Muslims in the West are today stereotyped and subject to various discriminatory practices, while their religious symbols are denigrated and insulted. Thus the Report emphasizes the dangerous repercussions for world peace and security caused by Islamophobia, the difficult situation of Muslims in the West and the defamation of Islam. While demanding national European legislation and international instruments to combat these misdeeds, the Report acknowledges that Western governments, NGOs and representatives of civil society have taken serious note of the importance accorded by the Muslim world to the defamation of Islam.

The Report, however, postulates the inadequacy of these initiatives, the lack of clear-cut terms for addressing this problem and the absence of punitive legal measures with which to charge Islam-haters and to limit the abuse of freedom of expression. It should be noted here that any European defending his or her national or cultural values or religious convictions that are based on the Bible could be accused of Islamophobia, racism and xenophobia. Theoretically, it would be enough to say that Abraham was not a Muslim prophet in the Judeo-Christian tradition and that Isa, the Muslim Jesus of the Koran having preached Islam in no way resembles Jesus of the Gospels—or the transformation of Jews into monkeys and pigs by Allah as stated in the Koran and taught to Muslim children in the West is hardly credible.

On September 2, 2008, Doudou Diène presented his Report on contemporary forms of racism, racial discrimination, xenophobia, and on the manifestations of defamation of religions and in particular the serious impact of Islamophobia on the enjoyment of all rights.[34] In this text he expands on the violence against Muslims since 9/11/2001 and states that at the Council's request he gave priority to examining Islamophobia, even though he adds that antisemitism and hatred of Christians ought to receive equal attention as Islamophobia. One can therefore ask why for years the Commission on Human Rights and the Council have accorded special attention to this aspect that in broad terms also involves the rights of illegal immigrants in foreign countries, while those of natives and legal, non-Muslim foreigners are subject to much more serious violations in countries governed by *shari'a*. And this is not to mention the negation of the historical, political, cultural and human rights of Israelis in their own country, the genocidal threats they face, the defamation of their humanity as monkeys and pigs, and of their religion constantly on media in the Arab/Muslim world. Does not this partiality, in favoring one sector, attest to certain discrimination in respect of others; is it not an indication of the OIC's domination over the Human Rights Council and the UN in general?

It is true that the Rapporteur also denounces the recrudescence of racist violence and xenophobia in the world against religious, ethnic and cultural communities. However, he is only speaking of extremist, neo-Nazi and nationalist groups, namely of the West (§7). The Islamists and jihadists operating in Europe and in most Muslim countries, including Turkey, Egypt, the Levant, Africa, and Asia, are forgotten, exactly like those who in Europe attack, in violation of its laws, Muslim apostates and free thinkers.

One of the manifestations of Islamophobia, according to Diène, is the exclusion of Muslims in Western countries from key political and social spheres (§19)—a point the OIC strives to correct. Although there are many cases that disprove this allegation, such exclusion could also be explained by the refusal of some new immigrants to assimilate in their host countries and their hostility to a culture they reject. In their countries pre-Islamic Jewish and Christian religious and ethnic minorities are despised, banned from senior positions and suffer gross discrimination when they are not simply persecuted or massacred in churches. It is noteworthy that recent Muslim immigrants to the West occupy more ministerial or other important positions than their Christian, Jewish, Berber, Kurd or Hindu opposite numbers who managed to survive the religious and ethnic cleansing in their Islamized home-lands. We also note that Article 12 of the Islamic Declaration on Human Rights limits travel or immigration as part of *shari'a*.

Speaking of the causes of Islamophobia (§20), Diène mentions the cru-sades as a landmark but not the jihads that over a prior period of four hundred years had Islamized Christian, Hindu and Buddhist countries. He also cites an identity crisis in the West created by non Western multiculturalism with a strong Muslim element. He acknowledged thus the considerable pressure of Muslim immigration to impose multiculturalism on populations who did not want it. Diène explained that to these Islamophobia factors are added the polarization of the Israeli-Palestinian conflict, oil crises and the "materializa-tion of political movements that legitimize the use of violence by Islam." The victims of terrorist attacks in many European cities for forty years, those taken hostage, air and maritime piracy are forgotten. The threats of global jihad, terrorism, general insecurity, rioting in the suburbs and crimes of hon-or do not appear in this picture of victimization.

The Special Rapporteur severely criticized freedom of expression, the jewel of Western culture. He again denounced the programs for fighting terrorism, the defense of national identity and security, which trivialize and legitimize Islamophobia (§23). Diène recalled that throughout his mandate (August 2002–2008) he had emphasized that the question of Islam's place in Europe constituted a central issue in building a new European identity. As we have seen, this is the position of the OIC, ardently defended by Ekmeleddin Ihsanoglu, its Secretary General, and which the EU has been forced to satis-fy. Which is why, warns Diène, the political and economical scope of the European enterprise must not obscure that of the multicultural identity recon-struction of the new Europe (§26). In other words, this reconstruction of the new Europe must include Islam. This obligation determines the contemptu-ous condemnation of those identities where Islam is absent.

In his analysis of antisemitism, Diène underscores its resilience in its historical lands of origin, in Europe. However, this is an erroneous and biased opinion. Excepting the Iberian Peninsula (modern-day Spain and Por-tugal), Christian antisemitism first manifested itself in the Byzantine lands of the Orient and North Africa, Islamized in the seventh and eighth centuries. It developed in Europe most especially at the time of the Crusades and the great Muslim conquests of Europe's eastern flank (eleventh through sixteenth cen-turies). In Christian countries that had been Islamized, Judaeophobia twinned with Christianophobia was incorporated into the body of Islamic jurisprudence from its very beginning (eighth and ninth centuries), and was based on its holy texts, written in Arabic.[35] Jews and Christians were expelled from the Hejaz (Arabia) in 640 and forbidden to live there. In their Islamized countries they were expropriated, forced into special quarters, and from the eighth century subject to a degrading status as established by Muslim jurists. It is thus incorrect to attribute Judaeophobia to Europe alone, as does Diène, and to cover up its Islamic aspect. What is more, he claimed that reference to Judeo-Christian roots is antisemitic, whereas these roots are an historical reality, denied by Muslims who claim, based upon the Koran, that Jesus was a Muslim Prophet. Muslims categorically refute any allusion to a Christian line of descent from Judaism, considering Islam to be the source of Christianity. Diène expands on antisemitism in Europe and America, but hardly mentions it in Muslim countries, thereby presenting a biased picture.[36]

His examination of hatred against Christians in Muslim countries attributes its contemporary causes to colonialism, the association of the West with Christianity, the conflict of civilizations theory, proselytizing by Evangelists, and the aggressiveness of European secular dogma. This potpourri type of analysis does not explain the murder of Copts, the kidnapping and rape of their daughters and wives, the burning and destruction of their churches, the massacres in Iraq of Assyrian Christians and others if they refuse to pay the *jizyah*, a Koranic tax that is obligatory for non-Muslims—attacks that are in no way related to the causes enumerated by Diène. In fact, according to this report, the causes of the hatred against Christians displayed by Muslims would seem to stem from Christians themselves.

In all these accusations, some justified, others less so but presented in a tendentious manner, can be seen the OIC plan decided at the 2005 Mecca Summit and other later meetings: to carry the fight against Islamophobia into international and national forums and force the West to proscribe the criticism of religions and blasphemy, obsolete ideas in Europe. In the West such policies represent serious breaches of freedom of opinion and belief of Westerners. What is more, the denunciation of legitimate attachment by Europeans to their national identities, cultures and histories, and the denunciation of anti-terrorist measures and illegal immigration at the Council seek to impose multiculturalism and insecurity on Europeans.

Multiculturalism allows immigrants who refuse to integrate into their host countries to impose their identities and laws on an equal footing with those of Europeans, notwithstanding the considerable contradictions in terms of freedom of expression, the status of women and of the family. Between these groups the difference of interpretation of human rights and the criteria for objectivity in teaching and culture appear to be insurmountable. Further, Muslims' obedience to *shari'a* in every aspect of their lives, as required by the Cairo Declaration on Human Rights in Islam, their rooting in the Koran and the Sunna, demanded by the OIC that arrogates to itself a right of protection, make their integration in a post-religious, libertarian and secular Europe extremely problematic.

On March 27, 2008, the OIC succeeded in getting one more resolution on "combating the defamation of religions" adopted by the Human Rights Council. This Resolution subjects freedom of expression to respect for religion and belief and removes *shari'a* laws and all religions from any criticism. It considers the fight against terrorism to be an aggravating discriminatory factor against Muslim minorities and obliges the state to take appropriate steps to protect respect for religions and to fight against their defamation. At the subsequent session, on June 16, 2008, the President of the Council, Romanian Ambassador Doru Romulus Costea was forced by several OIC representatives to stop David G. Littman from reading a three-minute joint statement on violence against women in Muslim lands. The statement from two NGOs, the Association for World Education (AWE) and the International Humanist and Ethical Union (IHEU), mentioned the words *shari'a* and *fatwa*.[37] He was stopped on sixteen points of order, half from OIC countries, and the meeting had to be suspended for forty-five minutes.

Finally, on March 25, 2010, the Human Rights Council adopted with a small majority the OIC proposal against the defamation of religions, co-sponsored by Pakistan.[38] The Resolution endorses the OIC's decisions taken at the 2005 Mecca Summit and the subsequent ones in relation to the defamation of Islam, its stereotyping by the media, and its linkage with terrorism. It adopts the OIC victimizing view after 9/11, alleging discrimination through ethnic and religious profiling, by the controlling and monitoring of Muslim communities in implied Western countries, although the location is not specified. The Resolution stresses several times the state duty to fight Islamophobia and protect Muslim communities worldwide in particular, especially in Western countries.

As this document supposedly embodies world concerns on religious persecutions, one might well ask why it is mute on Western and in general non-Muslim rights violated by Islamist terrorism (Israel, US, Europe, India, Africa), genocidal wars, killings, rapes and a campaign of incitement to hate and genocide against Israel in particular by Iran, Hamas (Gaza), the Palestinian

Authority, and Hizbullah (Lebanon). It is clear that although it is couched in general terms it intends to protect Muslim immigrants in Western countries by preventing any criticism of their own intolerance toward others. Paragraph 8 strongly condemned the ban on the construction of minarets of mosques that was decided by popular vote in Switzerland on November 29, 2009. It affirms that being a manifestation of Islamophobia, it could lead "to dangerous unintended and unforeseen consequences." One wonders why only minarets were mentioned in view of Egypt's banning Jews to pray in their oldest Cairo synagogue, the Palestinian riots in Jerusalem against the restoration of a nineteenth-century synagogue destroyed under the Jordanian occupation (1948–1967) and—in all Muslim countries—the severe restrictions on building or repairing religious non-Muslim places, and even in some countries the prohibition of any non-Muslim religious service. Moreover, the threats proffered by Turkish Prime Minister Erdogan against states and peoples recognizing the genocide of the Armenian people, assorted with the menace to expel the Armenian immigrants from Turkey,[39] are a violation of the right of the Armenians to preserve their own history, including its greatest tragedy.

Thus, the OIC has succeeded in imposing the decisions taken at the ministerial conference in Jeddah (March 15, 2006) that requested at a world level from UN bodies the proscription of the defamation of religions and religious symbols, blasphemy, denigration of all prophets, and the prevention in the future of other defamatory actions, as well as the planning of a global strategy to prevent the defamation of religions with the implementation of effective and appropriate measures. Its Second OIC (2008–2009) Observatory Report on Islamophobia will be examined in chapter 4.[40]

In the light of this development it is clear that the Human Rights Council is getting closer to the Declaration on Human Rights in Islam, which states in Article 22:

1. Everyone shall have the right to express his opinion freely in such manner as would not be contrary to the principles of the Shari'a.
2. Everyone shall have the right to advocate what is right, and propagate what is good, and warn against what is wrong and evil according to the norms of Islamic Shari'a.

3. Information is a vital necessity to society. It may not be exploited or misused in such a way as may violate sanctities and the dignity of Prophets, undermine moral and ethical values or disintegrate, corrupt or harm society or weaken its faith.

NOTES

1. *The Koran*, trans. with notes by N[essim] J[oseph] Dawood (Penguin Books: New York, 1987; 1st ed. 1956).

2. *Report on Islamic Summit 1974: Pakistan. Lahore*, February 22–24, Karachi 1974, see speech by al-Tuhami, 195–219, and Bat Ye'or, *Eurabia : The Euro-Arab Axis* (Madison, N.J.: Fairleigh Dickinson University Press, 2005), 75–77.

3. Bat Ye'or, *Eurabia*, 63–69.

4. www.isesco.org.ma/ english/strategy/documents/Strategy%20West.pdf (accessed January 6, 2011).

5. Before the 1974 law, migrants outside the EU could come only with a work contract, without their families and for a limited time.

6. www.isesco.org.ma/ english/strategy/documents/Strategy%20West.pdf (accessed January 6, 2011), 7.

7. www.isesco.org.ma/ english/strategy/documents/Strategy%20West.pdf (accessed January 6, 2011), 8, emphasis added by author.

8. 22.7.2000 EN *Official Journal of the European Communities* L 183/5, Common strategy of the European Council of 19 June 2000 on the Mediterranean region 83/5-/10.

9. *Council of Europe, Parliamentary Assembly, Discussion by the Assembly*, 19 September 1991 (11th session) (see Doc. 6497, report of the Committee on Culture and Education, Rapporteur: Mr. de Puig), Strasbourg, 1992. See also Bat Ye'or, *Eurabia*, 168–73.

10. Romano Prodi, left-wing Catholic, former member of the Christian Democrats, minister in Giulio Andreotti's government from November 1978 to March 1979, and twice Prime Minister of Italy.

11. *A Union of Values*, Final Text Agreed at the XIV EPP Congress, Berlin, January 2001, www.euractiv.com/en/culture/dialogue-islam-key-parteuropean-intercultural-year/article-169403.

12. For this Joint Memorandum, see Bat Ye'or, *Eurabia*, 89.

13. Jan Friedmann and Klaus Wiegrefe, "Study Highlights, German Foreign Ministry's Role in Holocaust," *Spiegel On Line International*, October 27, 2010. The study shows that Nazi criminals became diplomats and were posted in Arab countries, and that well into the 1980s they were protected by Genscher.

14. Commission of the European Communities, Proposal for a Decision of the European Parliament and of the Council concerning the European Year of Intercultural Dialogue (2008), presented by the Commission, Brussels 2005/aaaa (COD). This document is dated 2005, without further detail: ec.europa.eu/culture/portal/events/pdf/proposal_en.pdf (accessed January 6, 2011).

15. ec.europa.eu/culture/portal/events/pdf/proposal_en.pdf, 6.

16. ec.europa.eu/culture/portal/events/pdf/proposal_en.pdf, 7.

17. ec.europa.eu/culture/portal/events/pdf/proposal_en.pdf, 11. The original English text is unclear.

18. Decision No. 1983/2006/EC of the European Parliament and of the Council of December 18, 2006 concerning the European Year of Intercultural Dialogue (2008), *Official Journal of the European Union*, December 30, 2006, L 412/44–L 412/50.

19. Statement of His Excellency Prof. Ekmeleddin Ihsanoglu, Secretary-General of the Organization of the Islamic conference at the First International Conference organized by (OIC) under the theme: *Challenging Stereotypes in Europe and the Islamic World: Working Together for Constructive Policies and Partnerships*, Wilton Park Conference Center, London, May 2, 2006.

20. Co-presidents: Assia Alaoui Bensalah & Jean Daniel, members of the Group: Malek Chebel, Juan Diez Nicolas, Umberto Eco, Shmuel N. Eisenstadt, George Joffé, Ahmed Kamal Aboulmagd, Bichara Khader, Adnan Wafic Kassar, Pedrag Matvejević, Rostane Mehdi, Fatima Mernissi, Tariq Ramadan, Faruk Sen, Faouzi Skali, Simone Susskind-Weinberger and Tullia Zevi. www.iemed.org/documents/lindhgroupen.pdf (accessed January 6, 2011).

21. Euromed Report, 66 EN, Romano Prodi, President of the European Commission, "Sharing Stability and Prosperity," speech given to the Tempus Meda Regional Conference, Bibliotheca Alexandrina, Alexandria, October 13, 2003.

22. The Cairo Declaration on Human Rights in Islam Adopted and Issued at the Nineteenth Islamic Conference of Foreign Ministers in Cairo on August 5, 1990.

23. The conclusion of the Symposium was reproduced on a whole page as an advertisement by the Muslim World League in the *International Herald Tribune*, March 16, 2000.

24. For more details on this Foundation, see Bat Ye'or, *Eurabia*, chap. 17.

25. www.europarl.europa.eu/intcoop/empa/plenary_sessions/cairo_2005/cairo_03_05_final_declaration_en.pdf; see also the Barcelona Declaration.

26. Recep Tayyip Erdogan, Prime Minister of Turkey, called on the international community to declare the animosity toward Islam "a crime against humanity" at the celebration of *iftar* in Istanbul with Jose Luis Rodriguez Zapatero, see Thomas Seibert, "Enmity with Islam 'crime against humanity,'" *The National*, September 17, 2008. www.thenational.ae/news/worldwide/middle-east/enmity-with-islam-crime-against-humanity (accessed January 6, 2011).

27. Racism, Racial Discrimination, Xenophobia and all forms of racial discrimination: Situation of Muslim and Arab populations in various regions of the world. Commission on Human Rights, United Nations, Geneva, E/CN.4/2006/17, February 13, 2006. I thank David G. Littman for having provided me with the reports of Doudou Diène mentioned here.

28. Report of August 2005, A/60/283, 5–9, quotation marks in the text.

29. . Report of August 2005, A/60/283, 9.

30. A/HRC/2/3, Sept. 20, 2006 and A/HRC/6/6, August 21, 2007.

31. *Le Temps*, Geneva, May 24, 2007.

32. Cf. the text quoted above from the Mecca Summit, December 2005, § 49.

33. A/HRC/7/19.

34. A/HRC/9/12.

35. Elias Al-Makdisi & Sam Soloman, *Al-Yahud:The Islamic Doctrine of Enmity & the Jews*, Advancing Native Missions, P.O. Box 5303, Charlottesville, VA 22905, www.Adnamis.org, 2010.

36. On Islamic antisemitism, viz. Andrew G. Bostom ed., *The Legacy of Islamic Antisemitism, from Sacred Texts to Solemn History*, preface by Ibn Warraq (New York: Prometheus Books, 2008).

37. Information provided by David G. Littman. For further details, see David G. Littman, "UN Human Rights Council: Any mention of the word '*shari'a*' is now taboo," June 19, 2008, www.jihadwatch.org/archives/021461.php.

38. United Nations, Human Rights Council, Geneva, A/HRC/13L.1, Thirteenth Session, Agenda, item 9.

39. Suna Erdem, «Recep Tayyip Erdogan threatens to expel 100.000 illegal Armenians," The Times on line, March 18 mars, 2010, London (accessed April 9, 2010).

40. June 2008 to April 2009, issued at the 36th Council of Foreign Ministers, Damascus, Syrian Arab Republic, May 23–25, 2009.

Chapter Three

Multiculturalism, the OIC, and the Alliance of Civilizations

MULTICULTURALISM AND THE ALLIANCE OF CIVILIZATIONS

Spain, a country with a strong anti-Jewish tradition and which only recognized Israel when obliged to do so on joining the European Union in 1985, reacted to the March 2004 Madrid attack by increased allegiance to the Arab world. Subsequently, Prime Minister Zapatero insisted he be present at the 60th anniversary of the Arab League in Algiers (March 22, 2005), where he proposed the creation of an Alliance of Civilizations (AoC). This body would operate in the political and cultural spheres for the rapprochement of Islam and the West, thereby fulfilling the wishes of the OIC. At a packed plenum of Arab leaders he laid out his project, which encompassed the themes of the Barcelona Process and of the Anna Lindh Foundation. However, he placed it in a much more ambitious and larger context in international terms through its correlation with a multilateral system and at the UN. The rapprochement between the West and the Muslim world fell into a UN strategy on a worldwide scale.

Stimulated by his promise to do his utmost to eradicate the misunderstandings between the West and the OIC, Zapatero promoted the rather unoriginal idea of a constructive dialogue between peoples, religions and civilizations. Turkey and UN Secretary General Kofi Annan supported this project intended to fight divisions and prejudices between cultures, especially between Islam and the West. This project was not, in fact, Zapatero's but the OIC's—Zapatero merely became their European representative.

Personalities selected by Kofi Annan made up a High Level Group (HLG), responsible for resolving once again the clash of civilizations. In November 2006, in the name of the AoC, this group submitted its Report, the fruit of its much-vaunted skills.[1] The Report adopted the Islamic view of history and shifted blame to the West and Israel for the current conflicts that it claimed had started with European colonialism and Zionism, as if jihadist imperialism on three continents since the seventh century had been merely a pastoral stroll through uninhabited areas.

It is difficult to imagine a more simplistic and shallow text, replete with sleights of hand, than this Report drawn up by an organization that adorns itself with the grand-sounding title "Alliance of Civilizations."[2] How does it present the twentieth century? "For many, the last century brought unprecedented progress, prosperity and freedom. For others, it marked an era of subjugation, humiliation and dispossession."[3] The domination of totalitarian systems across Europe, Asia and Africa; the genocide of the Armenians, Greeks and Assyrians in the Ottoman Empire, the Caucasus, Balkans, Iraq, Syria from 1914–1933; two World Wars with over 20 million killed in the first, and over 40 million in the second; the unparalleled horror of the genocide of European Jewry, followed by the ethnic cleansing of Jews from Arab lands accompanied by pogroms, killings, rape, expropriations, arbitrary imprisonment and expulsions are all insignificant, as were the tens of millions massacred in the Soviet Union, Cambodia, Rwanda, Sudan and elsewhere. All these cataclysms of human barbarity vanish, replaced by the doctrine of the OIC "subjugation, humiliation and dispossession"—alluding probably to Palestinian Arabs, with no reference to the Jewish inhabitants of Judea, Samaria and Jerusalem who were expelled after the Arab League's war against Israel in 1948, with the invasion of five Arab armies and the active participation of the Palestinian Arabs. That is the HLG's wisdom on the unequaled high point of the great human tragedies of the twentieth century.

The text continues to pile up clichés about injustice, inequality and occupation (of whom, by whom?). Worldwide conflicts and terrorism are reduced to conflicts between the privileged and the poor, between the powerful and the weak, the rich and the poor, because—we are told—poverty leads to despair and alienation. In a nutshell, here we have the European, Marxist stereotypes dating back to the nineteenth century. As far as terrorism goes, we must seek out "its deep causes" while "recognizing the links between peace, security, social and economic development and human rights."[4] In other words, a plaster cast on a wooden leg, since the HLG sees the causes of conflicts in "persistent discrimination, humiliation, and marginalization," and in resentment caused by "increased humiliation or despair."[5]

The Alliance also proposes to reduce these conflicts through the affirmation of mutual respect between peoples, creating a relationship that gives "special attention to relations between Western and Muslim societies." This report recommends "a practicable program of action by states (at national, regional and local levels), international organizations, and civil society, which it hopes will assist in diminishing hostility and in promoting harmony among the nations and cultures of the world."[6] Today this action plan recommended by the Alliance and applied within the EU and in America, without the knowledge of its citizens, implements OIC interests.

The HLG endeavors to define principles to frame the promotion of a culture of dialogue and respect between all nations and cultures. Only "the rule of law and an effective multilateral system, with the United Nations system at its core," it declares, can regulate such an interdependent world, a strategy jointly supported by the EU and the OIC in order to oppose American President George Bush.

Invoking magic formulas such as laws, treaties, international rights, and human rights,[7] which the HLG abuses, sidesteps the central problem. Are we talking about the Universal Declaration of Human Rights, the International Bill of Human Rights, the Geneva Conventions and other UN Covenants pertaining to international law—or of human rights according to *shari'a* and jihad international law that contradict them all and many other international treaties? The same omission can be seen in the listing of terrorism, which excludes that of the PLO and Saddam Hussein's Baathist regime, and of the attempted genocide of Christians and Animists in Sudan through jihad and of the Darfur's African Muslims.

Thanks to its lavish efforts in numerous dialogues, the Alliance prides itself on a multi-polar, comprehensive approach in its analysis of global views and of relations between civilizations. However, it specifies that it focuses mainly on Western and Muslim societies. This leads it to affirm, counter to historical truth, a narrative of peaceful coexistence between "Christianity, Islam and Judaism from the earliest period to our day"—despite a few conflicts, more of a "political than religious nature."

The High Level Group notes that

during medieval times, Islamic civilization was a major source of innovation, knowledge acquisition, and scientific advancement that contributed to the emergence of the Renaissance and the Enlightenment in Europe. Historically, under Muslim rule, Jews and Christians were largely free to practice their faith. [8]

These clichéd assertions follow the Recommendations of the Islamic Conference in Mecca reproduced below (cf. above).

- *Promotion of the positive contributions of Islamic civilization in Spain to the West and to humanity in terms of tolerance, peaceful coexistence of the three Abrahamic faiths (Islam, Christianity and Judaism) and the development of science and technology by Muslim scholars and scientists.* [9]
- *Enlighten Western leaders and the public on: (a) the positive role played by Islam in the rise of modern Western civilization, and (b), the moral obligation they have to promote the socio-economic development of the South.*
- *Publish books on the heritage of the Islamic civilizations in Spain, the Balkans, Central and South Asia, and other regions of the world that focus on inter-religious harmony and tolerance, Muslim economic development, and the Muslim contribution to the development of modern science and technology.*

The HLG further enjoined people to fight those publications that contradict this version of history, because as claimed—flying in the face of the truth—they do not explain current conflicts or the increased hostility between Muslim peoples and the West.

The roots of these phenomena, the HLG explains, "lie in developments that took place in the nineteenth and twentieth centuries, beginning with European imperialism, the resulting emergence of anti-colonial movements, and the legacy of the confrontations between them." [10] The obligatory blaming of the West and Israel asserts an historical lie affirming that the root cause of Evil was the creation of the State of Israel, which

beginning [sic] a chain of events that continues to be one of the most tortuous in relations between Western and Muslim societies. Israel's continuing occupation of Palestinian and other Arab territories and the unresolved status of Jerusalem—a holy city for Muslims and Christians as well as Jews—have persisted with the perceived acquiescence of Western governments and thus are primary causes of resentment and anger in the Muslim world toward Western nations. This occupation has been perceived in the Muslim world as a form of colonialism and has led many to believe, rightly or wrongly, that Israel is in collusion with "the West." These resentments and perceptions were further exacerbated by Israel's recent disproportionate retaliatory actions in Gaza and Lebanon. [11]

To this assertion is added its twin,

It is the invasion of certain Muslim countries by Western military forces and their continued presence in these countries, combined with the suppression of political movements in the Muslim world, that are among the reasons for violent manifestations. As evidenced throughout history and across many countries, political repression as well as the prolongation of occupation help entrench violent resistance. [12]

We should first note that the terms *Israel's continuing occupation of Palestinian* and *other Arab territories* match the Islamic view that contradicts both history and geography, because the regions officially known as Judea and Samaria—until the end of the British Mandate in 1948—together with the Galilee, constitute the historic heritage and homeland of the Jewish people, whose millennial history in the Land of Israel was and remains the foundation of Christianity. The Report acknowledges the internal problems within the Muslim world caused by erroneous interpretations of Islam such as the repression of women, which is the only form of discrimination mentioned. It notes the existence of "intra-Muslim debates" about the nature of jihad. In fact, such debates take place in the West, because apart from a few, rare, Muslim critics, jihad in its original version of a war of conquest is the consensus. The HLG, ever faithful to the line set by the OIC at the 2005 symposium, attempts to rehabilitate jihad,

The notion of jihad is a rich one with many shades of meaning, ranging from the struggle between good and evil that is internal to every individual (often referred to as the "greater" jihad in Islam) to the taking up of arms in defense of one's community (the "lesser" jihad). [13]

One could ask what defensive wars were waged in Arabia, the Middle East, Africa, Asia and Europe by Arab tribes and then the Turkish tribes against peoples that had not attacked them or their countries in Arabia or Asia. The

HLG objects to the wrong interpretation of the word "jihad" by extremists to justify violence—the word "terrorism" is avoided—because when these exhortations to violence

> are picked up and amplified by media and Western political leaders, the notion of "jihad" loses the multiple meanings and positive connotations it has for Muslims and becomes only associated with violent and negative meanings which have been wrongly attributed to the term.

We can compare the HLG recommendations with those of the OIC reproduced below, to follow the thread of inspiration:

> *Promotion of the notion of peaceful Jihad in its many dimensions, such as economic Jihad, educational Jihad, intellectual Jihad, ecological Jihad, moral Jihad, Jihad against poverty, crime, drugs, AIDS, etc.*

Thus these proposals can be traced to the OIC recommendations in Mecca about the sanctity of jihad, the political aspects of the world *da'wa,* and accusations against Western media:

> *Work together to counter anti-Islamic propaganda in the international media.*

On this basis provided by the OIC, the HLG laid out its general policy to achieve an Alliance of Civilizations. As was to be expected, and ever in fealty to the OIC, it was the Palestinian question that required its urgent attention. It recommends "a just, worthy, and democratic solution," which in the Islamic interpretation of justice and democracy means the Hamas viewpoint. Israel, a true dhimmi state, should facilitate the creation of a viable Palestinian state at the risk of becoming unviable itself and as though Jordan had not been a Palestinian state since 1922—with more than 77 percent of its land area. Israel accordingly had to sacrifice itself, mutilate itself, and destroy itself—in the same manner as Europe is doing—in the name of jihad morality so as to enjoy peace and security in dhimmitude.

The HLG recommends drawing up competing narratives of the establishment of the State of Israel. It sees that as a most valuable instrument, as would doubtless be the rehabilitation of Nazism through competing narratives of the Holocaust. The HLG tells us that from the Islamic point of view, the restoration of the State of Israel is seen as an attack and occupation. However, the same applies to the decolonization from Islam of Spain, Portugal, Sicily, Cyprus, Serbia, Greece and the Balkan countries that were former

Arab or Ottoman colonies, just like Kashmir, India and other Asian countries—ancient lands of jihad and dhimmitude—not to speak of other citadels of the infidel that are destined for conquest.

"Competing narratives" about turning back Muslim colonists who were pushed out of their European colonies during centuries of warfare could largely justify the return of millions of their descendants and compensation for their goods and lands confiscated by Christians, whose own forebears had been expropriated, expelled and massacred in jihadist wars of conquest. The HLG creates a false equivalence between global jihadist imperialism and the liberation of dhimmi peoples; these latter had been dehumanized and expropriated by a war ideology conceding Islamic protection in exchange of territories according to the formula, the peace of dhimmitude in return for lands.

In fact, the only refugees expelled or obliged to leave their countries and omitted by the HLG were the civilian Jewish refugees from Arab countries, as most of the Arabs of Mandate Palestine fled from lands during a war of their own making: their own active collaboration in the invasion of Israel by five Arab armies in 1948.

In order to confer an appearance of respectability on the OIC's policy, the HLG recommended preparing a White Paper, which would present the competing narratives of the two parties.

> Such a document could provide a firm foundation for the work of key decision-makers involved in efforts to resolve this conflict. A levelheaded and rational analysis would make it clear to the Palestinian people that the price of decades of occupation, misunderstanding and stigmatization is being fully acknowledged, while at the same time contributing to exorcize the fears of Israelis. This effort would strengthen the hand of those who seek a just solution to this conflict while weakening extremists on all sides, as they would no longer be the champions of a cause they have been able to appropriate because its story had been left untold or deliberately ignored by the community of nations.[14]

Thanks to Europe, which to protect itself against terrorism had championed the Palestinian cause since 1973, the latter benefited like no other from world attention and especially from billions paid by Europeans straight down the drain. Without their knowledge, the EU was financing terrorism and hatred against Israel to ward off terrorism in Europe, thus buying security.

The forced departure of Jews from Arab lands and their dispossession were entirely ignored by the world and by the HLG, as were the history of martyrdom and the dehumanization of the dhimmis, including Palestinian Jews, who over the centuries suffered massacres, enslavement, deportations, ethnic and religious cleansing in their own countries. This White Paper, claiming to bring peace, sought to add yet another page to the defamation of Israel and to the Palestinian sense of victimization. This intention was confirmed by Ihsanoglu's declaration at the Dakar Conference (March 2008), demanding official documentation of Israel's crimes to have them judged in international courts, such as the newly created UN International Criminal Court.

One wonders about the motives that make the White Paper start with the restoration of the State of Israel, removing all previous Jewish history. Actually, it aims at writing under the aegis of the UN and the Alliance of Civilizations the memoir of the *nakba* (1948), the counterweight to the Shoah, to impose it upon Israel and the world in order to rehabilitate not just Nazism through the legitimization of Jew-hatred, but also the Muslim-Palestinian regime of dhimmitude in the Land of Israel over the centuries. The moral destruction of Israel's sovereignty, a central plank of Euro-Islamic antisemitism would pave the way for the return to Auschwitz, programmed for decades by Euro-Arab dialogues, and camouflaged under soothing words that promote peace and justice. This policy is hidden in the Declaration of the Nine in London (1979), followed by that of Venice (1980), obtained by the PAEAC[15] —all in order to satisfy the Arab League and the OIC.

A CONTINENT WHOSE INHABITANTS ARE NON-EXISTENT: THE PARTNERSHIPS' STRATEGY

The other general policy recommendations of the HLG repeat those of the OIC. They call for the development of multiculturalism in international institutions and mechanisms, especially the United Nations—which thereby strengthens the global power of the OIC. Others recommend migration and asylum policies in Europe, within a Western version of human rights. These recommendations emphasize the "central importance of the activism of civil society," in other words an intensification of propaganda to condition public opinion via the Alliance's networks.

The HLG demands a greater commitment in the "mechanisms for the advancement of its recommendations and, in particular, for the peaceful resolution of conflicts."[16] To this end the HLG recommends setting up and controlling various networks within the population. Intended to represent "civil society," they are the channels for promoting the OIC's policies in the West.

The High Level Group recommended, as part of the Alliance of Civilizations, the development of *partnerships* with international bodies that share its objectives. It also recommended the strengthening of the interaction and coordination of these partnerships with the United Nations system. The partnerships' strategy agrees with that of the OIC, which through the proliferation of dialogues manages to intimidate and control the EU's political and religious leaders. They are reduced to being its spokesmen in a Europe whose security depends upon the submission of its peoples.

The HLG sought to intensify cooperation between the partnerships and organizations that have already been cooperating with the High-Level Group of the Alliance of Civilizations, namely:

> the United Nations Educational Scientific and Cultural Organization (UNESCO), the European Union, the Organization for Security and Cooperation in Europe (OSCE), the Organization of the Islamic Conference (OIC), the League of Arab States, the Islamic Educational Scientific and Cultural Organization (ISESCO), United Cities and Local Governments (UCLG), and the World Tourism Organization (UNWTO), as well as other international and national organizations, public or private.[17]

These proposals closely paralleled those made by Ihsanoglu at the European Parliament in 2006 and in the recommendations of the Mecca Symposium (§1 and 2).

1. *Strengthen OIC relations with major international and regional organizations and make use of them to enhance the Islamic voice and advance Islamic causes.*
2. *Urge OIC member states to play a more active role within international organizations. OIC members should support the candidates from member countries for positions in international functions.*

Clearly the HLG has become the extension of the OIC policy, hiding behind puppets. The second part of the report examined the major means to set up these policies. Youth and education are crucially important sectors,[18] as are the media and migration. Education must develop "respect for different cultures through an understanding of shared values and ideals."[19] In education the HLG recommends that

> Governments, multilateral institutions, universities, education scholars and policy-makers should work separately and together to expand global, cross-cultural, and human rights education.[20]

To achieve this objective UNESCO and ISESCO, the main organ of the OIC, needed to cooperate with educational research centers and designers of study programs. The purpose was a regional distribution of school textbooks about human rights that would then be distributed by states.[21] Yet again confusion has been maintained between the Universal Declaration of Human Rights and the Islamic Declaration, which conformed to *shari'a*.

Thus the West should be inspired by the teaching methods of ISESCO, the Islamic organization for education, science and culture, whose skills can be appreciated in thousands of *madrassa* from Saudi Arabia to Pakistan. ISESCO publications develop the historical and religious version of the Koran. Biblical history never existed, all Jewish monuments are the monuments of Muslim prophets usurped by Jews; there was never a Jewish Temple in Jerusalem and Israeli archeological digs are criminal acts against the Muslim heritage.

Other HLG recommendations deal with collecting money from public and private donors to develop research on multicultural dialogue and understanding. It also advocates the involvement of religious leaders in the teaching of other religions. Thus:

> Member states and multilateral organizations such as the Organization of the Islamic Conference and the European Union should work together to implement educational efforts to build capacity for intercultural tolerance and respect, civic participation and social engagement.[22]

Would the EU manage to change verses of the Koran and *shari'a* law? The HLG invokes the Universal Declaration of Human Rights of the United Nations, pretending to ignore that the 1990 Cairo Declaration on Human Rights in Islam has effectively replaced it in Muslim countries.

The education of young people, a crucial element for the HLG, includes youth exchanges:

> The United States, the European Union, and the Organization of the Islamic
> Conference should set a joint goal of taking the number of youth exchanges
> that occur between their countries from the bottom of the list of inter-regional
> exchanges to the top. Priority should be given to extended-stay exchanges,
> group exchanges, and exchanges subsidized enough to allow participation
> from strata of society other than elite populations. [23]

This proposal promotes disguised immigration, camouflaged as a long stay, from OIC countries to the US and Europe. Decisions taken by the December 2005 Mecca Summit and confirmed at other OIC meetings recommended rooting the worldwide Ummah in the Koran and Sunna—a situation that would not fail to impact life in Europe through the immigrants protected and organized by the OIC, as advocated by the OIC Dakar 2008 meeting and by ISESCO.

The HLG proposed the planning of all structures and funds required for youth exchanges between Western and OIC countries. A cultural fund and a network department would put in contact

> young Muslim artists, writers, musicians, filmmakers, etc. with their Western
> counterparts and leaders in the culture industry.
> The objective would be to facilitate the dissemination of contemporary Mus-
> lim culture to other societies and, in doing so, to promote the cause of dialogue
> and understanding. [24]

These demands encourage Muslim immigration to the West, expand the scope of Muslim culture, and state the imperialist strategy of the OIC and the West's complacency in making itself the channel for *da'wa* (proselytism). It can also be asked why these exorbitant OIC demands are necessary for peace when peaceful and respectful relations with Japan, China, India and other non-Muslim countries do not require these conditions. Does not the constant reference to peace imply a terrorist threat if Europe refuses them? Conversely, this proposal omits the parallel need to disseminate Western culture in Muslim countries.

In the migration sector the HLG recommended taking steps aimed at reducing "social alienation of immigrant youth" in the West. It supported the fight in Europe against racism, xenophobia and discrimination of immigrant communities. The EU ought to provide immigrants with work, housing, social services, health services, education and more. It should encourage the emergence of immigrant communal leadership and of representative groups of "associations and networks that can serve as representational bodies to engage in cross-cultural and interfaith dialogues with other communities or with governmental agencies."[25] Rewards were even considered for societies that will have best combated discrimination. What will be the criteria for such a success? How many Muslim ministers or presidents should be at the head of European states? And who will distribute the rewards? Moreover, European and American leaders must promote the cultures of Muslim immigrants:

> *American and European universities and research centers should expand research into the significant economic, cultural, and social contributions of immigrant communities to American and European life. Likewise, they should promote publications coming from the Muslim world on a range of subjects related to Islam and the Muslim world.*
>
> Such research would support those in the political and media sectors seeking authoritative data on the integral roles played by immigrant communities. [26]

The HLG recommended Western leaders to extol immigrants in their public statements in order to reduce their sense of alienation. Such an approach would facilitate the "debate concerning policies of integration, while reducing to a minimum the specter of racist and xenophobic sentiments clouding them." The Report explains:

> developing a media campaign to combat discrimination through ongoing messages about immigrants and highlighting the benefits of the country's diversity, contributions of immigrants, and the danger of stereotypes is critical. The media campaign should also emphasize that all who live in the country have the right to demand and obtain good services, complain about discrimination, and seek appropriate redress. [27]

Clearly such measures are not envisaged for Europeans who are victims of violence, or for non-Muslim minorities in Muslim countries. In fact, these programs that plan at every level for the "deconstruction" of Western host societies have already been applied and are overseen by the Commission in the member states of the EU. The AoC program provides the software for the colonization of Europe.

Their appetites whetted by "rewards" offered to societies that best defended immigrants' rights and cultures, many European governments and political parties have promoted Muslim Europeans of immigrant origin to influential positions. The diversity plan or affirmative action in France announced by President Nicolas Sarkozy fits into this strategy.

If such appointments were motivated by qualities and skills they could be justified. However, if they are just following the *diktat* of the OIC, leavened by a reward, they are unacceptable. People belonging to religious minorities, such as Jews, Armenians, Greek Orthodox, Protestants, and Catholics among Protestant majorities or vice versa, have achieved political positions within European governments. However, they earned such distinctions based on their own skills and not at the request of an alien supra-national organization such as the OIC, which in addition proclaims itself the protector of the interests of all Muslims in the world and the guarantor of their loyalty to the Koran and Sunna, to which all Muslims must adhere. Such assertions have shocked many European Muslims.

The recommendations and rewards of the HLG follow the injunctions of the Ulamas who attended the 2005 Summit at Mecca. These meet their concerns about the political and human rights of Muslim minorities and of "the challenges they encountered in the countries in which they live." These thinkers had noticed the need to speed up and coordinate the efforts to protect the cultural heritage of Muslims in non-Muslim countries. The OIC set itself as the protector of their cultural and religious rights and their cultural identity (§49).

The Western media—frequently blamed by the HLG for having spread prejudice and ignorance in the news that should have been concealed—should, according to the Report, have foresworn the irresponsible exercise of their liberties. To fight extremism and the Islamophobia borne by the media, programs for youth and adults needed to be designed to teach methods to deconstruct disinformation. Not a word is said about anti-Western, anti-Israeli racism or the Jew-hating racism of the Muslim countries, or about the various aspects of the historical revisionism and denial of jihad, the Armenian genocide, the Shoah and the entire history of Islamic imperialism and colonialism.

The HLG noted that the events in "Palestine," Iraq and Afghanistan inform the Muslim world about the victimization of Muslim coreligionists and stimulate public sympathy and solidarity, whereas in the West "an appreciably more nationalistic and at times anti-Muslim tone has become evident in the news and commentaries, especially since the events of 11 September 2001."[28] The HLG recommended a package of measures for bringing the media under control and for the co-production of films. One of these co-productions, "Jenin, Jenin," would become an unfortunate example as it was nothing but a farrago of anti-Israel defamation and PLO propaganda.

The OIC had already stated its policy concerning extending the Internet to Muslim countries, and thus its spokesman, the HLG, recommends,

Governments together with international organizations, governments and technology firms, should collaborate to expand Internet access, with particular attention to predominantly Muslim countries.

The Organization of the Islamic Conference (OIC) could take the lead in articulating an ambitious but conceivable goal for its member states to pursue—i.e., there should be computers with Internet access in every primary, secondary, and university level classroom in the Muslim world by 2020—and convening the technology firms, investors, and other partners who could assist in the realization of this goal. Principal implementing partners of relevant existing pilot programs and technology firms with programs in developing countries should be consulted and lessons learned should be disseminated through the OIC to the governments of each of its member states. The OIC should also collaborate with the Internet Governance Forum, established in the wake of the World Summit on the Information Society in Tunis, to develop ways of accelerating the availability and affordability of the Internet in Muslim countries. In addition, collaboration with programs such as the One Laptop per Child initiative, which aims at improving the learning opportunities of millions of children in the developing world, should also be pursued.[29]

However, the computer is not an innocent, technological tool. Internet can become a formidable instrument of war and death through incitement of hatred and communications between terrorists.

The HLG urgently demands positive images of Muslims in Western media and films. Nothing is required of Muslim countries, because apparently everything there is perfect. In fact, the analysis and all the steps recommended only apply to Western societies, which is suggestive of their alleged responsibility for the conflicts and accordingly their obligation to solve them. Thus only anti-Muslim prejudices are mentioned, but not the prejudices of Muslim societies in respect of non-Muslims.

Infringements on Europeans' human rights, freedoms and security by Islamic terrorism figure nowhere. On the contrary, the report only addresses the obligation of Westerners to transfer to peoples in the South their knowledge and technologies, to finance their economic development, to accept their migrants and unemployed, to work for the political, economic and cultural advancement of Muslim immigrants in their host countries, to massage their sensitivities and fears in Europe caused by the discrimination and Islamophobia generated by 9/11 and that infringe their fundamental civil liberties. In the twenty-first century we are reliving a replica and restoration of the Islamic Caliphate of the seventh century, through the approval and pliability of Western leaders. One might compare these demands on the West with Article 23b of the Cairo Declaration on Human Rights in Islam, which stipulates:

> Everyone shall have the right to participate directly or indirectly in the administration of his country's public affairs. He shall also have the right to assume public office in accordance with the provisions of *shari'a*.

Here is a provision that reserves for Muslims versed in *shari'a* the management of public affairs and functions.

The general tone of the Alliance Report takes up the themes of Palestinian and Muslim victimization. It is full of grudges poorly disguised as "the double standards" that challenge Israel's sovereignty. The *nakba*'s transfiguration by the White Paper "will return its full meaning and every chance to the normalization again of relations between Islam and the rest of the world." Such phrasing masks the structural, religious realities of the Muslim world, for the conflict in Kashmir and terrorism in India and other regions of Asia are just as old and arise from the same ideological sources as the war against Israel. Europe, however, does not ascribe to their resolution "its full meaning" for the normalization of relations between Islam and the rest of the world. The stated objective is:

> It is essential for Palestinians as well as for the Arab-Muslim world and Muslims in general to understand and acknowledge the fact that we, the HLG, now know and take responsibility for ensuring everyone knows the price and weight of these sixty years of misunderstanding, stigmatization, as well as veiled and abused truths.[30]

Such accusations naturally relate to Israel and those who support its liberation in its ancestral homeland, and reject the dehumanizing, jihadist ideologies claimed by the Palestinian Arabs. The mission of the HLG is in a direct line from the Second International Conference of Support for the Arab Peoples (Cairo, January 25–28, 1969), at which the sponsors and participants solemnly declared,

> that all information media should be mobilized to enlighten world public opinion, kept in ignorance and confusion by deceitful propaganda on the part of Israel and its supporters. It is an incumbent moral and political duty of all

participants to this conference to reveal the truth and spread it through the press, the radio, television, demonstrations, visits of delegations, and the organization of seminars and conferences in the West and through all continents.[31]

Since then, all synagogues, Jewish cultural premises and Israeli embassies throughout the world have had to be provided with protection. Most media have censored opinions favorable towards Israel. Incitement to hatred and defamation has been resurrected in Europe. It is this meticulously planned mission by the OIC that the HLG has assiduously taken on.

Another falsehood peddled by the HLG is to maintain that the Palestinians are victims "of a story left untold and deliberately ignored for too long by the community of nations."[32] Whereas in truth the "Palestinian cause" is a world obsession that has supplanted all of humanity's other tragedies. This statement in fact just repeats one from 1969 quoted above:

> world public opinion [is] kept in ignorance and confusion by deceitful propaganda on the part of Israel and its supporters.

It expresses the OIC's determination to force all countries, whether they like it or not, to oppose Israel. Its withering by the "international community" would be for the Palestinians

> the first step on the road to recovered dignity and a newly found credibility that can restore the meaning and reality of a process that is likely to finally lead to peace.[33]

This is a process akin to dhimmitude in which the degradation of the dhimmis highlights the dignity of the Muslim, and to the language of Auschwitz, which called the extermination camps "labor camps." Similarly, the peace built from worldwide incitement to hatred of Israel as proposed by the OIC-HLG networks anticipates Israel's demise.

What can be thought of this unilateral Report that grants the United Nations, the OIC and international organizations the right to determine the policies, laws, culture and thought processes of 350 million Europeans? It could in fact be read as a treatise on dhimmitude about a continent whose inhabitants, like the Israelis, are non-existent. An international, multi-polar, fascist-type and totalitarian government that carries out such a cultural inquisition would replace their democratically elected national systems. Conclaves acting without the public's knowledge, insert their decisions by means of networks, partnerships and "representatives of civil society," who have been elected by no one but themselves and paid by mysterious humanitarian "foundations" aiming at world "peace and justice."

This report becomes clearer when studied in the light of the conferences organized by ISESCO to plan down to the smallest details the penetration and subversion of Western culture.

ISESCO AND THE MEDIA PLAN AGAINST ISRAEL

ISESCO is an official institution and one of the main organs of the OIC. It has conducted dozens of programs since 1982 on the Islamic and Christian holy sites in Israel. The most important of them were the international symposia, held in Rabat (1993 and 2002) under the patronage of the King of Morocco within the Framework of the Islamic-Christian Dialogue, and another convened in Amman in 2004 under the patronage of the King of Jordan. In the proceedings of the conference on June 7–8, 2002, the moderate King Mohammed VI stated in his introduction:

> The acts of destruction and distortion committed by the occupation authorities to distort the facts and truths of history cause serious damage to the Islamic and Christian holy sites and violate their sanctity and the values they embody for all the believers of the different religions. [34]

For the king, as President of the Al-Quds Committee affiliated to the OIC, such actions, including putting archeological artifacts in museums, constitutes an attack against all believers. However, Christian churches in Judea that had been reduced to ruins by the Islamic occupation were restored by Israel, because, contrary to *shari'a*, Israel has no laws prohibiting the restoration or construction of churches. It can also be noted that Morocco, like all of North Africa, is the region where virtually no vestiges of pre-Islamic Christian history remain.

In his speech Dr. Abdulaziz Othman Altwaijri, Director-General of ISESCO, went further, "The crimes against humanity committed by Israel have reached an extent of oppression, injustice and aggression that humanity has never witnessed, neither in this age nor in previous ages." [35]

A second international conference under the patronage of the Hashemite King Abdullah II and organized by ISESCO, took place in Amman on November 23-25, 2004. The official topic was again the protection of Muslim and Christian holy places in Palestine. However, this theme revealed a broad strategy for Islamic penetration of all economic, cultural, religious, political and media sectors within Western society under cover of the Palestinian war against Israel.

In his introduction, Altwaijri opened the conference "on the holy sites in this land of prophecy." This of course referred to the Hebrew prophets and biblical characters that the Koran had "Islamized," since Muhammad the Prophet of Islam had only lived in Arabia. He continued:

> Our responsibilities towards Islamic and Christian holy sites in Palestine spring from our commitment at the Islamic Educational, Scientific and Cultural Organisation to the Palestinian cause which we all believe to be the essence of all issues and the supreme task in the Islamic world and the Eastern Christian circles that are part of our Arab and Islamic civilisation.[36]

The publication of these conferences in Rabat and Amman in two volumes[37] represents a monument to hatred and anti-Jewish incitement that goes well beyond Nazi literature, with sentences such as, "Jews are the enemies of Allah, the enemies of faith and of the worship of Allah" (p. 253), translated in the French version as: "They are the enemies of God, the faith and other religions." According to the lecturer Mr. Adnan Ibrahim Hassan al Subah, president of the Palestinian Jenin Information Center:

> People familiar with the Torah, which we believe to have been distorted, know the extent of the evils they attribute to their prophets: corruption, treachery, fornication or approval of it. It is with these facts that we need to arm ourselves when we confront the Zionist propaganda in the world with tangible facts, as part of our defense of the faith and the faithful on earth, wherever they may be. (p. 254)

The lecturer had probably never read the Bible of which he speaks, since his allegations are fantasies. They are the seeds for fanning hatred among the illiterate, manipulating them and conditioning as he himself explains:

> [T]his approach is more likely to establish a bond between the faithful of the earth. In our information efforts, we need to target the simple Jew and expose the anti-faith Zionist regime.

Mr. Al Subah doubtless was unaware that the Hebrew Bible is part of the basic religious texts of Christianity and that his insults about the Torah are also insults against more than two billion Christians, believers and non-believers, if only through the excessive ignorance they reveal. The lecturer, who collaborates through ISESCO with the Alliance of Civilizations and the EU then made a recommendation for the UN and other bodies:

> To this end, it would be beneficial to call for the organisation of a conference of the world's faithful that would homogenize [sic] the perception of holy sites, pave the way for containing of Zionist movements and expose their shameful practices against Islamic and Christian holy sites. These practices should be exposed to the international community as a violation of human rights and a blatant breach of international conventions, treaties, and pacts, and of the civilizational values of modern societies. It would also be beneficial to urge the United Nations Organisation and other affiliated organizations to discharge their duty in defending the lofty principles for which they were created. [38]

These books of incitement to religious hatred were on display at the Palais des Nations in Geneva at a reception after a day's Conference organized by the OIC on December 19, 2008 to commemorate the 60th anniversary of the Universal Declaration of Human Rights.

THE MEDIA STRATEGY AGAINST ISRAEL: INFILTRATION OF THE WEST

The Rabat and Amman conferences organized by ISESCO represent a monumental case of historical mythomania that seeks to deny any trace of Judaism in the lands of the Bible and to prove its Arab and Muslim character since the third millennium BC. The Jews are accused of having "judaized" the Biblical prophets who were in fact Muslims and to have usurped the oldness of other peoples, since the Jews themselves have no history. The same could be said of the Christians, who have usurped Jesus, the Muslim prophet.

The objective of the Amman Conference was to establish a global strategy for the re-Islamization of Jerusalem (al-Quds), because, as one of the lecturers explained, "Jerusalem is the cornerstone of the spiritual edifice and the Zionist Jewish entity. Were it to be dislodged, the whole edifice and the Zionist entity itself would crumble like a deck of cards." [39]

The lecturers emphasized the major importance of Muslim-Christian solidarity in the fight to seize al-Quds and to drive Israel out of Islam's holy city.
They proposed a whole range of schemes, including the adoption of the
Muslim and Christian holy sites in al-Quds by all the mosques, churches,
monasteries, and Muslim and Christian institutions the world over. They
recommended a vast campaign at the United Nations, in the US and among
international NGOs. This joint Muslim-Christian media campaign on a global scale would expose the untruths of Israel—another point in common with
the Alliance of Civilizations. Promoting al-Quds would be by film, television, music and festivals, under the supervision of a special Muslim and
Christian group that would be working with all the rights tools. Such a
program is reminiscent of both the Anna Lindh Foundation and the Alliance
of Civilizations' policy for a Muslim-Western cultural union.

The campaign should be run through international bodies in a humanistic,
international manner and in the general interest, avoiding any appearance of
chauvinism or superiority complex. It needed to unmask the United States
and Israel and isolate them. It ought to communicate with the world's communities in their own language and mind set, because the media had to
influence the targeted audience, according to its culture, history and civilization. These involved prior knowledge of others, before starting any campaign. It had to be the same for the whole world, profiting from international
media support and the global platforms with selected profiles for each activity, such as knowing the audience's language and its mentality.

Action plans showed a media strategy that was meant to employ an attrac-
tive style and a scientific language. This information campaign would examine all the suffering since the establishment of the racist, Zionist entity in
1948, which paralleled precisely the plan of the Alliance of Civilizations in
its White Paper. The speakers stressed the crucial role and the utmost importance that could be played by the media in the fight against Israel. It was
recommended that the Islamic view should demonstrate an uncompromising
attachment to Arab and Palestinian rights, as well as the conviction that the
re-Islamization of Jerusalem would return to the city its spiritual position of
peace and harmonious, religious coexistence, the flourishing of faith and
make it an agent of culture and civilization (p. 175). Naturally, this picture in
no way corresponds to the Islamic history of al-Quds. It is a vision developed
a thousand years before Muhammad by the prophets and kings of Israel, who
spoke Hebrew and not Arabic and never preached Islam.

The Secretary-General of the Jordanian Royal Committee for Al Quds Affairs, Abdallah Kanaan, presented an elaborate strategy for ways of infiltrating Islamic policy into all Western cultural and media sectors invoking the Palestinian cause, and which matched perfectly the plan of activities decided upon by the Alliance of Civilizations.[40] Kanaan's plan first examined the European and American context and proposed turning the Muslim and Christian holy places in Jerusalem into a central world problem. A large number of conferences would be held on educational, scientific and cultural issues on a regional and international basis, especially in the West. The speaker laid out the various currents of opinion in Europe and the US in order to extract an action plan for maximum effect. He examined the media field in the West in order to unlock means for supporting the war against Israel. This plan recommended (1) clarity of the objective, (2) flexibility to achieve successful interaction, (3) a gradual approach to sow the plan's secondary objectives, then the advance toward execution of the ultimate objective through the division of the main objective into short, medium and long term targets, and (4) supervision of a media strategy entrusted to a single group that would anticipate local, regional and international developments.

In the short-term the author also recommended:

> 1) Publicizing the history of Jerusalem since its foundation by the Canaanite Jebusites [sic] to date. This would be achieved through a systematic and intensive process that is easy to assimilate by the Western public opinion and that demands little time, material and mental effort. It would be based on accurate and documented information that relies on archeological findings and credible documents or manuscripts, as well as on a rejection of the Torah-based history.
> 2) Popularizing Islamic and Christian holy sites in the same manner, starting with Al Aqsa Mosque which, according to the noble Hadith, is only forty years older than the first shrine ever created for humanity, Al Haram Mosque in Makkah.[41]

In enumerating the many themes of the media war waged by the OIC against Israel in the West, the speaker quoted arguments repeated *ad nauseam* by many Western journalists, intellectuals, ministers and heads of state, of whom we now know the source of their inspiration. Here are summarized some of the targets shared by European leaders and considered as short-term by the lecturer.

It was necessary to convince the European Union that a solution to the Arab-Israeli conflict was in its vital interest. It would thus free itself from the weight of history, especially Germany, and could expand its partnership with the Arab world and achieve full access to its markets. As long as the Palestinian Arab people did not have its own state, relations between the EU and the Arab world would remain unstable. It was also important to emphasize that the American pro-Israel position was in contravention of international law, threatened America's vital interests as well as of Europe's and was impacting on peace and security throughout the world. This argument, dictated to European leaders and journalists by the OIC, was hammered home by the Western media, and was the catalyst of European hostility towards America, in particular President Bush.

Another tactic proposed was to make Western public opinion aware of the threats facing Western interests caused by Israeli policy. The West, especially the US, had to be made to understand that the resentment of Arabs and Muslims toward Western policy stemmed from its support for Israel. This support had to be represented as one of the main factors in the violence against Western interests in the Middle East and even in the West by individuals who reacted emotionally to family tragedies.[42] Westerners had to be convinced that peace was impossible without recognition by Israel of the right of the Arab Palestinian people to self-determination, the creation of an independent, sovereign state in the entire territory "occupied" in 1967, with Al-Quds as capital, and the return of the "refugees." An Israeli withdrawal from all "Arab" territories had to be accompanied by Israel abandoning its Zionist, racist character. This tactic was successful in America and was invoked by American President Barack Obama to humiliate publicly Israel's Prime Minister Binyamin Netanyahu in March 2010.

Lastly the lecturer stressed the importance of making Western public opinion aware that the shared interests of Arabs, Muslims and the West could never be the same as those of Israel. The West had to be convinced that the only chance for peace lay in Israel abandoning its racist nature and its arms.

The speaker commended the argument ceaselessly promoted by Chirac, Prodi and European leaders, emphasizing that the American pro-Israeli position prevents its adherence to the resolutions of international legality, in which the United States of America had initially participated. He stressed that this position lacks balance, "undermines the vital interests of the United States of America and Europe, and influences the peace and security of the entire world."[43]

In laying out the medium-term targets the speaker presented a broad plan for the subversion and Islamization of the West. He recommended obtaining the support of certain intellectuals, *literati* and influential political movements that were capable of molding public opinion in the West within the context of the Arab-Israeli conflict and especially the issue of al-Quds. This campaign would refer to UN resolutions that formed the basis for the media plan. Here too, European Union policy to support the UN's "international law" is in fact strengthening world control by the OIC, whose influence with its allies, predominates in all international forums.

Another tactic proposed by the lecturer was to infiltrate the media as well as cultural, intellectual and economic circles that were influential in the West in order to expose them to the Arab point of view and to convince them that their country's policies were subservient to "the interests of the Zionist movement with its various formations and bodies and not of the interests of their own countries, in particular economic and vital interests" [sic].[44] Other themes were:

> 3. Discreetly and indirectly encouraging trends critical of Zionism and the Israeli judaization policies in Jerusalem within Western circles and in a way that would prevent the targeting, isolation and annihilation of these trends by the Zionists movement and its concealed and visible tentacles. This would make possible the use of these trends as a pressure tool in confronting the Zionist lobby and the coalition of Jewish and Christian Zionists (neo-conservatives)[45] in defending the vital interests of their countries.
>
> 4. Focusing on exposing anti-Semitic laws, such as the aforementioned Gatsio [Gayssot] Law in France and Bush's Anti-Semitism Law, as laws that have no bearing on the vital and non-vital interests of America, but are more of a mirror of Israeli and Zionist interests and serve as a decisive factor and tool in international policy orientations and contents, ultimately leading to the weakening of these countries and depriving them of the power to decide.
>
> 5. Transforming the question of Al Quds into a major domestic Arab issue instead of a subject for occasions and reactions.

The speaker then summarized the long-term objectives of the media plan, of which we mention two:

> Encouraging the European Union, as a central institution and as individual members, to shift positions from a negative stance imitative of the United States, to positive stances. The European Union should not leave the stage free for the United States, and must be able to forge its own visions and positions. These would be more in harmony with the international will vis-à-vis the

Arab-Israeli conflict, the Israeli occupation of Arab territories, including Jerusalem, and the right of the Arab Palestinian people to self-determination and to
the establishment of its independent state with Al Quds as its capital. Only in
this way can the European Union become a major player instead of waiting for
American instructions and guidance, as if these matters were the sole purview
of American administrations, and as if the EU countries can only undertake
what the United States of America sanctions. In other words, it is necessary to
curb the monopoly of the United States of America exercised over the Palestinian question, the issue of Jerusalem and the Arab-Israeli conflict with all its
dimensions and ramifications.

Kanaan stated that the EU needed to become "an independent player not
subject to the *diktats* of Washington under the pretext that the Middle East is
under American domination and that European countries cannot do anything
without the authorization of the American Administration." In other words,
he explained, "the target is to end US hegemony in the region and to termi-
nate the Americans' monopoly on handling the Israel-Arab conflict and the
Jerusalem question in particular."

The other target was:

> Transforming the Palestinian question and the Arab-Israeli conflict from inter-
> nal American issues to external issues primarily governed by the mutual inter-
> ests of America, the Muslims and the Arabs. This would break the immunity
> of the Israeli policies and force Israel to bow to the will of the international
> community and adhere to all of the UN resolutions. [46]

This reference to the United Nations demonstrates the hold of the OIC reinforced by its allies, the NAM, over the UN and announces that the new world
order, to whose development Europe has contributed so much, will be amen-
able to *shari'a* law.

The lecturer laid out the many mechanisms for carrying this out at the
local, regional and international levels. He mentioned the mobilization of
members of the Arab and Muslim communities in the West, especially in the
US. These Muslims should be encouraged to participate in political life in
their countries to achieve major political weight instead of remaining marginalized, without influence and neglected by candidates at election time. He
stressed that this Muslim community was made up of important scientists,
intellectuals and politicians, and could therefore exercise major influence in
the West. This type of strategy of seeking to extend the OIC's influence to

Western countries through immigrants and their growing weight in their host societies had already been alluded to by Ihsanoglu at the European Parliament in 2005,[47] and by the founders of the Euro-Arab Dialogue.

Another step was to block Western policy in Europe and the United States from prohibiting charity organizations, which according to the author worked in the humanitarian field, whereas in fact they were also fundraising for jihad terrorism.

The lecturer also mentioned the financial aspects and tools of this strategy, because they opened up several possibilities. He recommended:

9. Encouraging Islamic and Arab investments of Arab and Muslim capital in the media field in the West, most particularly in the United States of America, in the different forms of media, written, audio and visual, thus paving the way for breaking the Jewish monopoly over American media.

10. Encouraging Islamic and Arab investments in modern information and communication technologies such as the internet and the making of television and cinema documentaries which are likely to effect a change in Western public opinion spheres which rely on this type of educational and media sources in forming their opinions about nations and civilizations and cultures. (p.206)

Mr. Kanaan advised, "Encouraging Arab and Muslim communities to integrate as much as possible the societies where they live, in order to gain credibility," and to become involved with students and teachers at Western universities, especially in the US, and to create Friends of Al-Quds associations at their places of higher education together with their colleagues.[48] Various projects about the media and Western public opinion were presented, such as the creation of a multilingual satellite channel called Al-Quds, which "would be staffed with a media, information, intellectual and historical team knowledgeable about the question of Al-Quds and its various dimensions" [sic]. Arab and Muslim thinkers, ulamas and intellectuals living in Western societies ought to recommend to Muslims to reject extremism, fanaticism and violence "as this tends to be detrimental and generates negative reactions to Arab and Islamic issues."

The lecturer spoke at length about the possibilities of "utilising modern communication technologies, especially the opening of web sites dedicated to al-Quds, and encouraging Muslims to embark on an Internet-supported war for al-Quds to counterbalance the activities of the Zionist movement and its octopus-like formations, the most dangerous of which is Christian Zionism and its mastermind, the Neo-Conservatives." Arab radio stations and satellite channels such as Al-Jazeera, Al-Arabia and Dubai, should broadcast "weekly programs in English [about Al-Quds], targeting Western public opinion, benefiting from media personalities knowledgeable about the Western mentality and capable of influencing it to the benefit of the issue of Al Quds with the help of UN resolutions." Programs should be made about Al-Quds in English, French, Spanish, German, Russian and other languages.[49]

Friends of al-Quds associations in the US and European companies should be set up in working class and student circles, which would support the work of non-governmental organizations working for the cause of al-Quds at the Arab, Islamic and international levels. To this would be added the publication of "all that is issued by Americans, Europeans and Jews against Israel, its policies and Zionism." These booklets would be published again and distributed in various languages in the West in order to enlighten Western public opinion. Films should be produced "that reveal the barbarity of Israel, the dangers inherent in the policy of demolishing houses, murder and massacre of the Arab Palestinian people, and distributing these films as widely as possible in the Islamic world." (p. 208)

Finally, specialists and experts in Western affairs should be involved "in the discussion of the broad lines of the media plan in order to enrich it and guarantee all conditions of its success." Such experts would specialize in Western media, history of al-Quds, Western political issues and Western public opinion, psychology, religions, law, and Western culture. In two notes that appear in the French text but are omitted from the English book, the lecturer mentions "Zionist stories of alleged Nazi slaughters," and explains, "*Kristallnacht* was the night when Jews were persecuted by the Nazis and when the windows of their homes and businesses were broken."

As we shall see below, the networks sponsored by the UN that bring together the European Union, OIC, and its cultural wing ISESCO in the partnership's strategy would be charged with the responsibility of carrying out this policy in all Western countries.

The Christians living under the Palestinian Authority and in Gaza were made the strident megaphone for the OIC's policies in a document entitled *Kairos Palestine*, drawn up by Palestinian theologians and published in Bethlehem on December 11, 2009 by the World Council of Churches, Geneva.[50] In the name of love, peace and justice, and making Israel the symbol of evil, occupation and oppression, they called on the Churches and the West to initiate a policy of economic strangulation and defamation of Israel.

On March 1, 2010, the Greek Catholic Melkite Patriarch of Antioch, Alexandria and Jerusalem Gregory III, wrote to Pope Benedict XVI concerning the synod scheduled for October 2010. This Synod planned to bring together the Catholic Churches of the Middle East to discuss the escalating problems for Christians in the region and to put a stop to their flight.

In his letter the Patriarch wrote that it was his duty to inform the Pope of the increased dangers in the region, particularly for Christians.

> There is a diffuse but sure rise of Islamic extremism, provoked by the threats of the Israeli government against Palestinians, Lebanon, Syria (and Iran), which is spreading throughout all the countries in the region. Even in Syria, where such extremism has been up to now very limited, its advance has become more and more evident, despite efforts from the government against it.

This extremism, the Patriarch states, does not hesitate to employ terrorist methods, especially against Christians, particularly in Iraq and Egypt. The Patriarch begged that:

> the Holy See's diplomacy redouble its efforts to persuade the Tel Aviv government, despite the views of its most intransigent wing—probably via the United States and those European countries which, having sponsored the birth of the State of Israel and supported it ever since, should be able to exert effective pressure on it—of the grave danger of this development which in the medium and perhaps short term, runs against the interests and future of the State of Israel itself, which needs peace in the region just as much as Arab countries, to be able eventually to live normally all together.

In accordance with the cycle of dhimmitude, Muslims massacre Christians, who put the blame on Jews, who have done nothing to them.

In June 2010, numerous Catholic organizations expressed their solidarity with the population of Gaza, which support Hamas, its genocidal charter and its continuous shelling of Israel's villages and cities. These were Justice et Paix, France; Mission de France; Pax Christi, France; Chrétiens de la Méditerranée; le Comité catholique contre la faim et pour le développement; and Le Secours catholique.

At the same time, bishops from across the Middle East and Vatican officials decried the plight of Christians in the region in a meeting with Pope Benedict XVI in Nicosia, Cyprus. The Pope presented a document which stated: "Today, emigration is particularly prevalent because of the Israeli-

Palestinian conflict and the resulting instability throughout the region."
While the document indicted "Israeli occupation," it remained silent on persecutions of Christians by Muslims.[51]

For its part, Europe lavished billions of euros on Palestinian NGOs and
representatives of "civil society," which called for a boycott and for the
demonization and delegitimization of Israel in schools, on the television and
radio, in Palestinian publications and on the international scene.[52] Since
2005, a Palestinian Week Against Israeli Apartheid takes place on campuses
and in the major cities in Europe, Canada and the US, calling for disinvest-
ments, sanctions and boycotts of Israel. The latest was on March 1-10, 2010.
According to NGO Monitor in its comprehensive analysis, most of the speakers at these hate-filled demonstrations belong to NGOs financed by European
governments, the European Commission and the New Israel Fund, created
following Obama's election.[53]

On March 26, 2010, the Iranian Foreign Minister, Manouchehr Mottaki,
called on the world to save Jerusalem from Judaization, which was destroying churches and mosques; this was in accordance with the media program of
the OIC, of which Iran is a major member.[54]

On its website ISESCO indicates that the ISESCO/UNESCO cooperation
program for 2008-2009 contains 128 activities in the areas of education,
science, culture, communication, external relations and National Commissions. Presenting its action plans, ISESCO states that "The three-year Action
Plan for 2010-2012 constitutes the first part of ISESCO's action plans derived from its Medium-Term Plan for the years 2010-2018 [...] Countering
the aggressive campaign against Islam and Muslims represented a major
strategic objective for the outgoing action plan and the core of its action
during that period."[55]

The central strategic objective of the 2007-2009 Action Plan was focused
on the campaign against Islamophobia. ISESCO had a large number of programs and projects to maintain, since the fight against the anti-Islam and
anti-Muslims campaign would be a fixed strategic objective in its plans. The
partnership with international organizations and NGOs to fight Islamophobia
was another major strategic objective. The correction of the image of Islam
and Muslims in the West is one of the targets set for 2010-2012.

In the field of education and every aspect of culture, the action plan
accorded priority to Islamic education within the framework of cultural diversity and promotion of dialogue between civilizations. It emphasizes the
modes of expression of cultural diversity.

ARADESC is the UNESCO/ISESCO Arab Research-Policy Network on Economic, Social and Cultural Rights. It boasts about its beliefs that human rights are universal, indivisible and interdependent, and that cultural rights are, like other human rights, an expression and requirement of human dignity. It affirms its conviction that violations of cultural rights provoke tensions and identity conflicts and affirms that respect for cultural diversity, tolerance, dialogue and cooperation are essential.

It calls for respect of freedoms and cultural diversity, which play a fundamental role in the buttressing of democracy. The Declaration commends respect for freedom of choice in cultural identity, freedom of belief, conscience and religion, freedom of opinion and freedom of expression, including the corresponding values and the exercise of cultural activities that conform to the principles of human rights and democracy.

What to think of such language issued by tyrannical regimes intolerant of their pre-Islamic minorities, some of whom practice torture and slavery? These words are addressed to the West in its own language to defend the rights of Muslim immigrants in their Western host countries.

In spite of these noble commitments, ISESCO, which has adopted the Islamic Declaration on Cultural Diversity, does not recognize the cultural rights of Israel, Jews and Christians whose religious and cultural historic sites have been Islamized. In the same way, the Jewish holy sites in Iraq commemorating the prophets Ezekiel and Daniel were Islamized, as was the alleged tomb of Joseph in Shechem. In October 2000 Arab vandals torched and burned down a large part of the ancient synagogue remnants in Jericho, and the Ecumenical Orthodox Patriarchate is dying in its ancient capital, Constantinople.

On March 3, 2010, Dr Abdulaziz Othman Altwaijri, Director General of ISESCO, wrote to Mrs. Irina Bokova, UNESCO Director-General. He urged his counterpart in UNESCO to take immediate action to stop Israel's continuous falsification of Islamic history in Palestine and reiterated his request that UNESCO ask Israel to revoke its government's decision to annex Al-Haram Al-Ibrahimi and Bilal Ibn Rabah Mosque to the list of Jewish archaeological sites "as it is at odds with international law."[56] The sites referred to by Islamized names are the Hebron tombs of the Hebrew Patriarchs Abraham, Isaac and Jacob and their wives (Machpelah) being of Herodian construction (1st century), and Rachel's tomb near Bethlehem, built on former Jewish sanctuaries. From 1266, Muslims prohibited Jews and Christians from entering the Machpelah; after the British conquest of the Holy Land in 1917, Christians but not Jews were allowed to visit it. Only in 1967 after the Six Day War, could Jews pray again at their millennial shrine.

In its request 184 Ex 37, the UNESCO Executive Council complied with ISESCO's request and asked that Rachel's Tomb and the Cave of Machpelah not be counted among Israeli national heritage assets.

NOTES

1. Cf. the report on this topic, *Alliance des civilisations?* in *Controverses*, no. 9, November 2008 (Paris: Editions de l'Eclat, 2008).

2. *Alliance of Civilizations*, Report of the High level Group, www.unAOC.org, November 13, 2006 (New York: United Nations, 2006).

3. *Alliance of Civilizations*, Report, 3, §1.1.

4. *Alliance of Civilizations*, Report, 6, §2.6. See the Mecca Symposium, §4.

5. *Alliance of Civilizations*, Report, 10, §3.13.

6. *Alliance of Civilizations*, Report, 4, §1.5, author's emphasis.

7. *Alliance of Civilizations*, Report, 5 and 23.

8. *Alliance of Civilizations*, Report, 11, §4.2. These opinions are now repeated by American journalists.

9. Parentheses in the text.

10. *Alliance of Civilizations*, Report, 12, §4.3.

11. *Alliance of Civilizations*, Report, 12, §4.4.

12. *Alliance of Civilizations*, Report, 13–14, §4.12.

13. *Alliance of Civilizations*, Report, 15, §4.17, parentheses and quotation marks in the original. Mentioning the historical jihad is now considered to be Islamophobic.

14. *Alliance of Civilizations*, Report, 18, §5.7. The novelist James Caroll developed this pattern of equivalence between shoah and nakba in an article in the *Boston Globe*, "New talks, old wounds," reprint in the *International Herald Tribune*, September 8, 2010.

15. As stated in its brochure titled *1974–1994*, 34.

16. *Alliance of Civilizations*, Report, 20, §5.17.

17. *Alliance of Civilizations*, Report, 21, §5.18.

18. See the report of November 8, 2002 presented to the European Parliamentary Assembly by its Committee on Culture, Science and Education by the Rapporteur of the Spanish Socialist group, Lluis Maria de Puig, assembly.coe.int/Documents/WorkingDocs/doc02/FDOC9626.htm (accessed January 6, 2011) and Europe's Parliamentary Assembly, Recommandation 1590 (2003) Cultural cooperation between Europe and the countries to the south of the Mediterranean. assembly.coe.int/Documents/AdoptedText/TA03/FREC1590.htm (accessed January 6, 2011) See also the goals of the Anna Lindh Foundation.

19. *Alliance of Civilizations*, 25, §6.4.

20. *Alliance of Civilizations*, 33, §1, italics in the text.

21. *Alliance of Civilizations*, 33.

22. *Alliance of Civilizations*, 35, §5, italics in the text.

23. *Alliance of Civilizations*, 36, §2, italics in the text. This proposal was accepted by President Obama in his Cairo speech, June 4, 2009.

24. *Alliance of Civilizations*, 37, §4, italics in the text.

25. *Alliance of Civilizations*, 39, §5.

26. *Alliance of Civilizations*, 39, §7, italics in the text.

27. *Alliance of Civilizations*, 40, §7.

28. *Alliance of Civilizations*, 31, §6.24.

29. *Alliance of Civilizations*, 35 §6, italics in the text.

30. *Alliance of Civilizations*, 53.

31. For more details, see Bat Ye'or, *Eurabia*, 45, chap. 4.

32. *Alliance of Civilizations*, Report of the High Level Group, 54.

33. *Alliance of Civilizations*, Report of the High Level Group, 54.

34. *Protection of Islamic and Christian Holy Sites in Palestine.* Publications of the Islamic Educational, Scientific and Cultural Organization–ISESCO–1425H /2004. Proceedings of the International Conference organized by ISESCO in Rabat, June 7–8, 2002.

35. *Protection of Islamic and Christian Holy Sites in Palestine*, 15.

36. *Protection of Islamic and Christian Holy Sites in Palestine.* (Proceedings of the Second International Conference) Amman, November 23–25, 2004. ISESCO, 1428H/2007, 18. The French translation is somewhat different.

37. I thank David G. Littman for having brought these publications to my attention.

38. Adnan Ibrahim Hassan Al Subah, president of the Jenin Information Center,"Role of Palestinian civil society in the protection of Holy Sites in Palestine," ibid., p. 254.

39. Ibid., p. 195.

40. Dr Abdullah Kanaan, Secretary General of the Royal Committee for Al Quds Affairs, Amman, Hashemite Kingdom of Jordan, "Media Plan for Publicizing the Cause of Al Quds Al Sharif in the West, and Mechanisms for its Implementation," ibid., pp. 187-208.

41. These are Muslim traditions; ibid., 201.

42. This and the preceding arguments were often pronounced by Romano Prodi, Jacques Chirac and left-wing European politicians to explain away the antisemitic fever of the years 2000–2005 in Europe.

43. Ibid., 202.

44. Ibid., 204.

45. Parentheses in the text. James Caroll published a violent diatribe against Christian Zionists, in which he accused them of harming America and Middle East peace interests, "Onward, Christian Zionists," *International Herald Tribune*, August 26, 2010.

46. Kanaan, op. cit. p. 205.

47. Viz. his speech §6.

48. See Robert Spencer, *Stealth Jihad. How Radical Islam Is Subverting America without Guns or Bombs* (Washington, D.C.: Regnery, 2008).

49. Al-Quds Underground (AQU) is funded by Cordaid (Holland), the Anna Lindh Foundation and SICA, another Dutch organization. It organizes intimate encounter with the inhabitants of Arab Jerusalem at secret locations to celebrate the beauty of "diversity," yet refusing Jewish presence.See also November 26, 2009, NGO Monitor.

50. Put online by Menahem Macina, February 22, 2010, www.debriefing.org/30011.html (accessed January 6, 2011).

51. Rachel Donadio, "Pope highlights plight of Christians in Mideast," *International Herald Tribune*, June 7, 2010.

52. Gerald M. Steinberg, Europe's Hidden Hand. EU Funding for Political NGOs in the Arab-Israeli Conflict. Analyzing Processes and Impact. NGO Monitor Monograph series. April 2008.

53. www.ngo-monitor.org/article/israeli_apartheid_week_ngo_involvement (accessed April 3, 2010).

54. www.jihadwatch.org 2010/3 (accessed March 27, 2010).

55. www.isesco.org.ma/english/actionPlan/action.php?idd=TDD_REF_ACT (accessed April 2010).

56. www.iina.me/english/news.php?go=fullnews&newsid=105 (accessed April 2010).

Chapter Four

The Destruction of
the Nations of Europe

Europeans for the most part have not yet understood that their governments have deliberately broken up their sovereign, national structures. They still believe they can impact their national destiny through the democratic system they had chosen themselves. In fact, decision-making power at the national level over internal and external policies has eluded them. Today, the populations of the EU are affected in political, cultural and information fields by transnational and international organizations such as the Anna Lindh Foundation and the Alliance of Civilizations—and in the immigration, education and social policies of the OIC and ISESCO. These bodies overlap in networks that spread global governance, where the influence of the OIC at the UN is paramount.

The transfer of power from local, national spheres of the EU member states to international organizations takes place through instruments called "dialogue," "partnerships" and "multiculturalism," linked to networks nominated by the states. Besides the numerous transnational systems linked to the UN, these networks are, in the Mediterranean interregional sphere, the Euro-Arab Dialogue, Medea, Barcelona Process, the Mediterranean Union, Anna Lindh Foundation, Alliance of Civilizations, the Euro-Mediterranean Parliamentary Assembly (EMPA), UNRWA, and others linked with EU funding Middle Eastern NGOs, as well as Arab cultural, political and economic projects. With their sub-ramifications they spread a wide web and pass on instructions to sub-networks, to myriads of NGOs and to representatives of "civil societies" that they themselves choose, activists promoting Palestinianism, boycotts of Israel, immigration and multiculturalism. The network of political institutes, think tanks, often financed by the European Commission, convert such directives into public opinion by injecting them into the media, publications, films, propaganda, a bottomless pit for billions.

Europeans are hemmed in by a game of multiple mirrors, which radiate at every level and into infinity, prefabricated opinions in accordance with political and cultural agendas of which they know nothing and often disapprove, but which they finance by their taxes. This is the principle of coherence of the European Council's Common Strategy that commended a partnership policy with the Southern neighbors, and stating in Article 26 that the Council, Commission and all member states of the Union must ensure the coherence, unity and effectiveness of the Union's strategy.[1]

This opaque, elitist system undermines democracy. It also lacks visibility, doubling and multiplying itself like a hydra into networks and sub-networks. Dictated by economic interests, global Islamist terrorism, energy requirements and high finance, it speaks in humanitarian and moral language. European politicians and intellectuals, discredited by their fellow citizens, are put back into the circuit through OIC networks to carry on their work of termites. This transformation of a "Europe of Nations" into a unified Europe that is integrated with international organizations such as the UN, UNESCO, OIC and others, fits the globalist strategy of the EU, especially in its Mediterranean dimension.

The rout of European nationalisms, discredited by two world wars in the twentieth century and by socialist, pacifist and universalist movements, made it easier for pan-Islamic ambitions that had been aroused by petrodollars. Already in the 1950s, Said Ramadan was soliciting funding from the Saudis to spread Muslim Brotherhood centers throughout Europe. In 1973 this expansion policy was strongly confirmed at the OIC conference just as European nationalisms were falling to pieces, sapped by the construction of Europe, immigration and the march towards globalization.

This view drives the shared policies of the EU and OIC in opposing both the cultural nationalism and local European identities, although each for different reasons. Globalization promotes multiculturalism and the internationalization of a European population that is destined to change and disappear through the union of the two banks of the Mediterranean. Such a goal condemns to disintegration the very idea and awareness of a specific European civilization developed over more than 2,000 years. Meanwhile, national and cultural European identities assimilated to racism are fought bitterly by

EU member states and at the UN. The OIC follows a similar approach, organizing itself as a transnational force. However, unlike the EU, it asserts itself through rooting the Ummah in the Koranic religious and cultural traditions and in the historic heritage and the globalist ambition of the caliphate.

CONVERGENCE OF EU AND OIC IN DOMESTIC POLICIES

The Ninth Islamic Summit Conference in 2000 at Doha (Qatar) adopted an Islamic cultural strategy for the West. The following year ISESCO published this strategy in a booklet entitled *Strategy of Islamic Cultural Action in the West* (later called *The Strategy for Islamic Cultural Action outside the Islamic World*). This manual explains the motives, objectives, methods and concepts of a vast, unified strategy implemented across Europe and beyond, throughout the West. This concern of the OIC is nothing new. Since 1974, when immigration through family reunification relaunched *da'wa* in Europe, the OIC had been discussing the advantages of immigration and the ways to protect Muslims from Europe's devilish influence. The booklet laid out a clearly defined strategy. It was to keep the second and third generation immigrants within their original culture, root them in the Islamic faith and subject them to the commandments of the Koran and *shari'a* while providing them with the tools needed to achieve Islam's objectives in Europe.[2]

Recognizing the incompatibility of Western values and laws with Islamic precepts, the authors recommended a series of steps to prevent the integration and assimilation of Muslims into European culture. The methodology required ending inter-Muslim divisions to facilitate the emergence of a unified European Islam within a wider Islam. The plan for a unified Islamic culture would consolidate Muslims' identity with all the Islamic nuances and would urge immigrant communities to organize themselves strongly with its system of values, their life being guided in accordance with its precepts (p. 31).

This unifying approach for all European and Western Muslims involved membership of a shared identity that would be forged through the mandatory knowledge of Arabic, the language of Revelation and the Islamic faith, together with the learning of Islamic history and civilization. To this end, a vast network of Islamic teachers, schools, institutes and universities would be given the task of spreading this teaching from the cradle, accompanying men and women in youth and adulthood throughout their working lives, providing the necessary support by planning an educational, cultural and social program (chaps. 4 and 6).

Teaching immigrant Muslim children the greatness of their heritage would allow them to realize the fullness of the borrowing from Islam in every aspect of Western civilization. Islamic identity would govern and organize every facet of life and would define both behavior and interpersonal relationships. Muslims should be also interested in Western cultures as they are rich sources for Islamic culture and do not contradict the fundamentals of Islam. "Emphasis should be placed on the harmony of the contents of Islamic culture, its values and principles in their comprehensive and universal directions with the common human principles and values" (p. 82).

Such planning sought to strengthen the presence of Islam in the West, activating the role of Islamic culture in safeguarding and immunizing Islamic identity (p. 49 §9), re-establishing Islamic collective memory, reactivating and unifying it throughout Europe in order to release the relevant elements and procedures capable of guiding "the blessed Islamic awakening" (p. 49 §8). The dwindling infatuation with Western civilization and its criticism is a "blessed awareness" that ought to lead to a straightforward affirmation of an irreversible Islamic presence in Europe and "to the ratification of the civilizational project as an alternative that relies on true Islam and the positive acquisition of human civilization" (p. 70). This Islamic presence can play its noble role and pursue its goals only if it is in harmony with the spirit of Islam (pp. 70–71). The reinforcement of Islamic culture should create a new perception based on the reconciliation of Muslims with the others "and by respecting their traditions and customs in such a way as to create a sense of trust and tranquility [sic]" (p. 71 §a).

The current impact of Muslim immigration on European societies covers several pages. The authors observe that as the Islamic presence is irreversible and definitive, Europe is restructuring itself into a multi-ethnic and multi-cultural society, losing its harmonious and monolithic character based on "a specific historical, economic, social and cultural lineage" (p. 52). Becoming a multi-ethnic, multi-cultural and multi-religious society, Europe offers a unique opportunity for Islam and the Islamic world, which must help and support its presence in the West.

As far as European schools were concerned in the medium term, they would be asked to amend their curricula and teaching system to open up to the children's culture in order to be in harmony with the children of immigrants (p. 65). The booklet attributes the scholastic setbacks to the refusal of schools to adopt a policy of openness towards the culture of Muslim children and to impose the culture and values of the West. It blames the assimilation-ist role played by European schools, the setting for cultural conflict caused by the resistance of Muslim students to European teaching (p. 64). To correct this situation the educational strategy needed to protect the Muslim student against "the cultural encroachment, intellectual assimilation and educational hegemony" of the West (p. 69), and to endeavor to introduce Islam into school subjects and curricula and the teaching of history. The European authorities responsible for education needed to improve Islam's image in European textbooks and history lessons (p. 77).

Teaching of Arabic language and Islamic culture is a major obligation since Western schools "planned to destroy the unconscious referential struc-ture of the immigrant child through organized destructive strategies of the values he has brought with him from the family and original culture" (p. 65). The booklet's authors accuse the educational system of refusing to open up to the cultures of others and of admonishing society to reject anyone who does not adopt European culture and values. This system treats immigrants as though they had neither roots nor Islamic reference points, while ignoring their religion, language and culture. Europe was responsible for the failings of Muslim students and needed to give up the principles of integration and assimilation, while accepting on its soil that a Muslim population would settle within a multicultural framework.

Setting up Islam in Europe had to be the constant priority of Muslim communities and their leaderships, the authors affirm. They needed to devel-op a jurisprudence that incorporated Islamic principles and a strategy that would allow Muslims to play a decisive role in every social field. Attempts at political action through organizations and established political structures have proven efficient, and many Muslims have been able to head some municipalities and supervise them in the host countries. Muslims have voted for Muslim members of parliament or those sympathizing with the Muslim community in legislative assemblies. This achievement will make the voices of Muslims heard, and their religious and cultural requirements respected. However, bad Muslim economic planning led to the weakening of the power of the political and financial influence that Muslims should possess. The strategy should aim to create a new culture with a style "characterized by dialogue, exchange of expertise and coordination of efforts among all the parties involved so as to achieve these goals" (p. 81).

These measures altogether—the educational, cultural and social strate-gy—are but the agent of a long-term vision whose success opens the way to the universal Muslim mission (*da'wa*), of which European and Western Is-lam, supported by the entire Ummah, is the carrier. In order to serve the universal message of Islam, to revive its eternal heritage rooted in the belief in Allah, the Koran and the Sunna of the Prophet, it is necessary to set up plans and programs to train media experts and specialists, and

> the creation of a radio and satellite station which broadcasts round the clock programs in several languages, intended mainly for Muslim communities and societies in Europe. There should also be concern with the Islamic heritage and its production in the form of interesting radio and television programs, Islamic art and literature included in programs targeting to the new generations of Muslim communities in Europe, and ways to achieve cooperation, comple-mentarity, coordination and the exchange of technical expertise in the field of media production to serve the message of Islamic media. (p. 84)

A mission on this scale, intended to spread the call of Islam for the conver-sion of the West, requires strong and adequate leadership with which the entire Ummah could relate. In the short term the plan also provided for the creation of a Higher Council for Education and Culture at Western levels. It would be made up of qualified members elected by Islamic institutions in Europe and helped by specialists appointed by ISESCO and by committees in each European country. The Higher Council would be responsible for drawing up a teaching method and unified educational program that com-plied with Islam's intangible principles and the European situation. It would lay down the objectives and the broad lines of a unified method for the entire West (pp. 89–96).

This Council would be appointed as the body to deal with the European education authorities for the teaching of children in Muslim communities, at both the regional and national levels. It would try to obtain government aid from Muslim countries, from the OIC and all the other Islamic organizations involved. This support is intended for Islamic centers and bodies in Europe and for setting up Islamic schools for the children of the Muslim commu-nities. A call would also be made to European institutions, the European Council and Parliament for educational and cultural projects of Islamic estab-lishments and for setting up a common methodology (p. 89).

The method formulates several projects. The one for first generation immigrants seeks to make them aware of Islamic culture, and fight illiteracy with ISESCO's help and with finance from Islamic governments. The project for second and third generation immigrants includes the teaching of Arabic and Islam, support for Western intellectuals and educationalists who try to obtain from Western education authorities the inclusion of Islamic studies in official Western school curricula. This follows the examples of Belgium, Austria, Holland, Spain, Alsace and some districts in Germany. The report goes back to 2000 and this list must certainly have become considerably longer since then. During an official visit to Turkey in March 2010, German Chancellor Angela Merkel accepted the establishment of Turkish schools in Germany where, according to official figures, over three million Turks reside.

Other claims address the inclusion of Arabic as one of the existing modern languages to be included in the curricula of the school systems, the development of Islamic and Arabic language teacher training for non-Muslims, and the encouragement of scientific research in this field. This list includes the promotion "of the culture of the Muslim child by publishing good-quality children's books and stories about Islamic issues, in European languages" (p. 90). This project has already been carried out. In European cities can be found children's books describing the metamorphosis of Jews into monkeys and the Islamization of the Hebrew prophets and of Jesus.

In the medium-term the project proposed the following measures:

2.1 Preparing the legal, organizational and educational requirements to establish Islamic regular schools geared especially for the Muslim communities in Europe, and inviting European countries to contribute to financing this important project.

2.2 Preparing a plan to train educational staff that will be in charge of teaching at private Islamic schools, by establishing a teacher training faculty in Europe.

2.3 Working towards creating an Islamic fund for the financial support of private Islamic schools, collaborating [sic] with Islamic governments and charities.

2.4 Setting up a scientific body under the supervision of the Higher Council that will be in charge of preparing the Islamic educational curricula for private schools.

2.5 Establishing an Islamic Observatory in Europe to track the development of education for children in the West, and setting up a data bank so as to improve the cultural, educational development of the Muslim communities. (p. 90)

The main objectives of this mission within the European context are to anchor the Muslim firmly in submission to Allah alone (*tawheed*) and to reinforce the faith in Allah, the Koran and the message of the Prophet Muhammad. The preacher should be taught the methodology of guidance, sound polemics and the adoption of a moderate approach in preaching; he should avoid ways of generating apathy and adverse reactions. He should stress the tolerance of Islamic legislation and the necessity to abide by its limits.

The *da'wa* (proselytizing) methodology emphasizes the special characteristics required for the right preacher, who should adapt his discourse to the target audience. It underlines the need for the preparation, training and qualification of preachers and the organization of *da'wa*.

The examination of the ways to apply the mission is followed by an analysis of the information issues. Already in the preceding pages, the authors had frequently denounced the West's unfair and tendentious prejudices toward Islam, demanding their punishments by their respective governments. To neutralize nuisance by the media, coordination between European politicians and the OIC was required. The dialogue between civilizations and educational, cultural, social and religious planning would facilitate preventing Islamophobia and drawing a link between Islam and terrorism. As part of the mission, information activities had to serve Islam; the right to knowledge is respected but within the ambit of *shari'a*.

The Islamic information strategy in the West intended to serve the world message of Islam, to bestow its perennial heritage to generation upon generation, in order to instill in their hearts and minds the Islamic principles. It plans to establish an Islamic cyberspace channel working around the clock and broadcasting in several languages and designed for Muslim communities and societies in Europe. A world Islamic Academic Institute and a center for training senior technical staff would specialize in training Muslims with the purpose of achieving worldwide complementarity, cooperation, coordination and the exchange of technical expertise in the field of information production, as well as circulation of materials, records and Islamic films.

This Islamic *Strategy* intended for the West was published in 2001. No European politician has ever mentioned it. Besides its main topics analyzed here, other features are noteworthy. First comes the constant proclamation of

Islamic perfection and tolerance, a characterization that was strongly insisted upon later at the 2005 Mecca Summit. Through repetition, this statement of the Islamic creed has succeeded in being widely accepted in Western society. Their political and cultural elites confirm its revealed truth by constantly repeating it. The other points relate to the means advocated in the methodology: interculturality; proliferation of dialogues and partnerships at all levels and in every sector as channels for Islamic penetration into Western society; lobbying European politicians sympathetic to Islamic issues; and infiltrating existing Western political parties to promote Islamic interests. As this strategy develops within the *da'wa* mission, it is recommended to use moderate and open-minded language, emphasizing common Western and Islamic values and the conformity of Islamic principles with universal human values.

From 2001 and especially following the 9/11 jihadist terrorist attack, organizations for Islamic-Western dialogues proliferated in the West. Many Western politicians publicly adopted the OIC vision, according to which Islamic terrorism was the result of Western aggression and only involves a minute fringe of Muslims, who themselves are victims of poverty and are indignant at the injustices of the West. Europe considerably increased its aid to Arab countries, hardened its anti-Israel policy and stoked the sense of guilt of its networks. At the internal level, these multiple networks for dialogue and rapprochement between Islam and the West endeavored to carry out the recommendations of the *Strategy of Islamic Cultural Action in the West*. In inter-religious dialogues Christian theologians felt the political pressures of their governments, which were working towards reconciliation between the West and the Muslim world. This political interference in religious areas led Christian theologians to introduce Koranic interpretations into biblical texts that were contrary to their original meaning, in order to show the congruence of Christian and Islamic values as claimed in the *Strategy*. The creeping Islamization of Christian theology created divisions that weakened even further the Churches faced with a monolithic Islam convinced of its own perfection.

In April 2008 the Parliamentary Assembly of the Council of Europe discussed a package of measures dealing with immigrants, including Muslims.[3] Since poverty, discrimination and social exclusion provided the fertilizer for extremism, the Resolution invited European governments to consider them seriously and to rigorously combat Islamophobia (§5). Member states of the Council of Europe were recommended to take concrete steps to allow immigrants and their descendants, including members of the Muslim communities, to integrate into society through access without discrimination to employment, education, professional training, housing and public services. European governments and society, as a whole, needed to adapt to social diversity and remove the obstacles to the integration of immigrants and people of immigrant origin into society in order to create inclusive and participative citizenship, with their active collaboration in public and political life (§7).

Among the many recommendations issued, the Assembly asked the member states of the Council of Europe to fight discrimination in every field, Islamophobia, incitement to hatred, and the removal of schoolbooks that stereotype Islam as a hostile, threatening religion. It urged the states to encourage information projects about Islam's contribution to Western societies in order to overcome stereotypes. There was a need to advance people of immigrant origins in political parties, trade unions and NGOs, and encourage a public, open debate about the repercussions of foreign policy on the whole issue of radicalization. This affirmation transferred the cause of radicalism from its Islamic matrix to European policies that it subjected to the approval of the OIC and Muslim immigrants.

The Assembly asked the states to encourage Muslims to play a full role in society without questioning the secularity of the society and institutions of the countries in which they lived; to officially approve the European Convention of Human Rights and Fundamental Freedoms, even though it differed from the Islamic Declaration. The Assembly asked Muslims to promote the transmission of basic European values within the Muslim communities, especially among the youth, *emphasizing their compatibility with the Muslim religion*,[4] and to ensure that basic European values be taught in Muslim religious schools. These misleading recommendations appear intended to conceal the submission of the Assembly to the OIC.

Article 6 of the Treaty of Maastricht stipulates that the European Union is based upon the principles of liberty, democracy, respect for human rights and basic freedoms, law and principles shared by the member states. It mentions neither the Koran nor *shari'a* as foundations of the EU. The OIC's ambition to integrate them into the basic European principles will lead to a collision, or rather to an acceleration of the rout already well advanced.

On June 9–19, 2009, the Supreme Council for Education, Science and Culture for Muslims outside the Islamic World convened in Rabat (Morocco) its 10th Meeting, with representatives from Europe, Russia, Latin America and the Caribbean, Pacific and Southeast Asia. Several decisions were taken covering the training of imams and religious guidance within the framework of ISESCO; the intensification of strategic relations with the Council of Europe and the European Union in the fields of education, science, culture and media cooperation; and the creation of radio stations in Eastern Europe in local languages. It was decided to draw up a comprehensive plan for the development of the activities of Arab Islamic schools outside the Islamic world; to create in Europe a league of Arab Islamic schools under the supervision of ISESCO; to consolidate the Islamic cultural identity of Muslims and their children outside the Islamic world; to commend the establishment of ISESCO's Dialogue and Peace Chairs at Mecca and Cairo Universities, at the university of Rotterdam (Netherlands) and to set up other chairs outside the Muslim world.

SECOND OIC OBSERVATORY REPORT ON ISLAMOPHOBIA
(2008–2009)

At the 36th Session of the Council of Foreign Ministers held in Damascus (Syrian Arab Republic) on May 23–25, 2009, the OIC presented its Second OIC Observatory Report on Islamophobia (June 2008 to April 2009).[5] This Report starts with Ekmeleddin Ihsanoglu's Foreword reiterating that the common values of mankind must be based on a firm commitment to human rights, as well as the recognition of the inherent dignity of all human beings. The speaker underlined that human rights and fundamental freedoms should be recognized as essential safeguards of tolerance and non-discrimination, which are indispensable elements of stability, security and cooperation.

Ihsanoglu stressed that Islamophobia in all its forms and manifestations could endanger global peace and security and needs to be addressed urgently and collectively by the international community. It constitutes a major threat to friendly and peaceful relations not only among states, but among peoples as well. For this reason the OIC had pioneered the cause for a Dialogue among Civilizations since 1998 and enjoyed the unanimous backing of the international community by declaring 2001 as the International Year for Dialogue among Civilizations. The speaker recalled that the OIC initiated various interfaith and intercultural dialogues that reflected the Muslim World's commitment to engage the West in a constructive dialogue with a view to defeating intolerance and inducing harmony among diverse religions

and cultures. This led to the establishment of the UN Alliance of Civilizations—an enterprise that Zapatero strongly promoted after the Madrid terrorist attack in March 2004.

The Report again invokes 9/11, symbol for the West of a jihadist massacre perpetrated in America. But this date is, however, derailed from its true
meaning and becomes the symbol of Islamophobia of which Muslims in the
West are victims. Hence the resurgence, especially after September 11, of
racist tendencies and Islamophobia challenge the exercise of fundamental
human rights and freedoms particularly in Western countries. This situation
contributes to misunderstandings and misperceptions about Islam in non-
Muslim societies and results in the rise of discriminatory treatment, negative
profiling and stereotyping of Muslims living in or visiting Western countries.
In spite of tangible progress achieved in eliminating institutionalized forms
of discrimination, many countries still experience—according to the Report—new and mounting waves of bias, exclusion, stigmatization, alienation,
hate and racist violence.

The Report denounces a systematic, motivated and sustained campaign
against Islam and its followers during the period under review. It catalogues
some worrying trends, particularly active in many parts of the Western
world; incitement to hatred, discrimination and intolerance against Islam and
the Muslims; creating misperceptions by distorting its values; and insulting
its symbols.

The domain that needs particular redressing is, according to the Report,
the institutional Islamophobia that exists in schools and educational institutions. Key knowledge about Islamic civilization is omitted in textbooks and
curricula from kindergarten through university. Educators and academics
who urge students to become more familiar with Islam as a moral and progressive force that shaped European history over a millennium of Islamic
civilization, are attacked. Islamophobia is fueled by negative images of Islam
and Muslims either through disinformation, or by focusing on selective
events without reference to historical context, as well as media coverage and
misrepresentation.

The Report denounces the denying of funding for university research in
the study of contemporary religious and social issues related to today's Muslims; cutting back teacher training in the areas of multiculturalism and social
integration. Schools downplay incidents of slurs, bullying, or verbal and
physical abuse motivated by the victims' religion; they deny the need to

confront and address the issue of Islamophobia in the classroom (pp. 11–12). Prejudices and discrimination against Muslims are felt in housing and employment. To this can be added:

- Lack of proper places of worship and burial facilities;
- Headscarf ban in restaurants and other such public places;
- Police practices—search and arrest; customs entry procedures, etc;
- Harassment, vandalism and attacks.

Islamophobia had adversely impacted the image, the honor, the cultural identity and the self-esteem of Muslims the world over, eroding their fundamental human rights.

Through numerous dialogues and contacts, the OIC has been working closely with its international partners, especially with Western countries and the Alliance of Civilizations toward intercultural understanding and defeating the propagators of hatred and intolerance. Hence the Report formulates a common strategy that would associate the Muslim world and the West. The main points here summarized stress that, the international community must first recognize the problem and be ready and willing to combat Islamophobia. The importance of the intellectual front in the fight against intolerance and discrimination against Muslims requires the planning of a sound strategy and adjustments in Western value systems and perceptions. The political will of Governments should show an unambiguous commitment to pursuing the dialogue as a key factor toward a global strategy to combat Islamophobia. The political leadership must underline the importance of correct and unbiased discourse and refrain from hate speech and other manifestations of extremism and discrimination.

On the local level, the Report underlines the following points:

- According the same official recognition to Islam as is given to other mainstream religions in the European states;
- Regarding the national legal systems, with particular reference to the countries/regions with a high incidence of Islamophobia; clear criteria for reporting and registering of hate crimes must be established and reporting of hate crimes must be encouraged;
- Capacity building of Muslim communities and civil society organizations in the Western societies with a view to enabling them to work with local and national authorities is an issue that must be addressed;

- Providing—especially the younger generation—a revised educational syllabus on both sides, particularly in key disciplines such as history, philosophy, social and human sciences with the aim of presenting a balanced view of other cultures and civilizations that would foster tolerance, understanding and respect for "the other." Officials should be trained in law enforcement;
- Fighting terrorism and extremism based on a clear understanding of its root causes and different dimensions to avoid misinterpretation and targeting of innocent individuals or organizations. (pp. 24–26)

With President Obama, America is engaging more radically along such a path. The Report quotes the recommendations made by Admiral William J. Fallon for engagement with the Muslims:[6] listen to their side of the issues and discuss with them the challenges; demonstrate U.S. interest in peace and stability with the majority of like-minded Muslims by engaging in the Middle East peace process and outreach initiatives across the world; put action to words; assist the less developed countries with economic, health, education and security issues (as in the December 2005 Mecca Summit); fix the bureaucratic process in obtaining US visas and avoid embarrassing delays (as recommended by the Alliance of Civilizations); and build trust by personal engagement and treating people with respect (pp. 23–24).

This last point recalls the deference required from the dhimmi, but is devoid of reciprocity as shown by Erdogan's arrogant contempt toward former dhimmis, both Israel and the Armenians, as well as toward Parliaments in the world willing to recognize the genocide of the Armenians.

The recommendations by Admiral Fallon are clearly the same as those of the OIC, especially in pressuring Israel to make concessions detrimental to its security and which deny Israeli's human and historical rights in their own homeland. Both Europe and the Obama administration have adopted the Islamic view of dhimmitude towards Israel. So while they bow and scrape to the followers of jihad ideology, they inflict outrages internationally against the Jewish State that will only prove detrimental to them. It should be noted that the human rights policy claimed by the OIC in Europe for Muslim immigrants has never been applied in any OIC country—because the West and the OIC are not speaking of the same human rights. At the religious, cultural or historical levels, the OIC does not in fact recognize the human rights of those peoples whether their countries were Islamized or not, while those of Muslims are enjoyed strictly within the framework of *shari'a*.

The Report, which is verbose about the evils of Islamophobia in the West, never mentions Islamic terrorism against the West, air piracy, economic boycotts, holding hostages to ransom, and in the Asian and African countries of the OIC the massacres of non-Muslims, slavery, expulsions and dhimmitude. Mentioning such facts comes under the heading of Islamophobia.

In the recommendations of the OIC to rid the West of Islamophobia can be easily recognized those of the *Strategy of Islamic Cultural Action in the West* and of the program of the 2005 Mecca Symposium. The Report refers to the system of collaboration, collusion and partnership of the leaders of the EU with the OIC, which in this book is analyzed in the context of multilateralism and multiculturalism. Islamophobia in education as denounced in the Report can be interpreted as a legitimate resistance in certain European circles to the OIC's demographic and cultural imperialism in their countries, which has been carried out with the connivance of their own governments. Such interference, expressed by way of political pressure, replaces the democratic process with authoritarianism.

The accusation of Islamophobia manifests the confrontation between the scientific criteria of European cultures and Islamic religiously cultural notions brought into Europe by the requirements of mass immigration supported by OIC pressure. The interpretation of jihad, whether a war of invasion or a justified war of Muslim land re-appropriation, is an example, as are the Islamization of the Bible, the teaching of the Armenian genocide, or the Shoah—or rather the refusal to teach them. This is a long-term struggle between, on the one hand, the European masses kept in ignorance of what is at stake by the EU-OIC networks and partnerships, and on the other hand the OIC, which is set upon bending Western governments until its targets have been achieved.

EU-OIC CONVERGENCE AND PARTNERSHIPS IN FOREIGN POLICY

In those areas that concern Israel, America and the Arab-Muslim world, a strong convergence can be noted between the policies of the EU and OIC. This is hardly surprising since the instruments of the Euro-Arab Dialogue and its later developments had set their sights on this strategic union. From the start, European and Arab policy coordination was ensured by the European Parliamentary Association for Euro-Arab Cooperation (PAEAC), which passed on to the European Council and its Commission the Arab League's demands concerning immigrants and European foreign policy. These concerned granting Muslim immigrants social services, professional and educational training, cultural facilities, changes in schools and university textbooks about Islam, promotion of the splendor of Islamic civilization, and the nomination of Muslim immigrants to influent and visible positions in the universities, the media and politics.

At the session on the Euro-Arab Dialogue held in Tunis (February 10–12, 1977), the Arab side proposed the creation of a joint Euro-Arab Commission for political consultation (§11).[7] It is probably this cell, working in concert with the Arab League, like all the other Commissions of the EAD that brought compatibility to the European and Arab League political positions. PAEAC had great influence over the spread of antisemitism/anti-Zionism, the development of multiculturalism, and the Islamization of the roots of European history. Supported by the Commission it functioned as the European instrument of Islamic *da'wa*. This advocacy stands out clearly from PAEAC's numerous reports on its activities.

Such policy has been the very marrow of the *Common Strategy of the European Council on the Mediterranean Region.* The entire security and defense strategy of the EU lies in the coordination of the *Common Strategy* with its Arab partners, members of the OIC. In his presentation at Helsinki on February 25, 2004, Javier Solana declared, "Closer engagement with the Arab world must also be a priority for us. Without resolution of the Arab-Israeli conflict, there will be little chance of dealing with other problems in a region beset by economic stagnation and social unrest."[8] He explained that future security would depend on a more effective multilateral system, "a rule-based international order and well-functioning international institutions." Europe would become stronger in building a stronger United Nations, and in being firmly committed to effective multilateralism.

This policy, intended to strengthen the UN's power, was reinforced by a strategy aimed at weakening American national identity through drift leading in the same directions as the multilateral utopia that had entrapped Europe. At the international level the EU strove to wipe out Europe's national identities, seen as obstacles to the expansion of a globalized, international society subject to UN governance—whereas, pulling in the opposite direction, the OIC rebuilds the universal Ummah, by rooting it in its religious and traditional values, and pursues the Islamization of the UN.

The EU's Mediterranean policy has officially mainly been concerned with ensuring good governance, the rule of law, economic development, human rights in general and women's rights in particular, their social role and independence, respect for minority rights, the fight against terrorism, educating the youth of both sexes for a knowledge-based society. The partnership task consisted of promoting an understanding among the peoples of the EU and the Middle East and encouraging "mutual respect for these peoples' unique cultures."[9] However, the re-Islamization policy of the OIC states, which underlay the union of those countries, was radically opposed to the reforms promoted by the EU and demolished the very idea of a society based upon knowledge rather than faith. The billions of euros wasted on Mediterranean countries and the European anti-Israel strategy had no impact on the discrimination, plundering and massacres of the Christian minorities, which continue right up until today. The unequaled, worldwide campaign of hatred and antisemitism inspired by the OIC, contradicts, even in a Europe won over by this murkiness, the respect for Mediterranean cultures.

COMMON THEMES OF THE EU AND THE OIC

The preceding chapters have already recorded the policy and propaganda similarities between the EU and the OIC, whether in respect to the Arab-Israeli conflict or in the dual strategy of penetration and control of Europe by both the OIC and the growing EU standardization system. This can be seen in the Palestinization of EU foreign policy that mirrors OIC paranoia in immigration issues, the Islamization of thinking, culture and society (Western guilt, internalized dhimmitude, banking, *shari'a* courts, and Islamic customs), the increased insecurity and anti-Zionist hatred—that are all parts of multiculturalism and globalization. Such processes are weakening local sovereignties and replacing them with infiltration of the global governance networks affiliated with the OIC and linked to the political and cultural "Palestinization" of Europe. On account of the zero influence of the EU in the Muslim world, it can be said that the EU diligently fulfills the role of carrying out the OIC's orders in Europe. Here we shall summarize the main points of similarity that were adopted also by the Obama administration from the moment it took over.

(1) 9/11 constituted the start of the persecution of Muslims in the West. This theme keeps coming back in all the speeches of Ihsanoglu and Doudou Diène at international forums and reports of the EU-OIC networks made up of the Anna Lindh Foundation and the Alliance of Civilizations. It is then spread in Europe through the militancy of the representatives of the civil society that emerge from these networks. This theme blends in with the sense of guilt tactics for the infidel, in line with jihad theory.[10] Making the West feel guilty involves moral obligations that the 2005 Mecca Summit of the OIC emphasized in its recommendations for policy strategy:

> Stress the moral obligation of Western powers that have directly or indirectly contributed to injustice, to oppression, aggression involving Muslim peoples, to lend their socio-economic assistance to the eradication of poverty in the countries of the South.[11]

The evocation of all the evils that afflict Muslims always evades their own responsibility and that of their leaders which led to these results. This concept of justice that exonerates Muslims from responsibility for failures and conflicts conforms to the Islamic view of history, whereby only non-Muslims are blameworthy because they oppose Islam's message. The Mecca Summit underlined again the moral obligation of the West:

> Enlighten Western leaders and the public on: (a) Islam played a positive role in the rise of modern Western civilization and (b) they have a moral obligation to promote the socio-economic development in the South.[12]

(2) Joint affirmation by the EU and OIC that Islam is the root of European civilization and that it is part of Europe. This belief justifies its return to European soil.

(3) The coordinated fight by the OIC and EU to impose multiculturalism in Europe, with its entire religious context (punishment for blasphemy) and legal one (establishment of *shari'a* whenever possible).

(4) The replacement of Western criteria for knowledge by historical myths such as the Golden Age of Andalusia under regimes that implemented *shari'a* and have imposed since the 12th century under the Berber dynasties, forced conversions and expulsions for native Jews and Christians. The affirmation that European Renaissance and modern science emerged from Muslim civilization belongs to this same trend.

(5) The venomous relentlessness of the EU and OIC against the Bible, with the negation of its spiritual and historical nature. This movement comes from the antisemitic and anti-American hostility of a Europe that since October 1973 has deliberately opted to unofficially align itself with the Muslim world against the US and Israel. The loyalty of these peoples to their spiritual and national values that drives their fight against jihad horrifies politicians who have repudiated them to glory in their role as OIC mercenaries by carrying out its Palestinian mission as well as the promotion of *da'wa* at home. In accordance with the targets of the Islamic media strategy in the West, the EU has unremittingly disseminated the OIC's recommendation which consists of:

> Drawing the attention of the international community to the dangers posed by the influence of Zionism, Neo-Conservatism, aggressive Christian evangelicalism, Jewish extremism, Hindu extremism and secular extremism in international affairs and the "War on Terrorism."[13]

In other words, the danger comes from peoples' resistance to the policy of Islamization. Obeying these orders from the OIC, the EU-OIC networks multiplied their attacks against Israel and Judeo-Christian America, unrelentingly fighting the "war against terror" formula, as though Bush had invented Islamic terrorism. Blowing the OIC's horn, they proclaimed the ineffectiveness of military operations, namely populations armed in self-defense against terrorism. Only "dialogues"—professed by these lobbies—and the billions lavished in the fight against poverty and to correct injustice, self-flagellation and deference to Islam—in other words, humiliations, concessions and tributes extorted from the West—would possibly succeed in eradicating it.

These networks, through their media and intellectuals, prompted Westerners to consider the resistance by Israel and Bush's America to jihad to be the source of all conflicts. Those European currents that deride the "war against terror" but failed to mention jihad and claimed that Bush and Israel trigger terrorism belong to the OIC's networks. The Mumbai (Bombay) massacres in November 2008, to give but one example, demonstrate the existence of global jihadist terrorism. To deny it is to adopt the multicultural agenda chosen by Europe in 1973 in its collaboration with the PLO and its "dialogue" with a terrorist organization.

(6) The alleged central role played by Israel as an instigator of war, terror and injustice, in other words the essence of evil. This vision belongs to a political doctrine reiterated at every meeting or Islamic Summit of the OIC,

and constantly ranted and imposed by the leaders of the EU and their media. The Mecca Summit reaffirmed several times that the issue of al-Quds/Jerusalem and the Palestinian question constitute the central, key policy of the OIC and the Islamic Ummah. [14] This position was ratified at the meeting of OIC ministers in Kampala in June 2008. [15] The ministers condemned the "colonization" of Judea and Samaria (West Bank), the construction of the "racist wall," demanding the creation of a sovereign, viable and independent Palestinian state, which together with the Gaza Strip would make up a single entity whose capital would be al-Quds (Jerusalem)—an illegal position in international law, hammered home word by word by the EU representatives since 1980 in the Venice Declaration, issued as a counter-reaction to the Israeli-Egyptian peace accords and which reduce the State of Israel to indefensible dimensions in order to bring its demise.

The ministers of OIC countries emphasized that Israeli policies, machinations and expansionist plans did not just threaten Arab countries and the peace process, but the other Islamic states as well and endangered international peace and security—another classic declaration of Chirac's France, of the EU, especially under Prodi as President of the European Commission. This pathological obsession with Israel is implicit in the *nakba* White Paper that will "restore all its meaning and its chances to the restoring of normalized relations between Islam and the rest of the world." Would the carnage then, as in Mumbai, also miraculously cease?

The accusation that Israel is the source of terrorism rather than being its victim, that it is the origin of the *nakba* and injustice, expresses the jihadist view of transferring guilt for the Arab wars against Israel to its resistance. The same reason attributes guilt to an infidel West, as mentioned above. Being the essence of evil, Israel and the West have the "moral obligation" to lavish services on the Ummah, thus fulfilling the traditional, obligatory charges for dhimmis paid in gratitude for being spared the resumption of jihad.

The other shared themes of the OIC and EU harped upon in the Alliance Report are: (a) Israel is the only obstacle to peace between Islam and Christianity, even though they have thirteen centuries of incessant warfare between them before the rebirth of Israel; and (b) Israel is an occupying, apartheid, oppressor state.

In January 2008 Franco Frattini, the European Commissioner for Security, acknowledged in a lecture given in Herzliya (Israel) that for too long there had been too many misunderstandings between Europe and Israel, motivated by a certain anti-Israel preference by European Union leaders and public opinion.[16] For too long, he continued, Europe had ignored the legitimate fears and concerns of Israel about terror, fanaticism, and the refusal of most groups within the Arab camp to accept Israel's existence, let alone its legitimacy. For too long Israel's difficult situation had been ignored and denied, whereas Europe should have understood it earlier because its problems with terrorism were the same. However, too often, Frattini acknowledged, European critics refused to recognize the risks incurred by Israel, and for three years during the Second Intifada many in Europe refused even to accept that the hate-filled, violent tide in the Middle East could be antisemitism. This European sickness, he said, had taken on new roots and new forms. However, he promised, things had changed and such prejudice against Israel and the Jews should no longer exist in today's Europe. And contrary to Prodi, who excused antisemitic crimes, attributing them to political resentment caused by Israel, incriminating the victim rather than the guilty party, Frattini declared: "That is simply unjustifiable. Period." He added: "Terrorism is a global threat. The whole world is concerned."

With the election of Silvio Berlusconi, Franco Frattini became Foreign Minister. Speaking in Berlin to a forum on Euro-Israeli relations, Frattini reiterated his criticism of the EU's unbalanced policy towards Israel, acknowledging that sometimes it confused legitimate political criticism with antisemitism.[17]

Were Franco Frattini's observations justified? A brief summary is called for.

In 1973 the European Community created a new people and a new nationalism that had not existed until then, Palestinism. Up until 1973 the Arabs of Palestine had seen themselves first as Arabs in British Mandate Palestine and subsequently as Jordanians following the occupation of Judea and Samaria by Transjordan in 1949. During this occupation by a foreign state that had invaded another country, all Jewish inhabitants were expropriated and expelled by the Jordanian Arabs who seized all their lands, homes and possessions.

The creation by Europe of a new Arab nationalism occurred in the 1970s when the EC, led by France and Germany, allied itself with the Arab League against Israel through unofficial accords known as the Euro-Arab Dialogue.[18] This approach did not seek to solve the Arab-Israeli conflict, but to perpetuate it through the artificial creation of a people who, rather than integrate into Jordan/Palestine, was dedicated to the destruction of Israel.

This process was clearly explained to Europeans by Chadli Klibi, Secretary General of the Arab League. Speaking to the diplomatic press corps in Paris on December 6, 1979, Klibi recalled the decision of the General Committee of the Euro-Arab Dialogue that met in Tunis (February 10–12, 1977) to launch an intensive media campaign in Europe to replace the term "Palestinian refugees" in UN Resolution 242 (1967) with "Palestinian people."[19] The Arab League gave Europe, with France as its motor, the key role of imposing this idea on international public opinion, especially American public opinion. France also invented a new formula: land for peace.

The entry in 1973 of the UK and Ireland into the EEC strengthened the European, pro-Arab policy and the anti-Israel policy of the Euro-Arab Dialogue (1975). In the 1970s the EEC hardened its position: recognition for a Palestinian people; Israel's obligation to withdraw to the 1949 armistice lines; the mandatory participation of the PLO in peace negotiations; the division of Jerusalem; and the return of Arab refugees displaced by the wars launched by the Arab League and five Arab states against Israel on 15 May 1948, and before, by Palestinian groups.

In 1977 the EEC demanded the application of the 4th Geneva Convention to the Administrated Territories, even though they did not represent an independent state and that the expulsion of its Jewish population and the prohibition on its presence under Jordanian occupation, were illegal. Then the application of the Convention was not requested. The European Community decreed, on its own initiative, the illegality of a Jewish presence in Judea and Samaria, alleging that it represented the colonization of Arab lands. But this inexact statement created and imposed by the EC in the 1970s under the pressure of Palestinian terrorism that was then cowering Europe, along with the oil embargo, itself constituted an imperialist expropriation of another people.

In the following years it insisted that peace talks take part within the framework of the UN, of which ex-Nazi Kurt Waldheim was Secretary General at the time. As Italian President Cossiga noted, Europe allowed Palestinian terrorists unrestricted use of its territory while placing an embargo on arms to Israel. It refused at the time to recognize the peace agreements between Israel and Egypt (1978–1979) and in 1980 issued the Venice Declaration, which publicly aligned its policies with those of the PLO and Arab League.

The European Community continued a pro-Palestinian policy that threatened Israel's vital security interests, applying economic sanctions, threats and boycotts. It championed Palestinian demands, attempted to distance the US from Israel and facilitated its contacts with the PLO. It supported the Intifada in 1987, adopted a policy of economic retaliation against Israel, and endeavored to paralyze its defenses against Palestinian terrorism and to limit as far as possible Israeli control and presence in the "Territories," trying to get it replaced by Palestinians. On the international scene it worked to favor Palestine, to provide it with political, economic and strategic support, upheld by hate-filled propaganda spread by its lobbies.[20]

In 2004, following jihadist attacks in the United States, Madrid and London, the Council of Europe issued its Declaration on the fight against terrorism.[21] However, this struggle excluded Israel since Europe was promoting Palestinian terrorism and had been sheltering it on its soil since 1973.

After World War II this anti-Israeli policy prolonged the Nazi war against the Jews and Zionism resuming, behind closed doors, the Palestine-Nazi alliance. Europe only recognized Israel after the US and the USSR, each country in its own good time, with Greece and Spain in 1980 and the Vatican about ten years later. Having fought Zionism, the European Community invented a new stratagem. It legitimized the PLO, gave it a country and a capital, fixed the frontiers of this new colony, invented for it a history and legitimacy, created its institutions and financed this undertaking almost single handedly. The financing of Palestine as well as the Euro-Arab and Euro-Israeli anti-Israel lobbies is a bottomless pit for billions funded by European taxpayers.

No European minister has gone as far as Italian Foreign Minister Frattini in the acknowledgment of Europe's wrongs towards Israel, though the elections of Angela Merkel and Nicolas Sarkozy ushered in a breath of warmth, dispersing the miasmas of EU-Israel relations that had been blown by Anna Lindh, Chirac, Prodi, Schröder, Solana, Patten and others. De facto, Europe took pleasure in treating Israel as the enemy, and enjoyed presenting to its own public opinion the tiny state with a population of seven million as a peril threatening its own enormous territories and colonies, with a population of about half a billion. In a word, Europe had donned Islamic spectacles to flatter the OIC. Today, the EU fiercely reproaches Israel for still existing. It considers it an obstacle in the way of its honeymoon with the Ummah, which doles out its favors stingily to succeed in its role as Israel's gravedigger.

EU-Israel relations, even if they seem now friendlier, have evolved in form but not in substance. Europe keeps its conditions aligned with those of the OIC in the imaginary peace process. Yet if it would ever try to change, it could not. It is tied by its Arab commitments dictated under the threat of Palestinian terrorism in the 1970s and has muzzled itself through all its joint security strategies conceived by Solana, a great admirer of Arafat and the prophetic visionary of the common Euro-Arab destiny under the universal caliphate of the OIC.

A "Palestinized" Europe that has voluntarily accepted its guilt continues to provide financial, diplomatic, political and media support for Palestine, but withholds its favors from Israel. Much of its media extols in every possible way Palestinian victimhood and innocence. The EU, having already Arabized and Islamized its history and culture and Palestinized its politics, has no qualms with doing the same to Israel. In this continuity the EU has refused to improve its political and economic relations with Israel outside of the Palestinian context, even though it is not so particular about human rights among its Palestinian protégés and Arab partners, especially Egypt, which is home to open war against Copts, apostates and Bahais.

In January 2008, the EU, which strives to stifle Israel's economy, announced considerable financial aid to Palestine and offered it in the first instance nearly seven and half billion dollars. Carried away by such generosity, the European Commission launched a new instrument, the PEGASE[22] mechanism, to channel EU and international assistance as a contribution to build the Palestinian State and as a follow-up to the current Temporary International Mechanism (TIM). PEGASE will support a broad array of activities in the four priority sectors of governance, social development, economic and private sector development, and public infrastructure. Benita Ferrero-Waldner, Commissioner for External Relations and European Neighborhood Policy, stressed again that the European Commission was the largest donor to the Palestinians.

On June 16, 2008, the 27 foreign ministers of the member states of the EU declared that Europe wished to develop a closer partnership with Israel, but only if Israel gave birth to the Palestinian state under the terms prescribed by the EU-OIC, in other words if Israel winds itself up. Curiously on December 8, the twenty-seven Foreign Ministers of the EU unanimously decided to raise their relations with Israel without strings attached. Salam Fayyad, number two after Abu Abbas, protested: "The political process in which the European Union wishes to be a key actor has the objective of creating a

Palestinian state."[23] Following Israel's defensive operations against Hamas terrorism in January 2009 and the violent reactions of the EU-OIC networks, the EU courageously renounced its decision.

In June 2010 a flotilla made up of Turks, Arabs, Germans and other European partisans of Hamas' genocidal policies set out for Gaza to break the blockade applied by Israel and Egypt following the firing of thousands of missiles by Gazans onto Israeli towns and schools for seven years. It was sponsored by IHH (Insani Yardim Vafki), an organization based in Turkey, linked to the Erdogan government and accused by various countries of pro-terror activities. The boarding of the largest ship, the MV *Mavi Marmara* by Israel resulted in casualties on both sides, the people on board making use of iron bars, coshes and knives while yelling jihadist, genocidal war cries. According to international terrorism experts, IHH was collaborating with al-Qaida and Turkish-Bosnian jihadist organizations involved in the war against the Serbs in the early 1990s.[24]

This episode aroused a chorus of exaggerated international condemnations of Israel, demonstrating the well-oiled media campaign planned back in 2004 at the ISESCO Amman conference. It contrasted with the media's indifference to Kurdish victims of Turkish raids, Turkey's blockade of Armenia since 1993, and the occupation of northern Cyprus by Ankara since 1974, and demonstrates European submission to Ottoman Jihadism in the Balkans.

The European Parliament condemned Israel by a crushing majority, showing its massive support for Hamas, the incarnation of Nazism in its Islamic avatar, created by the Palestinian branch of the MB under Amin al-Husseini, who like Hitler advocated the genocide of the Jews. This specter, in its various forms, has not ceased to haunt Europe. Catherine Ashton, the EU's High Representative for Foreign Affairs and security policy, and Vice President of the European Commission argued that lifting the blockade would bring peace. But she forgot to mention that the abrogation of the genocidal charter of Hamas, the party democratically elected by Gazans, was an essential condition for peace, and not the lifting of the blockade.

Andrew Rettman reports in the EU *Observer* (Brussels) that on December 6, 2010,[25] a large group of former EU leaders and commissioners, including Javier Solana, Romano Prodi, and Chris Patten, sent a letter to EU capitals and the leaders of the EU institutions urging the Union to take sanctions against Israel. In this letter the group recalls the adoption by the Foreign Affairs Council of the European Union on December 8, 2009, of a set of twelve "Council conclusions on the Middle East peace process." The group asked EU foreign ministers at their meeting scheduled on December 13, 2010, to take concrete measures to implement the December 2009 conclusions as "Europe cannot afford that the application of these policy principles be neglected and delayed yet again."

The letter recalls the Council's conclusion 2 stating that "The European Union will not recognise any changes to the pre-1967 borders including with regard to Jerusalem, other than those agreed by the parties." Commenting on this decision, the signatories condemn Israel and recommend: "that the EU reiterate its position that it will not recognize any changes to the June 1967 boundaries, and clarify that a Palestinian state should be in sovereign control over territory equivalent to 100 percent of the territory occupied in 1967, including its capital in East Jerusalem."

The third conclusion of the Council (2009) states:

> *The EU stands ready to further develop its bilateral relations with the Palestinian Authority reflecting shared interests, including in the framework of the European Neighbourhood Policy. Recalling the Berlin declaration, the Council also reiterates its support for negotiations leading to Palestinian statehood, all efforts and steps to that end and its readiness, when appropriate, to recognise a Palestinian state. It will continue to assist Palestinian state-building, including through its CSDP missions and within the Quartet. The EU fully supports the implementation of the Palestinian Authority's Government Plan "Palestine, Ending the Occupation, Establishing the State" as an important contribution to this end and will work for enhanced international support for this plan.*

The signatories then underline "the impressive progress" made by the Palestinian Authority toward the development of the infrastructure of the Palestinian state and add: "EU support and assistance has been vital to this success. To date, the EU and member states have invested some EUR 8 billion in the peace process, primarily in the form of assistance to the Palestinian Authority, Palestinian institutions, and the development of infrastructure in the OPT. By continuing to be the primary donor to this work, the EU underlines the vital European interest in the establishment of a Palestinian state and the implementation of a two-state solution" (§3).

Regarding what the EU calls OPT (occupied Palestinian territories), the letter strongly emphasizes that: "The EU has stated unequivocally for decades that the settlements in the OPT are illegal, but Israel continues to build them. Like any other state, Israel should be held accountable for its actions. It is the credibility of the EU that is at stake" (§4 and 5).

Like the European Parliamentary Association for Euro-Arab Cooperation created in 1975 for OIC advocacy, the signatories strongly advice boycott and retaliations measures against Israel while lamenting that Israel's disobedience "undermines the EU and its credibility in upholding international law (§6). Such reference to "international law" is laughable in such a context. Which Middle East and African countries abide by international law? Does *shari'a* rules conform to "international law"?

The eighth conclusion of the Council states its deep concern about East Jerusalem which it has never recognized as a Jewish capital, nor even as a city and which should become for the first time in history a Arab Palestinian capital. The ninth conclusion deplores the closure of the Gaza Strip, deemed "unacceptable and counterproductive" but never mentions the Gaza terrorists attacks on Israel nor the 1989 Hamas genocidal charter. The signatories suggest that the EU could promote a process of Palestinian nation-building (§10) apparently blind to the contradiction between their Palestinian policy and their engagement in the deconstruction of the European nations.

After mentioning the twelve conclusions on the Council, the authors finish on a note whose cynicism and aversion toward Israel can hardly be equaled:

> In conclusion, our Group wishes to point out that EU investment in building the foundations for a two state solution over the past two decades was very substantial, not least in terms of EU tax-payers' money. The EU should take what measures it can to justify this investment and act in Europe's genuine interest, but if no political progress is made, further expenditure—apart from that on humanitarian purposes—would be nugatory. In these circumstances Israel should be required to shoulder its obligations as the occupying power. But wider issues matter more than wasted expenditure. At stake are not only EU relations with the parties directly involved in the conflict but also with the wider Arab community, with which the EU enjoys positive diplomatic and trade relations.

In other words Israel, guilty for existing, must bear the cost paid by the EU in a policy aimed at its demise. This is called the "peace process" which is "working towards justice and peace." At a time when the Middle East is sinking into chaos and the Christians in Muslim countries are hounded, these leaders are obsessed with harming Israel like the Nazi leaders filling up the death-trains when their empire collapsed. Have these leaders ever showed such determination in protecting persecuted Christians in Muslim countries?

What Conclusions Can Be Drawn from the Mediterranean Policy of the EC/EU?

Its alliance with Palestinianism has led it to deny jihad and dhimmitude and to mantle them with its moral authority. It continues to remain deaf and dumb in the face of the oppression of Christian and other minorities in Muslim countries. Hostile to biblical Christianity, it has tried to distance it from its Jewish origins in its rapprochement strategy with Islam. Its intense Mediterranean immigration policy has led it to forging the instruments of its own destruction, the fight against the historical, national European identities. While crushing them with multiculturalism, it works at creating new, all-Muslim nationalisms: Palestinianism, the Bosnian and its brother Kosovar-Muslim irredentism, with the latter two preparing for the return of Erdogan's Ottoman policy in former Turkish European colonies.

The Mediterranean policy has shaken Europe to its very foundations. It has undermined school and university education, already governed by some *shari'a* injunctions; democratic institutions are just a memory, while civil rights, constantly violated by insecurity and the terrorist threat have become virtual—decorations on pieces of paper. The Anna Lindh system hounds, eliminates and destroys freedom of criticism and neutralizes any defense. Banishing Islamophobia re-establishes prosecution for one's opinion. Even if the target that has been sought so persistently for decades by neo-Nazi European trends has been achieved (i.e., to turn America against Israel in order to totally isolate it), this success nevertheless has a bitter taste. Obama, a third-world man, despises a Europe in tatters, even if it had spared no effort to ensure his victory.

NOTES

1. "Common Strategy of the European Council of 19 June 2000 on the Mediterranean Region"
(2000/458/Cfsp), *Official Journal of the European Communities*, 22.7.2000, L 183/5.

2. For the significance in the Koran and *Hadiths* of Islamic immigration, see Sam Soloman and E. al Maqdisi, *Al Hijra, the Islamic Doctrine of Immigration*, 2009, www.pilcrowpress. com.

3. Resolution 1605 (2008). European Muslim communities faced with extremism. Text adopted by the Assembly on April 15, 2008 (13th session).

4. Author's italics. We note on this point the compatibility of the *Strategy* with the Parliamentary Assembly.

5. 2nd Observatory Report on Islamophobia June 2008 to April 2009, issued at the 36th Council of Foreign Ministers, Damascus, Syrian Arab Republic, May 23–25, 2009, original: English, OIC/CFM-36/OBS/ISLAMOPHOBIE-2/SG-REP www.oic-un.org/document_report/ Islamophobia_rep_May_23_25_2009.pdf (accessed January 6, 2011).

6. Fellow of the Center for International Studies Massachusetts Institute of Technology.

7. *Documents D'Actualité Internationale, Ministère des Affaires Etrangères*, Paris, n° 16–17, 1977, 319–24; Jacques Bourrinet, ed. *Le Dialogue Euro-Arabe* (Paris: Economica, 1979), 308.

8. Speech of Javier Solana at Helsinki, 2/25/2004, "The European Security Strategy—The Next Steps?" in *Cahier de Chaillot*, Vol.V, no. 75, *Sécurité et Défense de l'UE, Textes fondamentaux, 2004*. Institut d'Etudes de Sécurité, Union européenne, February 2005, Paris.

9. Ibid, 138–39.

10. Cf. above Bassam Tibi.

11. Final Recommendations approved by the Commission of the OIC of Eminent Personalities (C.E.P) at the 3rd Extraordinary Session of the Islamic Conference at the Summit of Makkah Al-Moukarramah—Kingdom of Saudi Arabia 5-6 Dhoul Qaada 1426/ December 7–8, 2005.

12. Ibid.

13. Ibid.

14. Final Communiqué of the Ten Year Plan of the Conference, §4.

15. Resolutions on the question of Palestine of the city of al-Qods Al-Sharif and on the Israeli-Arab conflict adopted at the 35th Session of the Council of Foreign Affairs Ministers *(Session on Prosperity and Development)* Kampala – Republic of Uganda 14–16 Jumada Thani 1429H (June 18–20, 2008).

16. Opening remarks by EU Commissioner Franco Frattini for the second EC-Israel Seminar on the fight against racism, xenophobia and antisemitism, "From the outside, looking in: international perspective on the Middle East. Israel at 60: test of endurance." January 22, 2008, Herzliya, Israel.

17. *Haaretz.com*, June 21, 2008.

18. See on this topic Bat Ye'or, *Eurabia*.

19. *Groupe d'études sur le Moyen Orient*, n° 80, Décembre 1979, Genève.

20. For a detailed study of European policy, see Roy H. Ginsberg, *The European Union in International Politics: Baptism by Fire* (Lanham, Md.: Rowman & Littlefield, 2001).

21. *Cahier de Chaillot*, Vol.V, no. 75, op. cit., p. 29 et seq., Brussels, March 25–26, 2004.

22. www.delwbg.cec.eu.int/en/index.htm. *European Commission launches PEGASE: A New Mechanism to Support the Palestinian People*. europa-eu-un.org/articles/es/article_7681_ es.htm (accessed January 6, 2011).

23. Michel Bôle-Richard "Le pari israélien de l'Union européenne," *Le Monde.fr*, 12/20/08, see also Ray Archeld, «UE-Israël : nouveau chapitre », *Guysen News International* www.guysen.com/articles.php?sid=8724.

24. *International Herald Tribune*, July 16, 2010.

25. Andrew Rettman, "Former EU leaders challenge Ashton on Israel," euobserver.com/9/31477, December 10, 2010, to see the letter and the signatories, www.usmep.us/usmep/wp-content/uploads/2010-12-10-EFLG-letter-to-EU.pdf.

Chapter Five

Networks of Global Governance

THE ROLE OF THE
EUROPEAN PARLIAMENTARY ASSOCIATION FOR
EURO-ARAB COOPERATION (PAEAC)

In his remarkable book, Ambassador Bourdeillette notes the French political shift after Israel's victory in June 1967 by a preventive strike to foil the simultaneous attacks by Egypt, Syria and Jordan. On November 27, General de Gaulle officially announced at a press conference: "Our policy of friendship and cooperation with the Arab peoples of the Middle East is one of the fundamental bases of our foreign activity."[1] Everything had been said. This sentence determined Europe's destiny.

In Paris Bourdeillette observed that supportive movements for Israel were denounced and discouraged. State antisemitism began creeping out as though the ground had been prepared in earlier years, provoking the French ambassador's indignation: "Arab propaganda had a free run. A campaign for Palestinian refugees was emerging. Arab statesmen found every door open, while not a single Israeli voice could be heard."[2]

In his study on the European Union government and policies, Neill Nugent explains that the networks' policy creates areas in which decision-makers and interests mix to balance out differences and the search for solutions.[3] He observes that the networks' composition determines their openness to outside influences and to the independence of the decision-makers vis-à-vis the general population. This structure defines accurately Euro-Mediterranean relations, carried out unofficially and discreetly throughout the 1970s–1990s, without the knowledge of the European public. The promoters of the networks policy deemed that the EU had adjusted completely to this system of government. Various factors contributed to that: the unofficial nature of the EU's political decisions, the multiplicity of interests seeking to influence the political decision-makers, and the power of the Commissioners. Nugent also refers to the heavy dependence of EU politicians on outside interested parties to obtain information and advice on handling and implementing policy.[4] And in fact the policy of anti-Zionism and dhimmitude in Eurabia results directly from the importation of Christian dhimmitude, especially the Judaeophobic Palestinian model.

The first of the European networks to play a major role in Arabization/Islamization was PAEAC. This Association carried out its activities at various European political and strategic levels, of which the main ones were: (1) Combined policy of immigration and the Arabization of European culture; (2) the Palestinization/Islamization influence in Europe and the return of antisemitism; (3) anti-Americanism propelled mainly by Communist and Leftist trends; and (4) support for the Arab League policy. This campaign extended OIC strategy into Europe, established and carried out by its European agents. However, PAEAC was not merely the tool of the OIC to inject its political interests into Europe. It also revived the dark alliances of Nazism and Fascism with the Arab Middle East, thereby perpetuating a trend that is firmly anchored in the European Arabophile and Islamophile political current. The PAEAC represents the hidden, shameful face of unofficial European policy, concealed from the general public and taken to the very highest levels of state behind closed doors. Without the approval, financing and media provided by the European Community and the Commission, namely the European Council, the PAEAC could never have successfully achieved its targets and the OIC's.

As has been seen, the Islamic Conference held in London in May 1973 had decided to finance and support Muslim cultural centers in Africa and especially in Europe. The following year in Lahore the Secretary General of the OIC mentioned this commitment, because "a great need was felt for propagating the tenets of Islam and helping Muslim communities in Europe to play this role effectively and fruitfully." Referring to the London Conference, he recalled that it had:

decided to establish an Islamic Council of Europe to serve as an organ of coordination among all Islamic institutions and centers. Besides, it will help
propagate the true teachings of Islam throughout Europe. Undoubtedly, the
convening of such conferences would result in stepping up the activities of the
Islamic Da'awa [proselytism] and propping [up] the Islamic Cultural Center.[5]

Several decisions were taken at that Conference, among which was the urgent convening of experts to propagate Islam at a global level and the establishment of a jihad fund as a first step for defining the tasks allocated to this
fund. There were no restrictions to subscription, and it was meant to proceed
at the pace of the action plan in all sectors of the jihad. Another goal focused
on supporting cultural centers and Muslim organizations in Europe as well as
setting up two cultural centers on the continent.

The PAEAC was the decisive instrument of this program's success in the
coming decades. At its meeting in Strasbourg on June 7, 1975, it asked the
Nine countries of the European Community to recognize the historic contribution of Arab culture to European development, and emphasized the contribution this culture could still make to European countries, particularly in the
field of human values. In its cultural section the Association objected to the
limited range of cultural relations between European and Arab countries; it
deplored the relative indifference toward the teaching of Arab culture and
Arabic in Europe and recommended that these be developed. The Association requested European governments to help Arab countries obtain extensive resources so as to let Muslims and their families who immigrated into
the European Community take part in Arab cultural and religious life. It
asked the governments of the Nine to approach the cultural aspect of the
Euro-Arab Dialogue in a constructive manner and to give the highest priority
to spreading Arab culture throughout Europe. These demands clearly match
those of the OIC.

Over the following years, in their recommendations to European governments, the delegates of PAEAC never ceased to petition for the creation of
joint European-Arab cultural centers for the spread of the Arabic language
and its teaching in European schools, universities and other educational institutions. Their requests included organizing trips to Arab countries and the
award of grants and scholarships for the study and development of Arab
culture. With faith and culture thus linked, one wonders about the motives of
European parliamentarians, supported by the Commission to encourage the
Islamization of their continent. The Recommendations of PAEAC at the
1983 Hamburg Symposium anticipate and schedule the program recorded in

2001 in the *Strategy of Islamic Cultural Action in the West.*[6] These two documents seem to be traceable one to the other. As can be observed, PAEAC had remarkable success in achieving its targets in the political, so-cio-professional and cultural sectors.

THE ANNA LINDH FOUNDATION

According to its website, the Anna Lindh Foundation (ALF) has a lean administrative structure, and operates as a network of networks for the thirty-five civil societies of the Euro-Mediterranean partnership. This group in-cludes the twenty-seven member states of the EU and the ten countries of the South which were members of the Barcelona Process: Algeria, Morocco, Tunisia, Lebanon, Israel, Jordan, the Palestinian Authority, Egypt, Syria and Turkey. These national networks represent the institutions or bodies chosen by each member of the partnership. Such bodies have the task of setting up within their societies action programs decided on by the Euromed Commit-tee, which brings together representatives of the 37 Ministries of Foreign Affairs. Thus, contrary to what one might have thought, these civil societies do not represent the people but rather are charged with molding public opin-ion to approve their governments' policies.

The Foundation's 2005–2007 three-year program focused on the idea of a dynamic intercultural dialogue based upon intellectual cooperation, human rights, democracy, sustainable development, education and information, gen-der equality and youth. Six of the Foundation's projects are included in this program and are for youth, in order to inculcate them with the concepts mentioned.

Among these projects the cultural program offered the globalization of culture through the "denationalization" of national cultures. To this end, the idea of national culture needs to be replaced by "creative diversity" on a global scale. Thus we would no longer speak about German or French culture etc, but rather of the cultural life in Germany, France or elsewhere. We would no longer speak about German culture and foreign cultures, but rather of "the participation of Germany in the dialogue between cultures and civil-izations." This new formulation ought to be adopted in cultural policies, scientific research, journalism and education.[7] The ALF's political approach to denationalize European cultures seeks to dissolve them in a Mediterranean magma. The eradication of European cultural identities would satisfy Muslim cultural imperialism that pretends to be Europe's cultural matrix. The Muslim expropriation of European culture bypasses the Koran's prohibition on adopting the customs and ideas of the infidel (III:66; V:56) while facilitating the acceptance of European modes of thought and technologies if they are presented as having a Muslim origin.

The Foundation's educational program was based on the new concept embodied in the Report of Jacques Delors, President of the World Committee of UNESCO and former President for a decade of the European Commission (1985–December 1994). This concept envisaged the creation of a school that would practice tolerance in teaching students to take into account the others' point of view. According to Delors, this "multiperspective" apprenticeship is an exercise that lets school students choose their priorities among the multiple ideologies seeking to attract them. In other words, the teaching of an intellectual discipline, based upon objective critical criteria, would be replaced by an equivalence of contradictions.

THE ALLIANCE OF CIVILIZATIONS

As has already been seen, the AoC was the reaction to the trauma of Muslim terrorism in Madrid. This 2005 response repeated that of 1973, which sealed the allegiance of the European Community to PLO terrorism, as acknowledged by former Italian President Francesco Cossiga. It was the founding act of the European-Arab alliance and of the construction of Eurabia. Unlike America, which when attacked by terrorism declared war on it, when Europe was attacked by terrorism in 2005, some countries repeated its 1973 strategy when it created the PAEAC. Surrendering to the OIC, as thirty-two years earlier to Arafat, they set up another Islamization network under the aegis of the United Nations at the initiative of the Spanish and Turkish governments, the latter a member of the OIC. In April 2007 UN Secretary General Ban Ki-moon appointed Jorge Sampaio as High Representative for the AoC.

The Alliance's Secretariat represents yet a further occult organization on an international scale. It works "in partnership with states, international and regional organizations, civil society groups, foundations and the private sector to mobilize concerted efforts to promote cross-cultural relations among diverse nations and communities."[8] Its operation is a gigantic lobbying machine on a global scale whose priority interests are the bodies affiliated to the United Nations, whose objectives match theirs. These institutions include the

United Nations Educational, Scientific and Cultural Organization (UNESCO), the United Nations Development Program (UNDP), and other international organizations and regional bodies, including the European Union, the Organization of the Islamic Conference, the Arab League, the Islamic Education, Scientific and Cultural Organization (ISESCO), United Cities and Local Governments (UCLG), and the World Tourism Organization (UNWTO).

The AoC presents itself as "a UN initiative on a global scale, with a global perspective, while giving priority to relations between Western and Muslim societies." Such priority is already suspect. Why no priority for Russia, India or China? Apparently because these powers do not have permanent conflicts with the West. Some members of the Secretariat are known for their activities in Islamizing European school textbooks (the Andalusian myth), their racist anti-Zionism (Israel = racism = apartheid), and their views that can be traced back to the OIC.

The Alliance is a true lobbying and pressure group at the international level, which seeks to encourage contacts and dialogues between political and religious personalities from the media and civil society in order to advance the shared targets of the Alliance of Civilizations and the OIC. It takes up Ihsanoglu's proposal in his 2005 Strasbourg speech and seeks a true intercultural dialogue at the national, regional and international levels, and in all media, news, literary works and even cartoons—a program similar to the ISESCO media strategy. To achieve these objectives the Alliance intends working at early and later stages in order to create favorable conditions for its pressure on the decision makers and to mobilize groups. The cards for such "dialogues" have however been stacked, because self-censorship and legal action on Islamophobia deprive them of all credibility.

Based on the recommendations of the High Level Group's Report, the High Representative of the Alliance can advance specific political initiatives if the situation justifies it. It is thus the High Level Group that no one has ever elected and which most Europeans do not even know exists that will be directing their countries' policy and accordingly their lives and their nations' destiny. It will be working through partnerships, project coordination and unification of targets to achieve a multiplicator effect in order to enhance both visibility and effectiveness. Here can be recognized the Prodi-Solana method from the 2000–2004 period and the unified action method of the

OIC. The Alliance is not very talkative about its objectives except for the promise "to act in the interests of all, to prefer concerted, effective action and to offer a vision of the future."

With the Anna Lindh Foundation and the Alliance it is quite clear that we have left the democratic arena to set up an international system of occult conclaves for pulling the strings. At the Copenhagen International Conference on Education for Intercultural Understanding and Dialogue (Copenhagen, October 22, 2008), the OIC Secretary General, Ekmeleddin Ihsanoglu, recalled that the OIC had been one of the first to launch the concept of Dialogue between Civilizations from the mid-1990s. It had been at the request of the OIC that the United Nations had declared 2001 to be the year of dialogue between civilizations. The Euro-Arab Dialogue, PAEAC, Medea, the Barcelona Process, the Mediterranean Union, the Euro-Mediterranean Parliamentary Assembly, the Anna Lindh Foundation and its twin the Alliance of Civilizations amplified the OIC's influence in the West in every cultural, social and political field.

To achieve its mission the Alliance gives priority to its efforts at "resource mobilization, partnerships building, implementation of internal and external information and on communication mechanisms, as well as advocacy in order to promote the Alliance."[9]

The implementation plan is in two parts. The first part contains the *Strategic and Structural Framework*. Here the key objectives are stated: the basic principles of the Alliance, the creation mechanism for partnerships, the protection of its interests, financing and setting its priorities. It also includes the *network of partnerships* intended to strengthen the UN system, the design of projects to *encourage partnerships about intercultural relations, especially between Muslim and Western societies*, in conjunction with the *youth, education, media and migration sectors.*[10]

Knowing the OIC's policies concerning education, the media and migration into Europe, we can deem the Alliance like its sibling the Anna Lindh Foundation as yet another instrument of "dialogue" and partnership that promotes the OIC's penetration of the West and its worldwide ascendancy.

The strategic Framework spells out the AoC's functions, the programs' targets, project preparation and implementation, communications strategies, organization of governance mechanisms and financing. It stresses that the AoC will demonstrate, "*a universal perspective.* At the same time, a *priority emphasis on relations between Muslim and Western societies*" will be main-

tained to guarantee international stability and security.[11] The AoC will act
within the UN system and globally to be a bridge-builder and a convener,
particularly between Muslim and Western societies.

This section ends explaining the ideology of the AoC, the organization of
its global power to be used for a specific policy and strategy.

> The AoC will facilitate communication and the *sharing of information and
> strategies* [author's italics] among leading international donor agencies, foun-
> dations, corporations and philanthropists who are working on building cross-
> cultural understanding (with a particular focus on relations between Western
> and Muslim societies).[12]

In the new Orwellian political language in which dialogue means persuasion
through threats, "cross-cultural understanding" is translated as submission.
The second section describes the Program of Action from May 2007 to May
2009 together with an assessment of progress achieved, an analysis of obstacles encountered and solutions to overcome them and update the Program.
This section includes the High Representative's Program, the Alliance's organization and secretariat, its special allocation funds and more. Also mentioned are the AoC's main forums and meetings, project development, implementation of the Alliance's global communications strategy and the outlook
for the future.

The Alliance seeks to become an archiving body for practices, documentation and resources on the cross-cultural dialogue and cooperation with the
four themes already mentioned: youth, education, media and migration[13] —
exactly the fields of action proposed by the OIC. Would the Alliance be the
nucleus of a government for a new, transnational, Euro-OIC continent? Am-
bassadors already represent it in various countries and at the offices of international organizations. It is quite clear that its archiving system, together
with its networks for indoctrinating young people, will represent a vast control scheme covering Europe and America, because allegedly only these
continents host xenophobia, racism and Islamophobia and therefore must
open up their borders and fight at home the obstacles to peace between
civilizations.

The Alliance's activities will be amplified by the Friends of the Alliance
Group, whose task is to support its activity through representatives of civil
society and partnerships. These activities will focus on dialogues, cross-
cultural and inter-confessional cooperation, educating the media and journalists, university courses, and initiatives to empower Muslim immigrants in the

US and Europe, and more. The latter initiative as well as the others confirms the OIC's demands as stated by Ihsanoglu and the program of the 2005 Mecca Summit. Nothing is said of Muslim countries, and it can only be inferred that racism and incitement to hatred are non-existent there. Clearly, the initiatives proposed below are exactly those demanded by Ihsanoglu:

1. Intercultural and interfaith dialogues
2. Media education
3. Teaching religion in schools.
4. Governmental, university and civil society programs and initiatives "that educate and empower Muslim immigrants in the US and Europe."[14]

In less enigmatic words, this means giving Muslim immigrants politically responsible positions, which is nowhere practiced in Islam for non-Muslim natives, not to speak of immigrants. This transfer of power in European societies to Muslim immigrants, carried out at the request of foreign powers, reproduces the previous dynamic of the Islamization of Christian lands around the Mediterranean governed by the caliphate.[15] Reduced to the status of dhimmi viziers, Christian leaders from Andalusia to Armenia worked within the glitter of their masters' palaces toward the destruction of their own society; they were cogs in the political and social changes of the transnational, universal and timeless extension of dhimmitude.

The social and political advancement of Muslim immigrants in Western societies reproduced the ISESCO strategy:

> Muslims in Europe, then, should set up a uniform plan for the prospects of the Islamic presence there. This strategy should be targeted at providing the necessary conditions for individuals from the Muslim communities to occupy the key positions within host societies, in the economic, cultural, political or information fields.[16]

The Alliance states that it is planning its activity using an international network of high-profile personalities, apparently iconic image above any criticism, who would be working in the intercultural realm. Their articles, explaining the tensions and intercultural dissension, would be translated into various languages and distributed by the main publishers of the print press. The extreme furor of the press campaign against Israel during its "Cast Lead" defense operation in Gaza (December 27, 2008–January 3, 2009) and the flotilla affair was probably fomented by the OIC-AoC and its transnational networks.

The numerous projects of the HLG include Abraham's Path. This initiative conceived at Harvard University consists of a permanent long-distance route of tourism and pilgrimage in the footsteps of the "prophet Abraham" in several Middle East countries.[17] It is clear that here it is the Muslim Ibrahim of the Koran, whose prophethood and story do not exist in the two other monotheistic religions. Since, according to the Koran, Abraham constructed humanity's first temple in Mecca together with his son Ishmael, it would be interesting to see if non-Muslims taking this route would be admitted there. The title of prophet instead of Patriarch, the general anti-Israel, pro-Palestinian tone, like the programming in Europe and the US only, of multiculturalism and affirmative action clearly indicate the predominant influence of the OIC over the Alliance of Civilizations.

On its website the Alliance defines its functions, both global and within the UN system, in the following capacities:

- A bridge builder and convener, connecting people and organizations devoted to promoting trust and understanding between diverse communities, particularly between Muslim and Western societies;
- A catalyst and facilitator aimed at reducing polarization between nations and cultures through partnerships;
- An advocate for building respect and understanding among cultures;
- A platform to increase the visibility of the bridges between cultures;
- A resource providing access to information on successful cooperative initiatives to be used by member states, institutions, organizations, or individuals.

To this must be added the group of "Elders" constituted by former heads of states like Jimmy Carter and Mary Robinson and other political figures: Martti Ahtissari, Kofi Annan—a total of twelve. Former South African Archbishop Desmond Tutu, the initiator of the world campaign of cultural and economic apartheid against Israel, chairs this committee. Desmond Tutu congratulated Turkey for having sent its flotilla of pseudo-humanitarians to Gaza in June 2010, and the Elders condemned Israel's reaction. The "Elders" have much international influence and considerable funds; they support pro-Palestinian jihadist aggressions against Israel under the cover of the humanitarian terminology "peace and justice." Faithful to their former policy, they represent Israel as the unjust and warlike party and the Palestinians as peaceful victims whose cause, the denial of Israel's right to exist, embodies justice.

THE MODERN ASSOCIATIVE CALIPHATE

The OIC is a religious and political organization. Close to the Muslim World League of the Muslim Brotherhood, it shares its strategic and cultural vision, that of a universal religious community, the Ummah, based upon the Koran, the Sunna and the canonical orthodoxy of *shari'a*. The OIC represents fifty-six countries and the Palestinian Authority considered a state, the whole constituting the universal Ummah with a community of more than 1.3 billion Muslims.

The OIC has a unique structure among nations and human societies. The Vatican and the various Churches are de facto devoid of political power, even if they take part in politics, because in Christianity as in Judaism the religious and political functions have to be separated. Asian religions too do not represent systems that bring together religion, strategy, politics and law within a single organizational structure. Moreover, none of these religions have a religious injunction to eliminate or subjugate all others.

Not only does the OIC enjoy unlimited power through the union and cohesion of all its bodies, but also to this it adds the infallibility conferred by religion. Bringing together 56 countries, including some of the richest in the world, it controls the lion's share of the global energy resources. The EU, far from anticipating the problems caused by such a concentration of power and investing in the diversification and autonomy of energy sources since 1973, acted to weaken America internationally in order to substitute for it the UN, the OIC's docile agent. In the hope of garnering a few crumbs of influence the EU privileged a massive Muslim immigration into Europe, paid billions to the Mediterranean Union and Palestine, the Trojan horse of its Islamization, weakened the European states, undermined their unity, and wrapped itself in the flag of Palestine's justice as though this was some protective system against the jihad, which it endeavored to focus on Israel.

Religion as the main aspect of the OIC emerges from its language and its targets. It seems that the OIC is restoring in the twenty-first century the Caliphate, the supreme controlling body for all Muslims. Thus the Dakar

Conference (March 2008) was called "The Conference of the Islamic Summit, Session of the Islamic Ummah in the 21st Century." At this conference the OIC adopted a new Charter, whose key points will be summarized here.

In the preamble the Member States confirm their union and solidarity inspired by Islamic values. They affirm their aim to reinforce within the international arena their shared interests and the promotion of Islamic values. They commit themselves to revitalizing the pioneering role of Islam in the world, increasing the prosperity of the member states, and—contrary to European states—to ensure the defense of their national sovereignty and territorial integrity. They proclaim their support for Palestine with al-Quds Al Sharif, the Arabized name for Jerusalem, as its capital, and exhort each other to promote human rights, basic freedoms, the state of law (*shari'a*), and democracy according to their constitutional and legal system, in other words compliance with *shari'a*. They also undertake to stimulate noble Muslim values, to preserve their symbols and their shared heritage, and to defend the universality of the Islamic religion, simply put the universal propagation of Islam (*da'wa*). They state that they are promoting women's rights and encourage their active participation in all walks of life, in accordance with the laws of the member states. They agree to inculcate Muslim children with Islamic values and to support Muslim minorities and communities outside of the Member States in order to preserve their dignity and their cultural and religious identity.

The first chapter details with some repetitions the objectives and principles of the Charter that bind together the Member States of the OIC, and their respect for the principle of non-interference in the affairs of each Member State. Underlining their solidarity, article I-4 claims: "To support the restoration of the complete sovereignty and territorial integrity of a member-state under foreign occupation." Such a principle could be applied to every jihad waged by Muslims in various countries to expand the reach of Islam and to install *shari'a* there, whether in Europe, Africa or Asia. As the November 26, 2008, carnage in Mumbai—as well as in many other places—has shown, jihad is not limited to the Israeli-Arab conflict.

It is true that international law and cooperation are invoked by the Charter to govern conflicts. However, in the last resort it is Islamic law that prevails over that of the infidels.

The Charter's strategic targets seek: "To ensure active participation of the Member States [of the OIC] in the global political, economic and social decision-making processes to secure their common interests" (I-5); and "To promote and defend unified position on issues of common interest in international forums" (1-17).

These decisions rapidly bore fruit. The OIC's control of the UN was seen with renewed violence on November 24, 2008. The President of the United Nations General Assembly, Miguel d'Escoto Brockmann of Nicaragua, launched from the podium an unbridled attack inciting hatred against Israel and inviting the whole world to take part in a lynching through a policy of apartheid. In the name of love for his "Palestinian brothers and sisters" who "are being crucified" by Israel,[18] Brockmann, a former Catholic priest, forgot in his Jew-hating passion Palestinian criminal terrorism against Israel, global Islamic terrorism, and the apartheid practiced against his Christian brothers in Arab countries and particularly in Gaza, where the Hamas government supported by the OIC was restoring Islamic punishments, including crucifixion as in Sudan. His accusations were taken up by the Rev. Edwin Makue, General Secretary of the South African Council of Churches. It is clear that for these two religious people, the Koran has already replaced the Bible.

Using his usual, sententious tone, former UN Secretary General Kofi Annan, active in the Alliance of Civilizations, noted that the International Day of Solidarity with the Palestinian People was "a day of mourning and sadness." To consider the liberation of Israel from dhimmitude under the Islamic yoke and the recognition of its sovereign rights in its own country where its prophets spoke Hebrew in the towns and villages of Judea—reported in the Bible and not in the Koran—as a day of mourning is to declare mourning for people's freedom and mankind's conscience worldwide.

On November 28, 2008, two days after Jews were savagely tortured in Mumbai, Brockmann—previously active in the Churches' Ecumenical Council—symbolized the triumphant return of the National Socialism and Palestinian jihad alliance of the years 1930–1940. He resurrected the cohorts of Islamized Christians, Patriarchs, ecclesiastics and ordinary individuals who destroyed their own peoples by keeping them in the shackles of dhimmitude. If the Alliance of Civilizations has in no way contributed to inculcating the minimum of respect for Israel, it has on the other hand blindingly exposed the submission of the UN to the OIC and its antisemitic paranoia.

Among its targets the OIC Charter specifies the propagation, promotion and preservation of Islamic teachings and values based upon moderation and tolerance, the spread of Islamic culture and the preservation of the Islamic heritage (I-11). Article I-12 promotes the protection and defense of the true image of Islam, the fight against its defamation, as well as encouraging a dialogue between civilizations and religions. The other objectives deal with protecting inherent Islamic family values (I-14), the preservation of rights, dignity, and religious and cultural identity of the Muslim communities and minorities in non-member States (I-16). This issue points to the OIC authority over immigrants abroad and its pressure on the governments of the non-Muslim host countries through the channel of dialogues, including the Alliance of Civilizations.

We have also seen how the OIC supports all the jihadist movements considered to be resisting "foreign occupation," including those in "occupied" Indian Kashmir, and condemns the "humiliation and oppression" of Muslims in India. The involvement in the Mumbai carnage of Pakistani terrorists trained in their own country and linked to the Pakistani intelligence services, something strongly denied by Pakistan, is part of the global jihad. Ever faithful to OIC directives that recommend a common front while facing foreign states, the Saudi press exonerated Pakistan. Y. Yehoshua, Director of Research at Memri, notes that,

> This fear is manifested in the Saudi press, which has unanimously rallied to clear Pakistan of any responsibility, aiming to prevent conflict between the two countries. All editorials in the Saudi dailies *Al-Hayat, Al-Jazirah, Al-Madina, Al-Riyadh*, and *Al-Watan* were devoted to this message. One article in the Saudi daily *Al-Yawm* even raised the possibility that the attacks had been carried out by Western, rather than Pakistani, elements—a message that was especially prevalent in the Syrian and Iranian press. [19]

Just like 9/11 was attributed to the CIA . . .

Article 2 of the Charter states, "The Member States undertake that in order to realize the objectives in Article 1, they shall be guided and inspired by the noble Islamic teachings and values and act in accordance with the following principles." These refer to the respect for the principles of the United Nations, without specifying the contradictions arising from secular and Islamic laws. These principles repeat the obligation of the OIC's Member States to avoid any conflict among themselves and to settle any disputes peacefully. In the current controversy over Iran's nuclear projects, Turkish Prime Minister Erdogan has repeatedly stated that Turkey wants a diplomatic solution to end the deadlock.

Article 3-2 provides the conditions for membership of the OIC: "Any State, member of the United Nations, having a Muslim majority and abiding by the Charter, which submits an application for membership may join the Organization if approved by consensus only by the Council of Foreign Ministers on the basis of the agreed criteria adopted by the Council of Foreign Ministers."

Chapter III stipulates the organs of the OIC:

1. Islamic Summit
2. Council of Ministers of Foreign Affairs
3. Permanent Committees
4. Executive Committee
5. Islamic International Court of Justice
6. Permanent Independent Commission of Human Rights
7. Committee of Permanent Representatives
8. General Secretariat
9. Subsidiary Bodies.
10. Specialized Institutions
11. Affiliated Institutions

Chap. IV, Art.1: The Islamic Summit is composed of Kings and Heads of State and Government of Member States and is the supreme authority of the Organization.

The Charter stipulates that the International Islamic Court of Justice shall become the Organization's main legal body (Chap. IX, Art. 14) and that: "The Independent Permanent Commission on Human Rights shall promote the civil, political, social and economic rights enshrined in the organization's [OIC] covenants and declarations and in universally agreed human rights instruments, in conformity with Islamic values" (Art.15).

However, this article contradicts the prohibition on interfering in the affairs of other member states of the OIC. Would the Pakistani terrorists of the Lashkar-e-Taiba (Army of the Pure) who perpetrated the Mumbai massacres come under the jurisdiction of a Pakistani court or the Islamic Court of Justice? According to the OIC, combatants against "foreign occupation"— India in this case—and against the humiliation of Muslims at the hands of

Hindus in India, are "resistants" whom the OIC has to support. Will it be Pakistan or the International Islamic Court of Justice that will try the leaders of the ISI (the Pakistani Intelligence Services), which according to both the American and Indian intelligence tolerated and even aided and abetted this terrorist group linked to a nebulous financial benefactor.[20] In point of fact, the ideological and tactical approach in the jihadist war against India is identical to that of the Palestinian jihad against Israel.

Despite Eurabia's efforts to make Israel the sole source of the war, it is clear that peace will only come when the OIC recognizes the human, religious, historical and national rights of the indigenous expropriated peoples, victims of past and present jihad and dhimmitude, and through the renunciation of this ideology. One can note that Sudanese President Omar al Bashir accused, according to Western criteria of justice, of genocide committed in Southern Sudan and Darfur, has not been troubled by the Islamic Court of Justice. His colleagues at the OIC do not consider him in any way a criminal and receive him with great respect, as does Erdogan.

The Islamic Court of Justice has an international mandate and could try foreigners, both Muslims and non-Muslims (blasphemers, apostates, resisters to jihad), who have broken the laws of *shari'a* anywhere. Moreover, the claim by the OIC to be the guardian and protector of Muslim immigrants living in all countries that are not members of the OIC implies an extension of its jurisdiction and political influence over all the Muslims of Europe, North and South America and the other non-member states. This situation exacerbates the danger incurred by non-religious European Muslims, whether atheists or free thinkers.

Within its organization the Charter presents characteristics similar to those of the EU, however, in terms of its spirit, functions, principles and objectives, it is its very antithesis. Even if it employs the language of international organizations, the meaning of the words is subverted by their being rooted in the conceptual world of the Koran, which contradicts the basis of secular, Western thought. Thus Article 32-2 states: "The Council of Foreign Ministers [of OIC countries] shall recommend the rules of procedures of the Islamic Summit." This implies an Islamic view and understanding on policy.

AL-QUDS: SEAT OF THE CALIPHATE

On several occasions the OIC expresses its determination:

to support the struggle of the Palestinian people, who are presently under foreign occupation, and to empower them to attain their inalienable rights, including the right to self-determination, and to establish their sovereign state with Al-Quds Al-Sharif as its capital, while safeguarding its historic and Islamic character, and the holy places therein. (Foreword of the Charter)

In accordance with jihadist law, this formula eliminates all history and the rights of indigenous people prior to the Islamic conquest. World history began with Islam in the seventh century. And Article 11 states that in order to achieve progress on matters of capital importance for the Organization and its Member States, the Organization had created standing committees, of which the first mentioned is the Al-Quds Committee.

Article 18 declares, "One post of Assistant Secretary General shall be devoted to the cause of Al-Quds Al-Sharif and Palestine with the understanding that the State of Palestine shall designate its candidate." In Article 21: "The Headquarters of the General Secretariat shall be in the city of Jeddah until the liberation of the city of Al-Quds so that it will become the permanent Headquarters of the Organisation."

Thus, while Muslims in general deny the Shoah and make Hitler their super hero, the obsession with Israel is such that the OIC has endeavored to impose on Europe the similarity between antisemitism and Islamophobia. It has already convinced it about the *nakba*, wept for by a planet in mourning, under the baton of Kofi Annan, Nobel Peace Laureate and a Grand Master of the Alliance of Civilizations. The OIC, the would-be universal caliphate, has fulminated against Israel with accusations of apartheid through its spokesman Archbishop Desmond Tutu, also a Nobel Peace Laureate and distinguished member of the Alliance.

Doubtless the OIC will line up a few European and American politicians rejected by their own citizens. It will find new jobs for them in the corridors and circuits of its Dialogues and Partnerships where far from the public eye they will continue their work, by now well advanced, of Europe's disintegration. The European channels and networks affiliated with the OIC have already stated that the oppression of Muslims in Europe is akin to antisemitism[21]

In his book on the caliphate Ali Merad[22] observes that for almost thirteen centuries, "the Caliphate represented for most Muslims the model par excellence of the Islamic state" (p.7). On March 3, 1924, Ataturk abolished this model.

Such a combined political and religious institution is at the very outer rim of Western thinking, anchored as it is in the separation between politics and religion. Even if interference between the two fields had persisted, the principle of such separation has facilitated emancipation in the intellectual and political arenas from religious authority and the development of critical thought. Hence, the present-day aspiration of the Ummah to submit to such a combined political-religious institution can only surprise Westerners and highlight the gap that separates them. Rooted in individualism, Europeans cultivate the search for happiness and cherish freedom of thought, of opinion, and of rational, scientific exploration, which are perceived as a human being's greatest privilege and finest adventure.

Conversely, aspiring to the caliphate indicates the longing for a supreme authority owing its infallibility to Allah and his human intermediary, Muhammad. By placing politics at the service of worldwide, religious expansionism, this institution—according to Ibn Khaldun—was created as instrument for the mandatory Islamization of mankind. Faced today with this political archaism, a divided and broken West seeks refuge in denial and grasps at the demise of tiny Israel as though at a lifebelt. Taking in water from every side, this West in abandoning its own identity for multilateralism and undermining its values by buying security—has little chance of survival.

In his book, which displays strong signs of the anti-Western prejudices of an old-fashioned Third Worldism, Merad provides us with an analysis of the various current trends from Asia to Africa that are striving for the emergence of a caliphate "without forgetting," he tells us, "the Muslim minorities in Europe and the Islamic diaspora in the New World." He continues:

> These peoples and communities are looking to affirm their presence on the international scene, to organize their own solidarity, and to give back historical visibility to the mother community (the Ummah), whose universalist vocation has for a long time been opposed by Western expansionism and hegemony. (p. 9)

Merad examines the re-creation of the caliphate as an associative structure, and he observes that: "the current Organization of the Islamic Conference appears to be moving toward the realization of such a paradigm" (p. 183). Referring to the discussions about the geographic location of the headquarters of the caliphate, he propounds the possibility of one of "the humblest countries—but also one of the most worthy of consideration—on the international scene" (p. 182). However, in its Charter the OIC has already stipulated which is this humble country so admired on the international scene: the future Palestine, with Jerusalem at its capital, that the West is endeavoring to detach from Israel. Crowned as the seat of the caliphate, guarantor of *shari'a* and world jihad, Al-Quds al-Sharif/Jerusalem will witness Christianity's demise.

It is by no means history's smallest irony that European determination to destroy Israel will destroy Christianity. The stages of this development led by Europe and now the US with its funding to which have been committed incalculable billions in economic assistance, media indoctrination, world-wide lobbies on every front to ensure the international popularity of Palestine—conducted inexorably over decades, and succeeding finally in roping in America—will culminate in a Jerusalem caliphate purged of Christianity. In other words, another Mecca. It is to this end that the blind termites in the chancelleries of Europe and America are today working so assiduously. Crowning achievement of almost a century of the Palestine-Nazi alliance, reminding us of the time when Christians followed Jews into the extermination camps.

Can this process be changed? I doubt it. With the election of President Obama in 2008, the machine has broken loose, and only popular awareness of what is at stake—outlawed by the OIC-EU nomenclature—could stop it.

EURABIA: THE JINGOIST ROUT

The development of the policies of Turkish Prime Minister Recep Tayyip Erdogan can be explained within the context of the emerging caliphate. The public humiliations he has inflicted on Israel, mixed with haughty demands for respectful gestures is a true return to the contemptuous behavior of the caliphs towards the dhimmis. This about-face by a decades-old ally, together with his support for Hamas and the Palestinians, won for Erdogan the most prestigious prize of the Wahhabi kingdom. On March 9, 2010, King Abdullah of Saudi Arabia awarded it to him for his immense services to Islam through the defense of the Islamic nation and in particular the Palestinian cause. In addition, he was a key element in the Dialogue of Civilizations, drew closer to Iranian President Mahmud Ahmadinejad, and on several occasions invited Sudanese President Omar al-Bashir.

While Eurabian ministers focus all the world's sins on Israel, Islamic history calmly continues its millenary progress, ever true to itself. The bloody chaos in Iraq between the Sunni and Shiite, Arab and Kurdish clans and tribes, of whom the Christians and other minorities are victims and hostages, attributed to Bush by the Eurabian press, is repeating the episodes of centuries of Islamization of conquered countries. Here can be found the bloody, inter-Muslim tribal wars, the devastations, fiscal exploitation, and massacres carried out by foreign invaders against native Jews and Christians, who have to buy their existence through onerous extortion.[23] When in February 2008 the Chaldean (Assyrian-Catholic) Archbishop Paulos Faraj Rahho stopped paying ransom (*jizya*) for the security of his congregation, he was kidnapped and his chauffeur killed. Two weeks later his body was found near Nineveh. It was thus revealed that all Iraqi Christians had to pay for their own safety, in accordance with Koranic law (Kor. 9:29). For years on end Archbishop Rahho through ruinous ransom had bought from Muslim insurgents and terrorists his community's right to live. After the US army had improved security, Rahho interrupted these payments, which had obliged his flock to go into debt. Threatened and kidnapped by terrorists, he begged his coreligionists not to pay the ransom demanded for his release.[24] His execution was just a trivial fact of millenary dhimmitude repeated in the anti-Christian atrocities in Iraq and Egypt (2010–2011).

Despite the OIC's promises, religious minorities in Muslim countries continue to be discriminated against by the laws of dhimmitude. Most retain the law that punishes apostasy with death without always applying it, although a blasphemy law has been recently reinstalled in Indonesia. Christian converts to Islam cannot return to Christianity. Those "denigrating" Islam are imprisoned. The Copts are constantly harassed, threatened, humiliated, even killed and have been obliged to abandon their ancient homeland. They are often attacked, their stores pillaged and Christian women kidnapped. The construction and repair of Christian churches require a license that is rarely issued. Jews originally from Egypt who return as tourists to places where Jews had lived for a thousand years are not even allowed to photograph the vestiges of their history. The Bahai religion, which came after Islam, is accordingly not recognized, and its pacifist adherents have been deprived of their most elementary rights. These thousand-year-old laws derived from *shari'a* are applied in all Muslim countries with more or less severity. Generally speaking, the in-depth Islamization of the OIC countries strengthens animosity towards religious minorities and non-Muslims.

The strategy of dialogue and partnerships—that is, of Western concessions—punctuated by internal jihadist terrorism and the politics of chaos (arson in French suburbs, demonstrations, threats, violence, terrorism) represents the jihadist tactics of penetration and jihad intimidation in the West, serving the expansionist interests of the universal caliphate. The dialogue networks are activated to whitewash and launder the OIC's tactics, to couch them in humanitarian, universalist, pacifist language formulated by the Europeans, academics, politicians, clerics, and movie-makers who press them on the Western public.

Tony Blair—during whose ten years as prime minister *shari'a* laws and *shari'a* banking were established in a United Kingdom crisscrossed by Muslim networks—pleads in an article about an alliance of values. [25] What were his arguments? Globalization is the future and: "To work effectively, globalization needs values like trust, confidence, openness and justice." Faith can provide an important help if it is open and not closed: "if it is based on compassion and help for others and not on the basis of exclusionary identity." For globalization to flourish, we need mutual confidence, which will give us confidence in the future. Spiritual capital is an important part of social capital. In the globalization era, multi-religious societies must practice not just tolerance but also respect for other religions. The key to respect is understanding, from which flows our need to learn and educate each other about our respective faiths. Values such as confidence, the ability to count on other people's word or the long-term outlook will create confidence. This proves that an interdependent world cannot function without values, which create the bonds of confidence. Obtaining peace between Israel and Palestine is very important; it has a major symbolic significance that will stop terrorism, as Ihsanoglu had preached so well. However, with all this faith and compassion, the ten years of the Blair government saw Britain becoming one of the most antisemitic countries in Europe, close behind Sweden and nearly surpassing Chirac's France, which says a great deal.

Blair concluded that in order to overcome the crisis, we needed to have faith—however, not faith in our traditions or our identity but faith in values, not just democracy and freedom, but for the common good, compassion and justice. Blair's article could in fact have been written word for word by Ihsanoglu. In his lecture in Copenhagen in October 2008 at the second International Conference for Education and Intercultural Dialogue, the OIC Secretary General called for cooperation and consensus, which would require empathy, compassion, understanding, respect, human rights and international law. However, contrary to Blair who recommends rejecting self-identity, the OIC endeavors to cement Muslims' identity in the Koran and the Sunna. Above all, wrote Blair, we need an alliance of values that recognize equality of dignity and the value of each individual. Blair would have to convince the OIC, which refers to jihadist terrorists as "resistants."

Apparently Blair's article fits in the Alliance strategy, which had provided for articles, books and films by celebrities to promote its policies, namely those of the OIC. Its subsidiary, ISESCO, explained it in its strategy of controlling and subverting Western culture. Already an avalanche of films, articles, books and advertising clips remind evil Europeans that their culture and territory did not belong to them but rather to the magnificent Islamic civilization that can be seen flourishing today in Afghanistan, Pakistan, Iran, Iraq, Syria, Lebanon, Egypt, Libya, Gaza, Somalia, Sudan, and elsewhere. Meanwhile, a ruined Britain would beg for its economic survival in Saudi Arabia, as did Prime Minister Gordon Brown while promising to support increased influence for the Saudi kingdom in international forums.[26]

In an article entitled "The Muslims and Us: How to Win Islam Over," Olivier Roy and Justin Vaisse advised against a lecture by Barack Hussein Obama to the world's Muslim leaders.[27] The purpose of such a lecture, they explained, would be to refute any idea of a war waged by America against Islam. It would explain US values and interests and would ask the Muslim bloc to eliminate terrorism in a joint effort. Yet this initiative that seeks to reconcile Islam with the West would be wrong-headed, these authors claim, irrespective of its good intentions. Actually, it would falsely imply that Islam and the West are two distinct entities with totally opposed values. Those who want to promote dialogue and peace between "civilizations" and "cultures" should not play into the hands of Osama bin Laden by their belief in the existence of different civilizations. Does the OIC say anything different? It states that Europe and the West are part of the universal Ummah and represent the same, single civilization, with Islamic civilization being the mother of Western culture.

Obama, the authors write, is the first post-racist president, which is an unfortunate turn of phrase as it implies that a white American president would necessarily be racist. In this capacity, Obama should not lose time with a fake war between Islam and America, but rather he should focus his entire power fighting the erroneous concept that a monolithic Islam would be the source of all the world's problems. Even the recent attacks in Mumbai, India, were not caused by religion, claim the authors. The terrorists were

operating out of Pakistan and simply wanted to make normal relations between Pakistan and India impossible. For the authors, neither Muslims nor
their leaders nor their Imams represent Islam. Moreover, such a lecture by
Obama would involve the incorrect idea of a natural link between Islam and
terrorism, which would annoy Western Muslims. Obama would also be putting himself in the strange position of implicitly representing Christianity or
secularity. And they conclude, "After all, Americans have just elected a
president whose middle name is Hussein. That name goes a long way with
many Muslims." In other words, Muslims rely on Obama to serve the interests of the Ummah and the universal caliphate to the detriment of American
interests. Clearly, within the concept of a single, universal civilization, the
interests of Americans should be those of the caliphate.

Curiously, Roy and Vaisse impugn an official Islamic body. Faced with
the OIC—a constituted political body, representing the universal Ummah, 56
countries and over 1.3 billion Muslims, with a Court of Justice, a Charter and
now a Human Rights Commission as well as specialized political and cultural institutions based upon the Koran and Sunna—they are blinded. The
question can also be asked how the acknowledgment of different civilizations
necessarily involves the idea of war. Such a correlation requires us to deny
our own identity and culture in order to melt into Muslim identity, just to
avoid war. We can certainly accept the special features of the Chinese, Japa-
nese and Indian civilizations without necessarily wanting to fight them because they are different. Notwithstanding this prudent advice, President Obama gave his speech in Cairo from the podium of al-Azhar. The word "terrorism" was not mentioned, and his lecture honored his first name, Hussein.

The Western press acts as a chorus for the OIC and could never find
invective strong enough to throw at President George W. Bush. A white
Christian president, he unveiled for the world the reality of the jihad that the
Euro-OIC alliance endeavored to hide behind their incrimination of Israel
and America. As we saw, these accusations were recommended by ISESCO
and the OIC. Even the terrible massacres during the second war in Iraq were
blamed on him, whereas everyone knows that they resulted from Muslim
tribes and religious factions killing each other. The Western media, linked to
Euro-OIC networks, cheers on Obama, linked by family ties to the Muslim
world and whose program of changes greatly resembles Europe's self-defeat-
ing policy of rapprochement. The EU elites, modest in their triumph, anticipated impatiently the abandonment of Israel for "justice and peace in Palestine."

Thus, while Somalia reverts to its old demons with piracy at sea and hostage trading, Europe, itself hostage to terrorism, introduces both *shari'a* courts and finance on its own territory. Under various pretexts it has already adopted all of Ihsanoglu's proposals, and presented them to the public, packaged and labeled as human rights and European colonial guilt. Puffing its chest on human rights principles, it prepared draconian laws against "racism, xenophobia and incitement to hatred." However, it dutifully provides its citizens' money to finance—through a myriad of NGOs—incitement to hatred against Israel. Simultaneously, it triggers the country's disintegration from within by financing its client Israeli NGOs.

Churches have already broken with a Bible guilty of testifying to Israel's rights in its homeland. They joined the Marcionite heresy preached by the Palestinian Sabeel Center, the very source of the export of dhimmitude into Europe. They celebrated the introduction of *shari'a* in Europe and the proliferation of mosques. However, they maintain a total silence about the disappearance of Christianity from its lands of origin, or else blame Israel for it. As in the past with Nazism, many European youth adorn themselves with Palestinian insignia, the promise of Israel's destruction, while it announces that of Europe.

During the December 2008 pilgrimage to Mecca, many Western televisions, cautiously joining the Islamic *da'wa,* presented Abraham's sacrifice as being that of his son Ishmael in Mecca and not Isaac in Jerusalem, obfuscating the biblical narrative. Following the Mumbai massacres and the torture of residents of a Jewish center, the press carefully stuck to the Islamic lexicon.

Muslim laws of *da'wa*, blasphemy and apostasy have reached Europe. Atheist and non-religious Muslims live under threat, some obliged to hide, others needing bodyguards, while having committed no crime other than the innocent use of freedom of opinion. Will they be threatened even more by Article 14 of the World Islamic League (Rome, February 25–27, 2000), which declared that it is obligatory for all Muslims, leaders and nations, to apply *shari'a* in every aspect of their lives? In September 2008 Great Britain officially accepted *shari'a* courts to hear civil cases and authorized the execution of their decisions within the legal system. According to British Professor Anthony Glees, Director of the Brunel Center for Intelligence and Security at Brunel University, eight universities, including Oxford and Cambridge, have accepted more than £233.5 million (over $400 million) from Saudi and Muslim sources since 1995. In addition, Gordon Brown turned London into the Western center for *shari'a* finance.[28]

The well-established principle in the UK, as well as in other EU countries, of delegating to Muslim intermediaries the task of forcing their coreligionists to obey national laws suggests that only the authority of a Muslim legitimizes the law. This process of channeling to Muslims authority over other Muslim émigrés confirms one of the main laws of dhimmitude, which forbids an infidel to exercise authority over a Muslim.

As far as blasphemy is concerned, updated today by the official practice of *shari'a* in Europe, it ensures the conviction of infidels and Muslims alike who, accused of this offense, are hounded and even murdered. This danger brings politicians and ordinary people, irrespective of their religion, to accept considerable sacrifices at the family, professional and social levels, should they refuse to submit to the rules of dhimmitude now introduced into their own countries by their own ministers. Today these free thinkers are the heroes of a freedom that is dying in increasingly destructured societies eaten away by multiculturalism.

The case of Geert Wilders, a member of the Dutch parliament and leader of the Freedom Party (the PVV), a major liberal party, illustrates this situation. A Jordanian organization called "The Messenger of Allah unites us" had him convicted by a Jordanian court, which ordered him to present himself within fifteen days. A refusal would involve a request to Interpol for an international arrest warrant—a policy ushering in the legal jihad, also known as "lawfare." A person living in his own country and not contravening the laws of that country might thus be convicted as a criminal if he is in breach of the *shari'a* practiced in another country. The risk of extradition of an innocent person to a Muslim country that would find him guilty under *shari'a* endangers freedom of movement and travel. In this obnoxious situation, Muslims who have chosen democracy and modernity, who are well integrated into all sectors of European society, are the most exposed.

On January 21, 2009, a Dutch court ordered the opening of legal proceedings against Parliamentary Deputy Geert Wilders, accused of having made insulting remarks about Muslims via his film *Fitna*. These steps, the result of OIC pressure on Dutch business circles, eliminate freedom of expression since any speech could perhaps irritate Muslims and thus might lead to prosecution. Such restrictions on freedom of expression, whose victims in Europe, both Muslim and non-Muslim, are already numerous, testify to the official importation of *shari'a* laws on the continent.

Thus, while the defenders of constitutional freedoms are hounded and receive death threats, the Dutch Minister of Health, Jet Bussemaker of the Labor Party, proposed giving more attention to the role played by Muslims in the liberation of Holland during the Second World War.[29] According to Martin Bosma, a deputy from the Freedom Party (PVV), this request is motivated by a desire to please Muslim electors. It also contradicts historical truth. Admiration for Hitler and Nazism in Europe's Muslim colonies, which continues until today, was one of the reasons for refusing access there to Jewish refugees.[30]

Bussemaker proposed including the part played by ethnic minorities during World War II in teacher training and school textbooks. He reckoned that the knowledge passed on by teachers to their students would ease their integration. According to Deputy Bosma, this is a question of "a multicultural, historical falsification." Will one day the EU adopt for teaching purposes Articles 16 and 22 of the Declaration on Human Rights in Islam (1990), confirmed by the OIC and ISESCO, which connect culture and faith, prohibit scientific, literary, artistic and technological opinions and knowledge that are contrary to *shari'a*?

In some schools with a majority of Muslim pupils, teachers do not teach about the Shoah or other topics despised by Muslim students hostile to such "European teaching." This situation is common throughout many European schools. Muslim students of foreign parents dictate school education on a major European and historical world tragedy that has determined the very conception and adoption of the UN Convention on the Prevention and Punishment of the Crime of Genocide (December 9, 1948), followed the next day by the Universal Declaration of Human Rights.

According to Frank Furedi, professor of sociology at Kent University (UK), some schools in Denmark refuse to accept Jewish students on the pretext that they disturb the Muslim students.[31]

Universities and teachers who dare make a dent in the *doxa* dictated by the OIC are often snubbed by their colleagues. In France, Sylvain Gouguenheim, Professor of History at the Ecole Normale Supérieure (ENS) in Lyon, had this experience when he published a scholarly study on the transmission of Greek culture through Greek and Latin channels during the Middle Ages. This highly specialized and uncontroversial field turned into a vicious battle, because his research contradicted the Muslim version which asserts an exclusively Muslim transmission of Greek science to Western Europe. Now diversity of opinion is akin to blasphemy, objective information is accused of racism, while Judeo-Christian and humanist values and both national and European cultural identities become xenophobia.

In September 2008 a small demonstration in Cologne, "Stop the Islamization of Europe," was banned with extreme violence by the authorities, on the orders of the mayor. However, in January 2009 almost all the capitals of Europe suffered their massive demonstrations of hate with complete impunity under the banner of Palestine. Countless demonstrators, mainly Muslim immigrants, organized and supported by the Euro-OIC networks and press, burnt Israeli flags and yelled genocidal slogans inciting to hatred against Jews and Israel in the name of Palestine. When Israel neutralized the Hamas gangs that had incessantly bombarded its villages for over seven years, while perfecting the tunnels for transporting weapons under houses and schools, Europe demonstrated in favor of the rights of terrorism against the right to fight it and defend oneself. Synagogues were attacked, windows smashed along with racist verbal attacks and calls for boycotts, Jewish students expelled from schools (Denmark), and an Israeli flag confiscated from an apartment by the police (Germany), indicating that the fine principles of Universal Human Rights might become a mirage in Europe. In Rome, Bologna and Milan, imams led the prayers of immense crowds of Muslims in public squares, some even in front of cathedrals. In central London near St James's Palace, police officers fled from hordes of Muslim demonstrators, who hurled projectiles and mocking insults, "Run away, scram, coward, nonbeliever." Throughout Europe the cries of conquest, "Allah ul Akbar" and death to Israel were raised.

The demonstration of strength by the caliphate and its representative, Hamas, the Palestinization of Europe, had become facts with undeniable evidence before the eyes of appalled Europeans. The only exception to this rout was in Rome, where one hundred parliamentarians braved the cold to join a vast throng with countless flags adorned with the Star of Israel, to bear witness to the right to live and not to kill. Ukraine followed.

The Western press, under the caliphate's pressure, harassed the public with the question it deemed essential for all humankind, would Obama throw Israel to the wolves? Could this tiny people, subject to persecution at the hands of Christianity and Islam, still attest to freedom over slavery, to the spirit over barbarism, and to courage over servility? Would Obama pressurize Israel? This burning question inflames the Western press and the entire world while countless peoples suffer from hunger, war, terrorism, poverty and sickness, especially in the vast territories overrun and colonized by the jihad.

The networks of the Alliance of Civilizations, ISESCO, and the Anna Lindh Foundation, all affiliated to the UN and the OIC, conscientiously draw up their accusations against Israel. Yet neither the EU nor the UN, never once since 1988, denounced the genocidal Charter of Hamas that is in breach of human rights, nor the crimes against humanity carried out with impunity for eight years with the non-stop rocketing of Israeli villages and towns by Gazans who had freely elected Hamas since they agree with its Charter and policies. Contrary to their claims to victimology, Palestinians, supported by fifty-six Muslim countries, the whole OIC policy and the EU, are responsible for their own choices and not victims.

During the Palestinian demonstrations of hate celebrated in their capital cities, dazed Europeans discovered the irreparable erosion of basic freedoms, the subversion of human rights, and the import into their own countries of a racist, Nazi, antisemitic barbarism that revolts them. They realize the treason of their own governments, incapable of preserving the custody of their own national security and of constitutional liberties and rights and who consider their own compatriots and fellow citizens to be the enemies.

Today Eurabian globalist and pacifist trends are obvious in the American Democratic administration under President Barack Obama. The policy of engagement and outreaching with the Muslim world, its support for a UN world order, were explicit in the booklet *Changing Course: A New Direction for U.S. Relations with the Muslim World* published in 2007 and 2008.[32] For a European familiar with EU surrender policy, President Obama's policy had no surprises. Western guilt, apologies, flatteries, tributes, anti-Zionism/anti-semitism, open-doors immigration, were all part of the dhimmitude paraphernalia.

OIC influence is easily recognized in Obama's speeches to the Muslim world, like the one at al-Azhar on June 4, 2009:

> On education, we will expand exchange programs, and increase scholarships, like the one that brought my father to America, while encouraging more Americans to study in Muslim communities. And we will match promising Muslim students with internships in America; invest in on-line learning for teachers and children around the world; and create a new online network, so a teenager in Kansas can communicate instantly with a teenager in Cairo.

On science and technology, we will launch a new fund to support technological development in Muslim-majority countries, and to help transfer ideas to the
marketplace so they can create jobs. We will open centers of scientific excellence in Africa, the Middle East and Southeast Asia.

These, as we have seen, are also the recommendations of the Alliance of
Civilizations. They were followed by the *International Professional
Exchange Act of 2010* introduced by Senate Foreign Relations Committee
Chairman John Kerry (D-MA). It planned a two-way professional exchange
program between the United States and some Muslim-majority countries to
promote career development and cross-cultural understanding for young to
mid-career professionals.

In his Ramadan August 2009 address Obama evoked "Islam's role in
advancing justice, progress, tolerance, and the dignity of all human beings."

CONCLUSION

While writing this study I was reminded of a question that greatly troubled
me twenty-five years ago when researching *Les Chrétientés d'Orient entre
jihad et dhimmitude* (1991).[33] How did Christian peoples and states, some
with powerful armies and the richest cultures of their times, collapse when
faced with the onslaught of jihad and dhimmitude from the seventh to the
fifteenth centuries? Now I no longer ask myself this question. The breakdown process that I used to study and documented in old chronicles I have
seen taking place in today's Europe. When I examined the past I saw it
repeated in the present, under my very eyes. Indeed, the present situation is
reminiscent of the one that followed the Muslim conquests. Keeping Christian officials in their positions maintained a semblance of continuity. Behind
their foggy screen, Islamization could penetrate within every stratum of the
vanquished societies. However, with time, the collapse of this edifice revealed the true role of these ministers, whose job was to enforce upon their
people the caliphate's orders, under pain of death. I was missing one essential link in the chain of events: the motivations of human beings that lead
them in an unswerving direction within the chaos of events, the undeviating
route toward an ultimate objective. Now this link is revealed in the mix of
fears, cowardice, corruption, hatred and short-term ambitions that within the
space of forty years have led Europe along the road to Eurabia, an interim
stage in an even more profound change.

Is there a moral to the story? For Judeo-Christian societies the answer is affirmative, because the Bible, the spiritual bedrock of these societies, grants man freedom and dignity, as well as their corollary: responsibility. The biblical meaning of good and evil having penetrated every aspect of Christianity, the latter could not survive its hatred of Israel any more than a self-inflicting poison.

Active in its pursuit of its own Islamization, Europe encouraged the rejection of the Hebrew Bible. Loyalty to their origins was a rear-guard action fought by heroic resisters. Pressured by governments, the Churches have supported the Palestinian heresy of the Sabeel Ecumenical Liberation Theology Center, professing an Islamized Marcionite Christianity, which has not only removed all Hebrew bible roots, but has also dispossessed the Jewish people of its own timeless heritage and transferred it to the Palestinians. "Arab Palestine" and no longer the Church has become the new Israel. This majority movement in Europe today is the weapon of the OIC. Cut off from its base, Christianity can thus be reclaimed for Islam. That would seem to be the mission of the Jerusalem Sabeel Center and the Arab Eastern Churches.

Beside a cult hatred for Israel and the Bible, there have been other dynamics involved in the disintegration of Europe. However, for me this aspect would appear to present one of the main elements in the Europe-OIC alliance, because the demise of Israel is essential for the OIC in its conquest of the Christian West. Israel was born from the liberation of men and women from slavery and with their freedom came moral responsibility—characteristics that are consubstantial with the meaning of Israel since antiquity. The rejection and even hate-filled divorce from that spirit of liberty opened up the way to the dhimmitude preached by the Arab Churches, and for Christians to a total rejection of their identity. The renewal of Euro-Arab alliances formed by fascists and Nazis gave substance to the Palestinian, Muslim-Christian cult of substitution for Israel. The fight against Israel, inherent in the choice of Palestine, provided the basis for the erection of Eurabia. This ideology determined the denial of jihad and encouraged the self-destructive policies of moral and ideological Islamization within Europe.

It is evident that such choices, which are endemic within Christian societies, represent permanent currents that will lead ineluctably to the destruction of Judeo-Christianity and Enlightenment values. It has determined the choice of servitude over freedom, as we are seeing it today. Because one cannot compromise on one's own identity and freedom unless one is already a slave . . . or a dhimmi.

Europe has lost its bet. A hostage to hatred of Israel, it thought it could salvage peace by its surrender to Palestinian terrorism since the late 1960s. Burnishing the instruments of its own defeat, it has argued that terrorism will not be defeated through the military option, but rather through dialogue, multilateralism and multiculturalism, the main argument of the coming Caliphate. It has made clever use of such instruments to justify the surrender strategy and to turn Israel's military victories into political defeats, running to the rescue of its implacable enemies in order to keep the conflict alive.

The Palestinization of Europe has brought the caliphate into the cities of Europe. It has advanced through the denial of the dangers and the obfuscating of history. It has moved forward on gilded carpets in the corridors of dialogue, the networks of the Alliances and partnerships, the corruption of its leaders, intellectuals and NGOs, particularly at the United Nations. The caliphate is already alive and growing within Europe, in the extinction of the basic freedoms, control over thought, opinions and culture, subverting democratic laws by *shari'a*, *fatwas*, self-censorship and fear—inseparable companions of dhimmitude.

The universal caliphate, for which Europe provided a stepping-stone at the UN, stands before us, bringing together political and religious power. It has set itself up as the protector of the Muslim immigrant masses in the world and requires that they remain firmly anchored in the Islamic traditions of the Koran and Sunna, following *shari'a* laws while the Europeans are called upon to abandon their historic values and even their identity condemned as Islamophobia. Today, muffled rumblings are arising from the peoples of Europe, announcing to those who created this situation that they will not escape the judgment of history.

NOTES

1. Bourdeillette, 246–47.

2. Ibid., 246.

3. Neill Nugent, *The Government and Politics of the European Union* (UK: Palgrave Macmillan, 2003), 490.

4. Ibid., 491.

5. *Report on Islamic Summit, 1974*, al-Tuhami's discourse, 195–219; extracts 198–202, 204, 215, 217. See Bat Ye'or, *Eurabia*, 76.

6. *Euro-Arab Dialogue: The Relations between the Two Cultures. Acts of the Hamburg symposium. April 11th to 15th 1983.* English version edited by Derek Hopwood (London: Croom Helm, 1983), 305–16. Extracts in Bat Ye'or, *Eurabia*, 296–301.

7. Program presented by Dr. Traugott Schoefthaler, Executive Director of the ALF, for *IEMED Mediterranean Year Book 2004*, www.iemed.org.

8. *Alliance of Civilizations. Implementation Plan, 2007–2009*, United Nations, 2–3.

9. Ibid., 3.

10. Ibid., 4.

11. Ibid., 5, bold in the text.

12. Ibid.,10, parentheses in the text.

13. Ibid., 14.

14. Ibid., 13.

15. Bat Ye'or, *The Decline of Eastern Christianity under Islam: From Jihad to Dhimmitude,* preface by Jacques Ellul (Cranbury, N.J.: AUP, 1996), chap. 4, "The Conquered Lands: Processes of Islamization."

16. www.isesco.org.ma/english/strategy/documents/Strategy%20West.pdf, 16.

17. *Implementation Plan, 2007–2009*, 15.

18. Ann Bayefsky, EYEontheUN.org www.eyeontheun.org/assets/attachments/documents/7245_Brockmann_GA.pdf (accessed January 6, 2011).

19. www.memri.org/bin/latestnews.cgi?ID=IA47808 (accessed January 6, 2011).

20. Jane Perlez, Eric Schmitt, and Marc Mazetti, "Pakistan raids camp of Kashmir militants, But Lashkar-e-Taiba has thrived with Islamabad's backing," *International Herald Tribune*, December 9, 2008.

21. Matthias Küntzel, "'Islamophobia' or 'Truthophobia'? Berlin's anti-Semitism center is going astray," *Wall Street Journal*, December 7, 2008.

22. Emeritus Professor at the New Sorbonne University, Paris III.

23. Bat Ye'or, *The Decline*; Mark Durie, *The Third Choice, Islam, Dhimmitude and Freedom.* Foreword by Bat Ye'or (Australia: Deror Book, 2010).

24. Andrew E. Kramer, "For Iraqi Christians, Money Bought Survival," nytimes.com, June 26, 2008.

25. Tony Blair, "Faith and Globalization: An Alliance of Values," *International Herald Tribune*, December 19, 2008. p.8.

26. Melanie Phillips, "Fortune Takes Britain Hostage," *Daily Mail*, November 10, 2008.

27. Olivier Roy and Justin Vaisse, "The Muslims and us. How to win Islam over," *International Herald Tribune*, December 23, 2008.

28. Melanie Phillips, *Daily Mail*, November 10, 2008.

29. The Hague, May 5, 2008, www.nisnews.nl.

30. André Chouraqui, *La condition juridique de l'Israélite marocain*, pref. by René Cassin (Paris: Presses du Livre Français, 1950); David G. Littman, "Jews under Muslim Rule, II: Morocco 1903–1912 ," *Wiener Library Bulletin*, vol. 29, n. 37–38 (1976): 3–19; Paul B. Fenton and David G. Littman ed., *L'exil au Maghreb. La condition juive sous l'Islam–1148–1912* (Paris: Pups-Sorbonne, 2010).

31. Frank Furedi, "Giving Voice to Anti-Semitism," *The Australian*, January 15, 2009.

32. *Changing Course. A New Direction for U.S. Relations with the Muslim World.* Report of the Leadership Group on U.S. Muslim Engagement (U.S.–Muslim Engagement Project: Washington, D.C., Cambridge Mass., 2008, 2009). See also *Shariah. The Threat to America*, The Center for Security Policy, 2010.

33. Translated as *The Decline of Eastern Christianity under Islam*, 1996.

Bibliography

GENERAL

"Alliance des civilisations?" Controverses, no. 9, November 2008, Paris: Editions de l'Eclat, 2008.

Archeld, Ray. "UE-Israël : nouveau chapitre,"*Guysen International News* www.guysen.com/ articles.php?sid=8724.

Al-Banna, Hassan. IkhwanWeb - Cairo, Egypt, *To What Do We Invite Humanity.* www.ikhwanweb.com/Article.asp?ID=804&LevelID=1&SectionID=117 (accessed September 19, 2010).

Bat Ye'or, *Le Dhimmi, Profil de l'opprimé en Orient et en Afrique du Nord,* éditions Anthropos, Paris :1980, translated into English as *The Dhimmi: Jews and Christians under Islam,* preface by Jacques Ellul, Cranburry, N.J.: AUP, 1980.

——. *The Decline of Eastern Christianity under Islam: From Jihad to Dhimmitude,* preface by Jacques Ellul. Cranbury, N.J.: AUP, 1996.

——. *Islam and Dhimmitude. Where Civilizations Collide.* Madison, N.J.: Fairleigh Dickinson University Press, 2002.

——. 'Le dialogue Euro-Arabe et la naissance d'Eurabia', *Observatoire du monde juif,* Bulletin n°4/5, dec. 2002, pp. 44-55. Translated into English as "The Euro-Arab Dialogue and The Birth of Eurabia," at www.dhimmitude.org/d_today_eurabia.html (accessed September 19, 2010).

——. *Eurabia: The Euro-Arab Axis.* Madison, N.J.: Fairleigh Dickinson University Press, 2005.

Bayefsky, Anne. Statement of H.E. Miguel D'Escoto Brockmann, President of the United Nations General Assembley, at the 57th Plenary Meeting on Agenda Item 16, The Question of Palestine: United Nations, New York, November 24, 2008. www.eyeontheun.org/assets/ attachments/ documents/7245_Brockmann_GA.pdf

Blair, Tony. "Faith and Globalization. An Alliance of Values," *International Herald Tribune,* December 19, 2008, 8.

Bôle-Richard, Michel. "Le pari israélien de l'Union européenne," *Le Monde.fr,* December 20, 2008.

Bostom, Andrew G., ed. *The Legacy of Islamic Antisemitism, from Sacred Texts to Solemn History*, pref. by Ibn Warraq, New York: Prometheus Books, 2008.

Bourrinet, Jacques, ed. *Le Dialogue Euro-Arabe*, Economica, Paris 1979.

Bourdeillette, Jean. *Pour Israël*, Seghers, Paris 1968.

Bulletin de la Ligue Arabe. Centre d'Informations Arabes, Geneva.

Cahier de Chaillot, Vol.V, no. 75, Brussels, March 25–26, 2004.

Caroll, James. "Onward, Christian Zionists," *International Herald Tribune*, August 26, 2010.

Cazzullo, Aldo. *Corriere della Sera*, July 8, 2008.

Changing Course. A New Direction for U.S. Relations with the Muslim World. Report of the Leadership Group on U.S. Muslim Engagement. U.S.-Muslim Engagement Project: Washington, D.C. Cambridge MA, 2008, 2009.

Chouraqui, André. *La condition juridique de l'Israélite marocain*, pref. by René Cassin. Paris: Presses du Livre Français, 1950.

Coudron, Stephanie. "Terrorism Phrase Book to Put Officials on Guard," *The Times*, London, April 2, 2008.

Cuppers, see Mallman.

Curtis, Michael ed., *Orientalism and Islam*, Cambridge University Press, Cambridge, 2009.

Diène, Doudou. Reports to the UN General Assembly on September 20, 2006 and August 21, 2007. A/HRC/2/3, Sept. 20, 2006 and A/HRC/6/6, August 21, 2007.

Documents d'Actualité Internationale, Ministère des Affaires Etrangères, Paris.

———. Report to the Council on Human Rights dated February 20, 2008, A/HRC/7/19.

———. Report on contemporary forms of racism, racial discrimination, xenophobia, and on the manifestations of defamation of religions and in particular the serious impact of Islamophobia on the enjoyment of all rights . . . September 2, 2008. A/IIRC/9/12.

Donadio, Rachel. "Pope highlights plight of Christians in Mideast," *International Herald Tribune*, June 7, 2010.

Durie, Mark. *The Third Choice, Islam, Dhimmitude and Freedom*. Foreword by Bat Ye'or. Australia: Deror Book, 2010.

Enyo, *Anatomie d'un désastre, l'Occident, l'islam et la guerre au XXIe siècle*, p. 238, Paris: Denoël, 2009.

Erdem, Suna, "Recep Tayyip Erdogan threatens to expel 100000 illegal Armenians," *The Times* (online), London, March 18, 2010 (accessed April 9, 2010).

EURO-ARAB DIALOGUE. The relations between the two cultures. Acts of the Hamburg symposium. April 11th to 15th 1983. English version edited by Derek Hopwood. London: Croom Helm, 1983.

Fasanella, Giovanni, and Priore, Rosario. *Intrigo Internazionale*. Milan: Chiarelettere, 2010.

Fenton, Paul B., and David G. Littman ed., *L'exil au Maghreb.La condition juive sous l'Islam—1148–1912*, Pups-Sorbonne, Paris: 2010.

Frattini, Davide. *Corriere della Sera*, August 14, 2008.

Furedi, Frank. "Giving voice to anti-Semitism,"*The Australian*, January 15, 2009, www.theaustralian.news.com.au/story/0,25197,24913868-7583,00.html.

Ganz, Menahem. *Israel News*, August 17, 2008.

Ginsberg, Roy H. *The European Union in International Politics: Baptism by Fire*. Lanham, Md.: Rowman & Littlefield, 2001.

Glick, Caroline B. "The Ironies of the West's Collusion with the Arabs and Iran," July 10, 2008, www.jewishworldreview.com/1008/glick100708.php3 (accessed September 20, 2010).

Groupe d'études sur le Moyen Orient, n° 80, December 1979, Geneva.

Haaretz.com, June 21, 2008.

El-Hudaibi, Mohammad Ma'mun, *The Principles of the Muslim Brotherhood*,www. ikhwanweb.com/Article.asp?ID=813&LevelID=2&SectionID=116(accessed May 3, 2009).

Ibn Warraq. *Defending the West: A Critique of Edward Said's Orientalism.* Amherst, N.Y.: Prometheus Books, 2007.

Ihsanoglu, Ekmeleddin. Speech of His Excellency Prof. Ekmeleddin Ihsanoglu Secretary General of the Organisation of the Islamic Conference at the First International Conference organized by (OIC) under the theme: "Challenging Stereotypes in Europe and the Islamic World: Working Together for Constructive Policies and Partnerships," Wilton Park Conference Center, London, May 2, 2006. www.wiltonpark/organization/uk/documents/conferences/WPS)6-27/pdfs/WPS06-27.pdf.

———. Speech . . . at the Eleventh Session of the Islamic Summit Conference, Dakar – Republic of Senegal, March 13–14, 2008. www.oic-oci.org/is11/english/SG-speech-sum.pdf.

———. Copenhagen Meeting. October 22, 2008. www.oic-oci.org/topic_detail.asp?t_id=1548&x_key= (accessed May 3, 2009).

International Herald Tribune, July 16, 2010.

International Islamic News Agency. "ISESCO/UNESCO: ISESCO Calls on UNESCO to take action to stop Israel's falsification of Islamic History." March 3, 2010. www.iina.me/english/news.php?go=fullnews&newsid=105.

Jihad Watch. "Expansion of Israeli settlements . . . shows the Zionist plans to accelerate Judaization of east Jerusalem," www.jihadwatch.org/2010/03/expansion-of-israeli-settlementsshows-the-zionist-plans-to-accelerate-judaization-of-east-jerusalem.html.

Johnson, Ian. *A Mosque in Munich. Nazis, the CIA, and the Rise of the Muslim Brotherhood in the West.* New York: Houghton Mifflin Harcourt, 2010.

The Koran, trans. with notes by N[essim] J[oseph] Dawood. New York: Penguin Books, 1987. First edition 1956.

Kramer, Andrew E. "For Iraqi Christians, Money Bought Survival," nytimes.com, June 26, 2008.

Küntzel, Matthias. "'Islamophobia' or 'Truthophobia'? Berlin's anti-Semitism center is going astray," *Wall Street Journal*, December 7, 2008.

Laske, Karl. *Le banquier noir. François Genoud.* Paris: Seuil, 1996.

Le Temps, Geneva, May 24, 2007. Article on 2007 report of Amnesty International.

Littman, David G. "Jews under Muslim Rule, II: Morocco 1903–1912 ," Wiener Library Bulletin, vol. 29, n. 37–38, 1976, pp. 3–19.

———. "UN Human Rights Council: Any mention of the word 'shari'a' is now taboo," June 19, 2008,www.jihadwatch.org/archives/021461.php.

Littman, David G., and Paul B. Fenton. *L'exil au Maghreb.La condition juive sous l'Islam— 1148–1912.* Paris: Pups-Sorbonne, 2010.

Al-Makdisi, Elias, and Sam Soloman, *Al-Yahud: The Islamic Doctrine of Enmity & the Jews*, Advancing Native Missions, P.O. Box 5303, Charlottesville, VA 22905, 2010.

Mallman, Klaus-Michael, and Martin Cuppers. *Nazi Palestine. The Plans for the Extermination of the Jews in Palestine.* New York: Enigma Books, 2010.

MEMRI. Discussion on Al-Jazeera: The Arab Rulers. www.memri.org/report/en/0/0/0/0/0/0/826.htm

Merad, Ali. *Le califat, une autorité pour l'islam ?* [The Caliphate, an authority for Islam?], Paris: Desclée de Brower, 2008.

NGO Monitor. November 26, 2009.

———. Israeli Apartheid Week 2010: NGO Involvement. www.ngo-monitor.org/article/israeli_apartheid_week_ngo_involvement (accessed October 6, 2010).

Nugent, Neill. *The Government and Politics of the European Union.* UK: Palgrave Macmillan, 2003.

PAEAC. 1974–1994. *Association Parlementaire pour la Coopération Euro-Arabe.*

Péan, Pierre. *L'Extrémiste, François Genoud, de Hitler à Carlos.* Paris: Fayard, 1996.

Priore, see Fasanella.

Perlez, Jane, Eric Schmitt, and Marc Mazetti, "Pakistan Raids Camp of Kashmir Militants: But Lashkar-E-Taiba Has Thrived with Islamabad's Backing," *International Herald Tribune,* December 9, 2008.

Phillips, Melanie. "Fortune Takes Britain Hostage," *Daily Mail,* November 10, 2008.

Prodi, Romano. "Sharing stability and prosperity." Tempus MEDA Regional Conference – Bibliotheca Alexandrina, Alexandria, 13 October 2003. europa.eu/rapid/pressReleasesAction.do?reference=SPEECH/03/458&format=HTML&aged=0&language=EN&guiLanguage=en.

Rauffer, Xavier. *La Nébuleuse: le terrorisme du Moyen-Orient.* Paris: Fayard, 1987.

Roy, Olivier, and Justin Vaisse, "The Muslims and Us: How To Win Islam Over," *International Herald Tribune,* December 23, 2008.

Said, Edward. *Orientalism,* Routledge & Kegan Paul, London, 1978.

Schoefthaler, Traugott. "The First Steps of Establishing the Anna Lindh Euro-Mediterranean Foundation for the Dialogue between Cultures." Written for the IEMED Mediterranean Yearbook 2004.www.iemed.org/documents/lindhstepsang.pdf.

Seibert, Thomas, "Enmity with Islam 'crime against humanity'," *The National,* Sept. 17, 2008. www.thenational.ae/article/20080916/FOREIGN/253853817/1011/NEWS&Profile=1011.

Shariah. The Threat to America, The Center for Security Policy, 2010.

Soloman, Sam, and E. al Maqdisi. *Al Hijra, the Islamic Doctrine of Immigration: Accepting freedom or imposing Islam?* Pilcrow Press, 2009, www.pilcrowpress.com

Solana, Javier. "The European Security Strategy—The Next Steps?" *Cahier de Chaillot,* Vol.V, no. 75, *Sécurité et Défense de l'UE, Textes fondamentaux,* 2004. Institut d'Etudes de Sécurité, Union européenne, February 2005, Paris.

Spencer, Robert. *Stealth Jihad. How Radical Islam Is subverting America without Guns or Bombs.* Washington D.C.: Regnery, 2008.

Steinberg, Gerald M. "Europe's Hidden Hand. EU Funding for Political NGOs in the Arab-Israeli Conflict. Analyzing Processes and Impact." NGO Monitor Monograph series. April 2008.

Tibi, Bassam. "War and Peace in Islam" in *Islamic Political Ethics. Civil Society, Pluralism, and Conflict,* ed. by Sohail H. Hashmi, with a Foreword by Jack Miles, Princeton University Press, 2002.

Today's Zaman. "Ankara to propose joint NATO-OIC conference in talks with Rasmussen." August 28, 2009. www.todayszaman.com/tz-web/news-185374-ankara-to-propose-joint-nato-oic-conference-in-talks-with-rasmussen.html (accessed October 6, 2010).

Védrine, Hubert. "To Paris, U.S. Looks Like a 'Hyperpower.'" International Herald Tribune. February 5, 1999. www.nytimes.com/1999/02/05/news/05iht-france.t_0.html (accessed September 21, 2010).

Waterfield, Bruno. "Don't Confuse Terrorism with Islam, says EU." *Telegraph.co.uk,* March 31, 2007. www.telegraph.co.uk/news/worldnews/1547133/Dont-confuse-terrorism-with-Islam-says-EU.html (accessed September 21, 2010).

World Council of Churches. "Kairos Palestine," drawn up by Palestinian theologians and published in Bethlehem on December 11, 2009 by the World Council of Churches, Geneva. Put on line by Menahem Macina, February 22, 2010, www.debriefing.org/30011.html.

EEC/EU DOCUMENTS

Joint Resolution of the Nine countries of the EEC, Brussels, November 6, 1973. www.ena.lu/ joint_statement_governments_eec_november_1973-020002394.html (accessed October 6, 2010).

Declaration of the Nine, London June 29, 1977. aei.pitt.edu/1410/01/London_june_1977.pdf (accessed October 6, 2010).

Venice Declaration, June 1980. domino.un.org/unispal.nsf/fd807e46661 e3689852570d00069e918/fef015e8b1a1e5a685256d810059d922? OpenDocument (accessed October 6, 2010).

Council of Europe, Parliamentary Assembly, Discussion by the Assembly, 19 September 1991 (11th session) (see Doc. 6497, report of the Committee on Culture and Education, Rapporteur: Mr. de Puig), Strasbourg, 1992.

Official Journal of the European Communities, "Common Strategy of the European Council of 19 June 2000 on the Mediterranean Region (2000/458/CFSP)." europa.eu/legislation_summaries/external_relations/relations_with_third_countries/mediterranean_partner_countries/r15002_en.htm (accessed October 6, 2010).

A Union Of Values, Final Text Agreed at the XIV EPP Congress, Berlin, January 2001, www.euractiv.com/en/culture/dialogue-islam-key-parteuropean-intercultural-year/article-169403

Council of Europe Parliamentary Assembly. Recommandation 1590 (2003) "Cultural co-operation between Europe and the south Mediterranean countries." Text adopted by the Assembly on January 28, 2003 (3rd Sitting). assembly.coe.int/Main.asp?link=/Documents/Adopted-Text/ta03/EREC1590.htm (accessed October 6, 2010).

Council of Europe Parliamentary Assembly. "Cultural co-operation between Europe and the south Mediterranean countries." Report of November 8, 2002 presented by the Commission on Culture, Science and Education by the Rapporteur of the Spanish Socialist group, Lluis Maria de Puig. assembly.coe.int/Mainf.asp?link=/Documents/WorkingDocs/Doc02/EDOC9626.htm (accessed October 6, 2010).

Communication from the Commission to the Council and the European Parliament," The European Union and the United Nations: The Choice of Multilateralism," Brussels, 10/9/2003 [COM(2003) 526 final—Not published in the Official Journal], eur-lex.europa.eu/LexUriServ/LexUriServ.do?uri=COM:2003:0526:FIN:EN:DOC (accessed September 21, 2010).

Dialogue Between Peoples and Cultures in the Euro-Mediterranean Area. Report by the High-Level Advisory Group established at the initiative of the President of the European Commission (2004). www.iemed.org/documents/lindhgroupen.pdf (accessed October 6, 2010).

A Secure Europe in a Better World: European Security Strategy, Brussels, 12 December 2003, p. 3.ue.eu.int/uedocs/cmsUpload/78367.pdf(accessed September 20, 2010).

Euro-Mediterranean Parliamentary Assembly (EMPA) held in Cairo March 12–15, 2005. www.europarl.europa.eu/intcoop/empa/plenary_sessions/cairo_2005/cairo_03_05_final_declaration_en.pdf.

European Commision. Proposal for a decision of the European Parliament and of the Council concerning the European Year of Intercultural Dialogue (2008). [SEC(2005) aaaa] ec.europa.eu/culture/portal/events/pdf/proposal_en.pdf

Council of Europe, 2005 Ordinary Session (Fourth part), Report Twenty-seventh sitting, Tuesday, October 4, 2005. assembly.coe.int/Main.asp?link=/Documents/Records/2005/E/0510041500E.htm#7 (accessed September 21, 2010).

Decision No. 1983/2006/EC of the European Parliament and of the Council of December 18, 2006, concerning the European Year of Intercultural Dialogue (2008), Official Journal of the European Union, December 30, 2006, L 412/44 – L 412/50.

Council of the European Union, Partial Declassification—Annex. June 6, 2007. register.consilium.europa.eu/pdf/en/07/st05/st05469-re03ex01.en07.pdf (accessed September 21, 2010).

European Parliament, Parliamentary Questions—Reply, September 27, 2007. www.europarl.europa.eu/sides/getAllAnswers.do?reference=E-2007-3587&language=EN (accessed September 21, 2010).

"European Commission launches PEGASE—a new mechanism to support the Palestinian people." europa-eu-un.org/articles/es/article_7681_es.htm

Parliamentary Assembly of the Council of Europe . . . Resolution 1605 (2008). European Muslim communities faced with extremism. Text adopted by the Assembly on April 15, 2008 (13th session).

Med Union: Empa Asks Foreign Ministers For More Powers (Ansamed) - Brussels, October 13, 2008.

Les institutions communes aux trois piliers–La Commission des Communautés européennes. See www.diplomatie.gouv.fr/fr/europe_828/union-europeenne-monde_13399/politique-etrangere-securite-commune_851/fonctionnement-pesc_15060/les-institutions-communes-aux-trois-piliers_15061/commission-communautes-europeennes_40924.html (accessed September 20, 2010).

Guide de la PESC, Ministère des Affaires Etrangères, Paris. www.diplomatie.gouv.fr/fr/IMG/pdf/pesc.pdf.

Les Objectifs de la PESC. Ministère des Affaires Etrangères, Paris. www.diplomatie.gouv.fr/fr/europe_828/union-europeenne-monde_13399/politique-etrangere-securite-commune_851/est-pesc_15055/les-objectifs-pesc_15102/les-objectifs-pesc_41284.html (accessed September 20, 2010)

A Secure Europe in a Better World—European Security Strategy. Brussels, December 12, 2003 [Not published in the Official Journal].europa.eu/legislation_summaries/justice_freedom_security/fight_against_terrorism/r00004_en.htm(accessed September 21, 2010).

The History of the European Union.europa.eu/abc/history/index_en.htm

ISLAMIC ORGANIZATIONS DOCUMENTS

Report on Islamic Summit, 1974, May 1973 the Islamic Conference held in London.

Report on Islamic Summit 1974: Pakistan. Lahore, February 22–24, Karachi 1974.

Cairo Declaration on Human Rights in Islam Adopted and Issued at the Nineteenth Islamic Conference of Foreign Ministers in Cairo on August 5, 1990. nifcon.anglicancommunion.org/work/declarations/cairo.cfm

The Strategy for Islamic Cultural Action outside the Islamic World, (former title: *Strategy of Islamic Cultural Action in the West*) Adopted at the Ninth Islamic Summit Conference held in Doha–State of Qatar, 2000. Publications of the Islamic Educational, Scientific and Cultural Organization –ISESCO–Rabat, Morocco, 1422H/2001 A.D. www.isesco.org.ma/english/strategy/documents/Strategy%20West.pdf.

Protection of Islamic and Christian Holy Sites in Palestine. Publications of the Islamic Educational, Scientific and Cultural Organization–ISESCO–1425H/2004. Proceedings of the International Conference organized by ISESCO in Rabat, June 7–8, 2002.

Protection of Islamic and Christian Holy Sites in Palestine. (Proceedings of the Second International Conference) Amman, November 23–25, 2004. ISESCO, 1428H/2007.

Final Recommendations approved by the Commission of the OIC of Eminent Personalities (C.E.P) at the 3rd Extraordinary Session of the Islamic Conference at the Summit of Makkah Al-Moukarramah–Kingdom of Saudi Arabia 5–6 Dhoul Qaada 1426/ December 7–8, 2005.

ISESCO, Implementation Plan, 2007–2009.

OIC. "Resolutions on the cause of Palestine, The City of al-Qods Al-Sharif, and The Arab-Israeli Conflict, adopted by the Thirty-Fifth Session of the Council of Foreign Ministers (Session of Prosperity and Development) Kampala-Republic of Uganda 14–16 Jumadal Thani 1429H (June 18–20, 2008)." OIC/CFM-35/2008/PAL/RES/FINAL. www.oic-oci.org/is11/english/SG-speech-sum.pdf (accessed May 3, 2009).

Statement of H.E. Miguel D'Escoto Brockmann, President of the United Nations General Assembley, at the 57th Plenary Meeting on Agenda Item 16, The Question of Palestine: United Nations, New York, November 24, 2008. www.eyeontheun.org/assets/attachments/documents/7245_Brockmann_GA.pdf

2nd Observatory Report on Islamophobia June 2008 to April 2009, issued at the 36th Council of Foreign Ministers, Damascus, Syrian Arab Republic, May 23–25, 2009, www.oic-un.org/document_report/Islamophobia_rep_May_23_25_2009.pdf

"The Three-Year Action Plan and Budget for the Years 2010–2012." www.isesco.org.ma/english/actionPlan/action.php?idd=TDD_REF_ACT.

Arab Interparliamentary union (UIPA) Arab Inter-parliamentary Union–News, at www.arab-ipu.org/english/ (accessed September 19, 2010).

reveil-des-consciences.over-blog.com/article-dr-said-ramadan--les-prieres-avant-le-pouvoir-37316496.html (accessed September 19, 2010).

Hassan Albanna, IkhwanWeb - Cairo, Egypt, *To What Do We Invite Humanity*, www.ikhwanweb.com/Article.asp?ID=804&LevelID=1&SectionID=117 (accessed September 19, 2010).

www.memriiwmp.org/content/en/report.htm?report=2877 (accessed September 19, 2010).

www.oic-oci.org/ex-summit/english/prep-docs.htm (accessed September 21, 2010).

The Third Extraordinary Session, Secretary General's Report, "New Vision for the Muslim World: Solidarity in Action," Presented at the Third Extraordinary Session of the Islamic Summit Conference.

www.oic-oci.org/ex-summit/english/sg-report.htm(accessed September 21, 2010).

Ten-Year Programme of Action to Meet the Challenges Facing the Muslim Ummah in the 21st Century, www.oic-oci.org/ex-summit/english/10-years-plan.htm (accessed September 21, 2010).

Final Communiqué of the Third Extraordinary Session of the Islamic Summit Conference. "Meeting the Challenges of the 21st Century, Solidarity in Action." www.oic-oci.org/ex-summit/english/fc-exsumm-en.htm (accessed September 21, 2010).

Recommendations of the OIC Commission of Eminent Persons (C.E.P) Saudi Arabia, 5-6 Dhoul Qaada 1426/ December 7–8, 2005. www.oic-oci.org/ex-summit/english/em-persons-rep.htm (accessed September 21, 2010).

OIC, The Executive Committee Meetings. www.oic-oci.org/page_detail.asp?p_id=193 (accessed May 3, 2009).

Final Communiqué adopted by the First Ministerial Meeting of the Executive Committee of the Organization of the Islamic Conference (OIC Troikas) Jeddah—Kingdom of Saudi Arabia, 15 Safar 1427h (15 March 2006). www.oic-oci.org/english/conf/exec/ OIC%20TROIKAS%20-%20En.pdf, §7 (accessed September 21, 2010).

OIC, 11th session of the Islamic Summit Conference-Dakar Declaration, March 13–14, 2008.www.oic-oci.org/is11/english/DAKAR-DEC-11SUMMIT-E.pdf(accessed September 21, 2010).

The Principles of the Muslim Brotherhood, www.ikhwanweb.com/Article.asp?ID=813&Level-ID=2&SectionID=116 (accessed May 3, 2009).

www.oic-oci.org/is11/english/SG-speech-sum.pdf(accessed May 3, 2009).

Resolutions on the cause of Palestine, The City of al-Qods Al-Sharif, and The Arab-Israeli Conflict, adopted by the Thirty-Fifth Session of the Council of Foreign Ministers (Session of Prosperity and Development) Kampala - Republic of Uganda 14 - 16 Jumadal Thani 1429H (June 18–20, 2008).www.oic-oci.org/35cfm/english/res/35CFM--PAL-RES-FINAL. pdf(accessed May 3, 2009).

Oic/Cfm-35/2008/Pol/Res/Final, Resolutions on Political Affairs adopted by the Thirty-Fifth Session of the Council of Foreign Ministers (Session of Prosperity and Development) Kampala Republic of Uganda 14-16 Jumada Al-Thani 1429H (June18–20, 2008) Resolution No.5/35-P on the Situation in Cyprus, pp. 15-18. www.oic-oci.org/35cfm/english/res/35-CFM-%20RES-POL-FINAL.pdf (accessed May 3, 2009).

Resolution No.6/35-P on the Aggression of the Republic of Armenia against the Republic of Azerbaijan, pp.19–22. www.oic-oci.org/35cfm/english/res/35-CFM-%20RES-POL-FI-NAL.pdf (accessed May 3, 2009).

Resolution No.2/35-P on the Jammu and Kashmir Dispute, pp.7–9. www.oic-oci.org/35cfm/ english/res/35-CFM-%20RES-POL-FINAL.pdf (accessed May 3, 2009).

www.todayszaman.com/tz-web/news-185374-ankara-to-propose-joint-nato-oic-conference-in-talks-with-rasmussen.html, August 28, 2009.

UN ORGANIZATIONS DOCUMENTS

"Racism, Racial Discrimination, Xenophobia and all forms of racial discrimination: Situation of Muslim and Arab populations in various regions of the world." Commission on Human Rights, United Nations, Geneva, E/CN.4/2006/17, February 13, 2006.

Alliance of Civilizations, Report of the High level Group, November 13, 2006, New York: United Nations, 2006, www.unAOC.org.

Alliance of Civilizations, Implementation Plan, 2007–2009, United Nations.

Statement of H. E. Miguel D'Escoto Brockmann, President of the United Nations General Assembley, at the 57th Plenary Meeting on Agenda Item 16, The Question of Palestine: United Nations, New York, 24 Novewmber 2008. www.eyeontheun.org/assets/attachments/ documents/7245_Brockmann_GA.pdf.

United Nations, Human Rights Council. OIC proposal against the defamation of religions, co-sponsored by Pakistan . . . March 25, 2010. United Nations, Human Rights Council, Geneva, A/HRC/13L.1, Thirteenth Session, Agenda item 9.

Diène, Doudou. Reports to the UN General Assembly on September 20, 2006 and August 21, 2007. A/HRC/2/3, Sept. 20, 2006 and A/HRC/6/6, August 21, 2007.

Documents d'Actualité Internationale, Ministère des Affaires Etrangères, Paris.

————. Report to the Council on Human Rights dated February 20, 2008, A/HRC/7/19.

————. Report on contemporary forms of racism, racial discrimination, xenophobia, and on the manifestations of defamation of religions and in particular the serious impact of Islamophobia on the enjoyment of all rights . . . September 2, 2008. A/HRC/9/12.

Index of People

Index of Organizations

Index of Places

About the Author

Bat Ye'or was born in Cairo. Her first major study (*Le Dhimmi,* 1980) appeared in English as *The Dhimmi: Jews and Christians under Islam* (1985). It is an essential introduction to *The Decline of Eastern Christianity under Islam: From Jihad to Dhimmitude* (1996), whose publication in French (1991), with a preface by Jacques Ellul, established the author's reputation as a pioneer researcher on "dhimmitude." With *Islam and Dhimmitude: Where Civilizations Collide* (2002) she opened up new ground, and her analysis in *Eurabia: The Euro-Arab Axis* (2005) was hailed as prophetic.

"Bat Ye'or has traced a nearly secret history of Europe over the past thirty years, convincingly showing how the Euro-Arab dialogue has blossomed from a minor discussion group into the engine for the continent's Islamization. In delineating this phenomenon, she also provides the intellectual resources with which to resist it. Will her message be listened to?" —**Daniel Pipes**

"No writer has done more than Bat Ye'or to draw attention to the menacing character of Islamic extremism. Future historians will one day regard her coinage of the term 'Eurabia' as prophetic. Those who wish to live in a free society must be eternally vigilant. Bat Ye'or's vigilance is unrivalled." — **Niall Ferguson**

"Ordinary people who are still in the dark about the way the Euro-Arab Dialogue is refashioning their lives may one day rebel, in which case Bat Ye'or and this book will seem prophetic. Or they may sink helplessly into dhimmitude, in which case Bat Ye'or will be ignored and her book unobtainable. Either way, she is a Cassandra, a brave and far-sighted spirit." —**David Pryce-Jones**